The Small College Guide to Financial Health

Beating the Odds

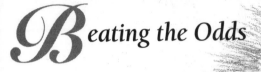

NACUBO
National Association
of College and University
Business Officers

By Michael K. Townsley, Ph.D.

The Small College Guide to Financial Health:
Beating the Odds is made possible by a generous
grant from Moody's Investors Service.

National Association of College and University Business Officers
Washington, DC
www.nacubo.org

Printed in the United States of America

ISBN 1-56972-023-1

Contents

List of Tables

Acknowledgments

I would like to thank my literary editor, Jennifer Lavelle, for substantially revising several drafts of this book without at all changing my original purpose. Her edits, rewrites, and organizational directions shaped my years of financial research into a more readable, broadly relevant form.

John Minter has helped me through long periods of doubt and trepidation about the financial data. He performed a minor miracle by building a very complex database. Most of all, he provided me with his keen insight into the financial structure and condition of higher education.

Also, Dana Keller made a large contribution by assisting in analyzing the data. He provided considerable support in dealing with data that could be unruly at times. His work kept the analysis on track.

This book was made possible because of the wisdom and insight of George Keller, John Nelson and Naomi Richardson of Moody's Investors Service, John Stevens of Kaludis Consulting, and Dr. Michael McPherson of Macalester College. I also thank Moody's Investors Service for contributing to the publication costs of this volume.

My wife, Susanne, and son, Andrew, deserve my deepest appreciation for helping me complete this very daunting task.

M. T.

Foreword

Higher education in the United States, and globally, is in transition. The dramatic shifts occurring in who is seeking higher education and how they learn have led some to say that we are in revolutionary times. Certainly, the evolution in the United States in the past 60 years has been profound, with enrollments escalating from 2 million in 1940 to 15 million in 2000.

Readers of this book can easily recite the drivers of change for today's campuses—among them an expanding but currently unpredictable economy, changes in student preferences, tuition that outpaces inflation, technology, and new forms of competition. In addition, higher education is moving from a producer to a consumer driven market and shifting from state and federal policy setting for the public good to policy for personal good. No sector of the college landscape has been more dramatically affected by these sea changes than the small private independent college. Leaders at these colleges face the difficult task of operating in a marketplace that is unsympathetic to their survival.

Michael Townsley has written an important book for all who are in these challenging positions of leadership at our nation's independent colleges with enrollments of 3,000 or fewer students. This is not just a book for chief financial officers. In fact, *The Small College Guide to Financial Health* can be argued to be even more important for college presidents, trustees, and chief academic officers, who must fit in understanding market forces as yet another skill they need to master as part of their busy agenda. The author provides college leaders with easy to understand models that spell out the key factors of economic success, or failure. As Townsley points out: "Small colleges can have a vibrant economic life if they understand the markets in which they operate….The board and president, if they want to foster a vibrant institution, must have a well-honed appreciation of all the markets that drive operations and decisions."

When Mike Townsley and I met last summer to discuss his ideas and outline for a book project, I learned that his experience as chief financial officer at Wilmington College, a college that struggled and then recovered, had led him to seek the answer to a burning question: Will small colleges go the way of community hospitals, small airlines, and local rail stations—sweetly remembered but devoid of the content that made them viable?

With this question in mind, Townsley conducted thorough research, talking with leaders at small colleges, rating agencies, accounting firms, consulting companies, and others, as well as obtaining data from John Minter Associates, IPEDS, and other sources. Armed with information and data, he could have easily written a "doom and gloom" book that answered his question and provided a few interested readers with a comprehensive, thoughtful analysis of the issues small colleges confront. Indeed, the working title of this project, "Financial Distress in Small Colleges," seemed to indicate that such a book might be the end result.

Instead, and fortunately for leaders at small colleges, Townsley has gone well beyond that working title. He proposes how small colleges can position themselves to avert economic disaster. In offering his straightforward solutions, he knits elements of finance and management with planning and strategy built around the reality of the marketplace for small independent colleges. He addresses strategies, structure, and operational performance measurements. In some ways, Townsley has written a gourmet cookbook for small colleges, with a detailed recipe for building an academically and financially strong small college. He points out that small colleges do have advantages in the marketplace if they are "planful" about strategy and disciplined in their expectations.

One of the greatest strengths of the American higher education network is the diversity of institutions. Townsley makes a strong and eloquent case for the survival and continuation of the nearly 1,000 small independent colleges that educate our nation's students. While the marketplace is certain to swallow up some small colleges in the years to come, small college leaders who read this book will be armed with powerful insights and tools to help them avert their institution's demise. Long may independent small colleges prosper.

James E. Morley Jr.
President, NACUBO

Small Colleges on the Brink of Financial Distress

Small independent colleges have been the backbone of American higher education since their inception. They contribute ingenuity, leadership, and academic integrity to the world's greatest education system. But changes in the current market are challenging their very existence. "Small" used to conjure images of an intimate, stable community of dedicated students and professors. Today small independent colleges struggle with susceptibility to economic shocks, rising expenses, spiking tuition, stagnant or falling enrollments, and competition in the marketplace.

Stock market and economic conditions from late 2000 through 2002 promise to undermine gift giving and endowment valuations, a harmful blow to many small colleges, which use these funds to cover annual operating deficits. As David W. Breneman points out, "the well-being of higher education is so closely tied to the well-being of the economy that planners can virtually ignore other conditions."[1] Small colleges that rely heavily on student revenue are the most vulnerable, not only to economic instability but also to competition, rising costs, and fluctuations in student demand. Poorly financed colleges are placed in the unenviable position of negotiating their standards to get and retain students, a situation that David Riesman has postulated.[2] Enrollments are less predictable as students "hop and shop" from college to college searching for courses to fit their schedules and budgets. As enrollments decline, those colleges may squeeze financial reserves to the point where liquidity disappears and they can no longer make short- and long-term debt payments. Independent colleges adapted to enrollment declines in the 1990s with new courses and services, aggressive marketing, and deep discounts, maintaining a fairly constant number of closings since then (less than 1 percent of colleges annually). Whether they can maintain deep discounts with increased spending in the current economy remains to be seen.

As colleges face decreasing enrollments, the competition for students intensifies, leading to increased spending and tuition rates. In the "field of dreams" syndrome, administrators scramble to satisfy the perceived demand of students for enhanced personal services and top-of-the-line technology and facilities. They finance huge construction projects with huge dollops of debt. As competitors begin plotting their own "fields," construction wars break out, leading to high debt loads with little or no payoff. Fierce competition comes not only from within the private sector, however. Public institutions with lower sticker prices are scrambling to fill their empty classrooms, and for-profit colleges are building market share with tough no-holds-barred marketing campaigns.

Will a flat economy, the stock market crash, changes in student preferences, tuition that outpaces inflation, and new forms of competition plunge small independent colleges into a sea of chronic financial distress? Will they go the way of community hospitals, small airlines, and local rail stations—sweetly remembered but devoid of the content that made them viable? Before we can begin to answer these questions, we must profile small independent colleges, focusing first on size and type, then on enrollments, growth, and income.

Since scale economy directly relates to size and operating efficiency, it offers a suitable mechanism for establishing rough boundaries for separating small and large independent institutions. Relevant literature suggests optimum scale economies for independent colleges is approximately 2,000 students.[3] This book addresses those with enrollments between 2,000 and 3,000 students. This definition captures most of the membership of the Council of Independent Colleges, whose members consider themselves to be small colleges. This group is divided into three subcategories: *small* (fewer than 2,000 students); *moderate-sized* (2,000 to 3,000 students); and *large* (more than 3,000 students). The large college category provides a benchmark for comparing performance. Chapter 7, which looks more closely at these colleges, uses a different set of enrollment categories.

Table 1.1 provides basic demographic and financial information about colleges in the three categories. This table excludes institutions that are self-identified in the Independent Postsecondary Education Data System (IPEDS) as one of the following Carnegie Commission types: health, art, law, and religious. The 593 colleges excluded represented unique missions and financial arrangements uncommon to traditional independent colleges and universities. Most would have been assigned to the first category; a large proportion of them reported enrollments of fewer than 50 students.

Nine hundred forty-four institutions fit the Carnegie classification criteria. Small and moderate-sized institutions identify themselves as primarily liberal arts institutions, while large institutions identify themselves as primarily comprehensive institutions. Most colleges in this group (58.7 percent) enroll fewer than 2,000 students. The moderate-sized category includes 152 colleges, or 16.1 percent of the total. Large colleges include 238 institutions, or 25.2 percent of the total. Although small colleges outnumber the others, they enroll only 22.1 percent of the students. In contrast, the largest institutions have three times more students than small colleges and twice the number of students as the combined enrollment

Table 1.1
Profile of Independent Colleges, 1988–96

	Small (fewer than 2,000 students)	Moderate-Sized (2,000–3,000 students)	Large (more than 3,000 students)	Total
Number of institutions	554	152	238	944
Percent of category	58.7%	16.1%	25.2%	
Typical Carnegie class	liberal arts	liberal arts	comprehensive	
Total enrollment	597,867	367,670	1,734,822	2,700,359
Percent of category	22.1%	13.6%	64.2%	
Average size	1,079	2,419	7,289	
Percent that grew	64.9%	71.1%	63.8%	65.8%
Percent that lost enrollment	29.4%	28.9%	36.1%	31.1%
Percent that closed	5.4%	0.0%	0.0%	3.2%
Growth rate	.65%	1.5%	1.0%	
Growth volatility	10.0%	4.2%	4.6%	
Volatility/growth rate	8.1	1.9	2.5	
Average net income	0.2%	1.1%	1.4%	
Net income volatility	4.6%	3.2%	1.8%	
Volatility/net income	19.2	2.9	1.8	
Expenses–50th percentile	$15,236,690	$32,377,067	$71,526,353	
Assets–50th percentile	$13,644,118	$42,935,105	$74,819,141	
Percent deficits and tuition dependency >60%	32.8%	23.2%	17.2%	
Percent reporting deficits 5 of 9 years	30.2%	13.4%	17.0%	

Source: "Sheet 10463025, Enrollment Level 1988–1997." (2001) NSF: WebCaspar database system; caspar.nsf.gov/.

of the low- and moderate-enrollment categories. Average enrollment also clearly indicates the size disparity among these colleges. Moderate-sized colleges were on average twice as large as small colleges, and large colleges were three times larger than moderate-sized colleges and seven times larger than small colleges. Table 1.2 also illustrates the relative enrollments and number of institutions for each size category.

Table 1.2
Number and Enrollment Comparison of Independent Colleges and Universities by Size

	Low	Moderate	High	Total
Number	554	152	238	944
Total enrollment	597,867	367,670	1,734,822	2,700,359
% with deficits	0.302	0.134	0.17	0.3575588
TDP >60%	0.328	0.232	0.172	
Expenses 50th percentile	15,236,690	32,377,067	71,526,353	
Assets 50th percentile	13,644,118	42,935,105	74,819,141	

Source: "Sheet 10463025, Enrollment Level 1988–1997." (2001) NSF: WebCaspar database system; caspar.nsf.gov/.

During 1988–96, enrollment increased 65.8 percent for all independent institutions. In the moderate-sized category, 71.1 percent of the colleges expanded; 64.5 percent of the small colleges grew; and 63.8 percent of the large institutions grew. Although more than a majority of independent institutions grew over the nine-year period, the compounded rate of growth was not particularly robust. Small colleges grew at a .65 percent compounded rate, moderate-sized colleges at a 1.53 percent rate, and large colleges at a 1.00 percent rate. Volatility (standard deviation) ranged from 10 percent for small colleges to 4 percent for moderate and large colleges. Volatility was 16 times greater than the compounded rate of growth for small colleges, while it was only twice as much for moderate-sized colleges and four times greater for large institutions. In other words, the rate of growth for a small college could vary (1 standard deviation) from a positive 10.65 percent to a negative 9.35 percent. Low growth rates and high enrollment volatility could pose a serious problem for small colleges that are tuition dependent.

The average net income as a percentage of revenue was lowest for small colleges—0.2 percent—and its volatility (deviation to average ratio) was also the highest at 19.2:1. The net income ratio was 1.1 percent for the moderate-enrollment category and 1.4 percent for the high-enrollment category. Net income relative to revenue increased with size, while volatility declined, suggesting that larger institutions have greater control over expenses or income flow. Spending at colleges in the low-enrollment category may be so minimal that those colleges respond to revenue shortfalls by making expense reductions. If they do, they risk cutting into the core of the organization.

Table 1.3

Comparison of Expenses and Assets for Independent Colleges and Universities by Size

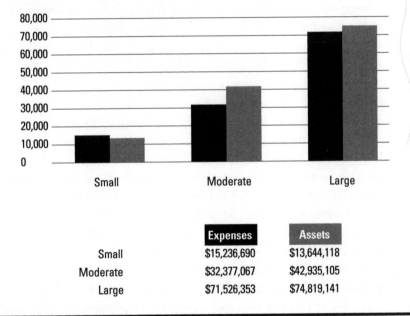

	Expenses	Assets
Small	$15,236,690	$13,644,118
Moderate	$32,377,067	$42,935,105
Large	$71,526,353	$74,819,141

The effect of size in these categories is reflected in the expenses and assets of institutions at the 50th percentile. Expenses double from moderate-sized to large colleges. Differences in asset size between low- and moderate-enrollment categories are more dramatic. The asset base of moderate-sized colleges is nearly three times greater than that of small colleges, and large institutions have 1.7 times more assets than moderate-sized colleges. But large colleges had 5.6 times more assets than small colleges at the 50th percentile. Given their relatively small asset base, small colleges may struggle to find the financial resources to invest in endowments since the plant may absorb most of the assets. The relative differences are readily apparent in table 1.1.

The most telling measure may be the proportion of institutions reporting deficits for five of the nine years. Thirty percent of the smallest colleges (167 institutions) reported five years of deficits, almost twice the rate for moderate-sized and large institutions. It is not unusual to have a deficit for one year or even several years over an extended period, but a college with at least five years of deficits is bobbing in and out of financial distress, barely keeping itself afloat.

The smallest colleges are the most problematic of the three categories for the period 1988–96. This category is the only one in which institutions closed, and it has the lowest net income ratio. Enrollment and net income volatility are many times higher than for colleges in the moderate-sized and large categories. The smallest colleges deploy the fewest assets and expenses to deliver instruction. Only colleges in this category report assets as being lower than expenses. The most shocking measure is the high proportion of the smallest colleges reporting deficits.

This combination of adverse conditions—volatile growth rates, inadequate asset bases, and deficits—could mean that many small colleges substantially depleted their reserves during the early 1990s. The strong economy of the late 1990s may have saved some institutions, but if they were unable to build financial reserves, they may have found themselves struggling again as the economy unwound in 2000 and 2001. Assuming that the 30 percent reporting five years of deficits are the most vulnerable, nearly 600,000 students could be affected—students who alone or with help from family have committed time, money, and federal dollars to these colleges with hopes of gaining a degree. Now students, parents, and the government find their investments in jeopardy.

Most small colleges have endured economic blows over the last 30 years that many believed would spell their demise. Despite the graduation of the baby boom generation, the inflationary cycle of the 1970s, economic weakness in the early 1980s and 1990s, and public outcry against the spiking rise in tuition, small independent colleges are still with us. But as threats to economic stability mount, small colleges will find survival more difficult. Indeed, most presidents and chief financial officers recognize that the financial condition of their small colleges is becoming less stable by the year.

Presidents and chief financial officers often shoulder the burden of keeping small colleges afloat. They are acutely aware of the circumstances—market and financial—that keep these colleges on the brink of financial distress. Presidents must raise new money or convince donors to carry the college one more year. They have the thankless responsibility of making the case for the college while boosting staff morale. Their personal resources can be drained as the struggle for survival weighs on them.

Chief financial officers carry a special burden because financial problems are readily evident to them. Vendors demand payment, students fail to pay bills on time, taxes and benefit withholdings are held to cover other financial problems, or the government threatens to hold financial aid disbursements. They are vigilant about avoiding mistakes because a minor financial error could be disastrous. When there is a problem—budgetary, policy, or some other area remotely dependent on money—the board turns to the chief financial officer for answers. The chief financial officer must also say no when the president's pet project is not financially feasible, and as a result he or she may eventually be seen as a naysayer and cut from the decision-making loop. The problems are compounded when the president does not understand basic financial concepts—for instance, that revenue is not the same as cash-in-hand. The daily grind of keeping finances in order can sap the energy of chief financial officers so that they only concentrate on immediate problems and lose sight of warning signs of bigger problems down the road.

Small colleges continue to believe that something will change—government funding, new markets, or new programs—to give them financial stability. For instance, some hope that the new tax-sheltered prepaid-tuition plans will help stimulate student revenue. However, small independent colleges may not be visible enough to benefit from these savings plans. William J. Baumol and Sue Anne Batey Blackman contend that America could easily live with education increasing its share of the gross national product from 9 percent in 1990 to 20 percent in 2040. They assert that total output measured by GNP will be so great that other efficiencies will offset the rising cost of education.[4] But it is hard to imagine the American electorate embracing personal financial sacrifices to support such a dramatic shift in the country's allocation of resources to education, especially to small independent colleges that represent such a small portion of total college enrollment. Though small colleges are the historic backbone of America's higher education system, they can not count on governmental assistance to cure their ills.

As we diagnose the financial condition of small private colleges and suggest how to strengthen their financial condition, we will explore several issues. Chapters

1 through 5 discuss how small independent colleges are bound by their history, economics, and financial structure. The history of small independent colleges is the history of higher education in America. Although they may play a minor role in higher education today, at one time they were the only option. You can trace the governance structure, economics, and finances of colleges and universities to small colleges' humble roots. Small colleges do it the old-fashioned way. Grants, gifts, and beneficences do not fill their coffers. Instead, students finance these colleges, and they survive by the good graces of the marketplace. To understand small colleges means understanding the economic and financial models that drive them. This book also looks at the major challenges that threaten to undermine the economic and financial base of small colleges in the 21st century.

Chapters 6 and 7 consider financial distress among small colleges. Chapter 6 describes a well-known model of financial distress. In chapter 7, case histories of several small colleges that have failed illustrate conditions that drive some colleges over the brink. Chapter 8 paints a broad picture of the financial condition of small colleges using financial data collected by the U.S. Department of Education. This chapter also suggests several basic measures to determine whether small colleges are encountering financial distress. Small colleges' financial condition is compared to that of larger independent institutions.

Chapters 9 through 12 weigh the roles of strategy, diagnostics, leadership, and business practices in alleviating financial distress, improving the future prospects, and pursuing excellence. Strategy encompasses both strategic planning and financial strategy. Diagnostics links marketing and financial management, since small colleges must know their place in the market and their financial condition before they can design an effective financial strategy. Leadership is essential to change and viability, so the principles and practice of leadership are significant parts of this book. In some ways, the future of many small colleges depends on simple business practices. Colleges in which everyday operations are chaotic and unreliable have a reduced capacity to deal with routine business, let alone the shock of the unexpected.

Small colleges must recognize that change entails more than a recipe. Change means that leadership must willingly contribute, in Winston Churchill's words, their blood, toil, tears, and sweat. There are no easy alternatives. If fact, some situations may require seeking partners, pursuing a merger, or closing the school. Heroic efforts may postpone such tough decisions, but the delay may have the deleterious effect of costing students a worthwhile education.

Chapter 13 examines the prospects for different classes of small colleges. Current economic news does not bode well for some institutions. Changes in the economy may have an adverse affect on some colleges given their place in the market and their financial condition. Others may have a better chance of responding to the economy, but it will take work to figure out how to make the most of their opportunities. On a more positive note, forecasts show that enrollment will grow over the next decade. Although government does bestow largesse on higher education, it continues to provide funds to independent colleges, and public institutions must confront the fact that state and local governments are cutting back on support.

In all likelihood, small colleges will have to deal individually with the consequences of their own vulnerability to changes in the economy. This book intends to provide the leadership of small colleges—board, president, and chief academic and financial officers—with a basis for evaluating their institutions' condition and establishing a thoughtful plan of action. In addition, government agencies, funding groups, and professional organizations can refer to this book for insight into small colleges and how they might grapple with their destiny.

Notes

1. David W. Breneman, *Liberal Arts Colleges* (Washington, D.C.: Brookings Institution, 1994), p. 31.
2. David R. Riesman, *On Higher Education* (New Brunswick, N.J.: Transaction Publishers, 1998).
3. Malcolm Getz and John J. Siegfried, "Costs and Productivity in American Colleges and Universities," in *Economic Challenges in Higher Education*, ed. Charles T. Clotfelter, Ronald G. Ehrenberg, Malcolm Getz, and John J. Siegfried (Chicago: University of Chicago Press, 1991), p. 355; Paul T. Brinkman and Larry L. Leslie, "Economies of Scale in Higher Education: Sixty Years of Research," *Review of Higher Education* 10 (fall 1986): 1–28.
4. William J. Baumol and Sue Anne Batey Blackman, "How to Think About Rising College Costs," *Planning for Higher Education* 23 (summer 1995), p. 6.

Historical Influences on the Economic Development of Independent Colleges

The deep pockets in the academic robes of medieval professors form the metaphoric core of the financial structure of today's small colleges. Those musty pockets, where learned men deposited their bargained teaching money, embody the essential economics of higher education—a price charged in accordance with market demand, student payment as the primary source of funds, and instruction as a handicraft. What was once a two-person transaction is now controlled by institutions.

English colleges and universities, the most direct ancestors of American colleges, were chartered by the king as corporations of students and masters that governed themselves—a *universitas*, or community, in this case, of scholars. The universities were endowed residence halls (colleges) for scholars (master and student) who elected the rector (president of the college). As independent corporations, the university and its colleges were granted the right to set their own rules of governance. Independence from the crown carried a price, however, as an institution was expected to finance itself through student payment of fees to masters. The entire university was at the mercy of its students, who, if dissatisfied, could form a new university in another city. Oxford, for example, came into being in the 12th century when disgruntled students left the University of Paris. Higher education in its earliest form was a marketplace where students and institutions negotiated the price and nature of instructional service.

By the time of the Black Death in the 14th century, Oxford and Cambridge—a collective corporate body of scholars—had developed strict standards of admission and a rigorous course of study that if completed successfully could lead to a promising career. Oxford and Cambridge only selected students who were "men of approved ability pursuing advanced studies under discipline." They offered students a "field of study . . . [that] includ[ed] the arts, the philosophy of Aristotle and theology" in the belief that "the diligent pursuit of the liberal arts sought to prepare young men for service in the world of affairs."[1]

Over time, the colleges embraced by the university assumed the routine business transactions of the professoriate, including but not limited to the collection of payments. Duties were delegated to one of the masters for a fixed term, and the professoriate retained ultimate control of business affairs and decisions.[2] When the American colonies founded their own colleges, they followed the English model and established self-regulating corporations. The colonial elite, seeking to emulate the society of their homeland, wanted to create institutions like Oxford and Cambridge that could train their young men in the finer points of being English gentlemen. The astute leaders among them anticipated that colleges could be the training ground for future social and political leaders, whether farmers or sons of the elite.[3]

Many colleges also rose and fell in response to geographic and sectarian interests.[4] Local interests' desire for local colleges would play out repeatedly during the colonial period. The sectarianism that was evident in the founding of Harvard led some men of faith and influence to doubt their alma mater's devotion to its denominational foundations. Such factional divisions drove Cotton Mather and Jonathon Edwards away from Harvard for its perceived lack of steadfastness to theology. They encouraged the establishment of Princeton as a counterweight to Harvard's irresolute character. How these founding intentions gave rise to higher education is the great story of independent American colleges, large and small.

Colonial Colleges and the Great Awakening

While the corporate charters for universities in England were awarded to a body of scholars, America's self-regulating educational corporations were placed in the hands of trustees, who governed the institution apart from the scholars. The first colonial colleges—Harvard in 1636, the College of William and Mary in 1693, and Yale in 1716—received corporate charters granting trustees authority to govern as a quasi-legislative body. In lieu of ownership, trustees usually assigned a permanent president the task of assuring the survival of the institution. Trustees with their presidents retained the freedom to establish new colleges, a prerogative that withered in England with the accretion of prestige, wealth, power, influence, and the drag of collegial governance.

Colonial colleges, neither public nor private in the modern sense, were public trusts under colonial regulation, with colonial legislatures retaining a direct interest in their activities and solvency.[5] Legislative involvement was not as intense as today's relationship between a public university and a state legislature. Unless expansion or extraordinary expenses required legislative intervention, colonial colleges were expected to balance their budgets without tax assistance.[6] The first American colleges, however, had the good fortune to receive a regular benefaction from the colonial governing bodies, thereby supplementing student revenue and undermining the power of dissatisfied students to whipsaw colonial colleges they way they did the first European universities.

In addition to the regular source of revenue from the colonial assembly, Harvard received 2,000 acres of land, a 100-pound tax levy, and rents from the Charlestown ferry. Virginia awarded William and Mary proceeds from a levy on skins and furs exports, a peddler's tax, and a tobacco tax; the city of Williamsburg extended to the college the use of its main commercial thoroughfare, the Duke of Gloucester Street. Connecticut offered Yale an alternative to direct subsidies by exempting students from taxes and military service. The future trustees of Yale prevailed upon Elihu Yale to support the new college using some of his fortune from his "magnificent orient plunder" from the East India Company at Madras.[7]

Though the mix of government and student funds set a pattern for independent college revenue that prevails today, other ties between state and college began to fray around the time of the Great Awakening in the late 18th century. New denominational colleges chose to separate themselves from the dictates of the state. Princeton was chartered in 1746 as a denominational college with a board of Presbyterian trustees. Congregationalists opened Dartmouth, Baptists founded the College of Rhode Island (Brown University) in 1765, and the Dutch Reformed in 1766 brought Queen's College (Rutgers University) into being. These colleges, though of sectarian origin, had broader dreams than producing a learned clergy. The College of Rhode Island, for one, saw itself producing men "duly qualify'd for discharging the Offices of Life with usefulness & reputation."[8]

The reality for most colonial colleges, though, was that they were small, enrolling relatively few children of the elite. Jencks and Riesman pose economic and practical reasons for the low enrollments. College graduates, unless they were ministers with an "intellectual bent," gained little of value from their market.[9] Coursework focused on individual character development and on studies of the eternal verities, through discourse in the ancient languages of Latin and Greek. Anyone seeking to move up in the economic pecking order had a better chance of doing so independently. Practically speaking, most colonies did not have the elementary and secondary schools necessary to form basic and advanced academic skills.[10] Those few colonists who could read and write were either autodidacts or home-tutored.

Postrevolutionary War Colleges

Colleges proliferated after the Revolution as new religious groups sought to impart their versions of faith. States were indifferent to supporting the new denominational colleges, promulgating the separation of church and state. Churches, while providing the impetus, the seed money, the trustees, and the early leaders for hundreds of new colleges, could no longer ensure their survival. The colleges of the Great Awakening soon discovered that freedom from state meddling meant dependence on students as underwriters of the institution. Denominational funds may have started these colleges, but the market would determine their success or failure—a phenomenon that prevails among independent colleges today.

Most independent colleges from the 17th through the 19th centuries were never entirely isolated from the vagaries of the market and its effect on their financial security. Great institutions like Harvard had to close their doors early in their histories. Yale University had to penny-pinch its faculty to survive. Colleges that had to rely primarily on students for their funds often found that students were quite willing to bargain them into penury. Colleges competed desperately for students, awarding perpetual scholarships through which students could receive virtually free educations. Lafayette, Wesleyan, Dickinson, Antioch, DePauw, and Columbia were only a few of the colleges caught up in this scheme, which led to increased enrollments without a concomitant increase in cash. (Today, this bargain is called tuition discounting, with the same devastating impact on the finances of many independent colleges.)

Several factors contributed to the unabashed competition for students. First, many new colleges entered the market—from nine at the time of the Revolution to 252 by the beginning of the Civil War.[11] These figures do not include the 700 colleges that tried and failed. Second, postrevolutionary citizens, many of whom were either illiterate or self-taught, continued to lack the skills required for college. In fact, legislatures debated the practicality of funding colleges given the high illiteracy rates. Most state governments preferred to fund common schools, believing it was more important to teach citizens basic skills so they could participate in the fledgling government. Third, the college curriculum, with its emphasis on the neoclassics, appealed only to the clergy or those young gentlemen of wealth seeking to become men of letters. Others with a practical bent, averse to the impoverished life of clergy or the sporting life of gentlemen, found the curriculum offered by the typical 19th-century college of little value.

The egalitarian spirit of postrevolutionary times caused state governments to challenge the independence of trustees as arrogant, aristocratic, and out of step.

The state vested its authority with trustees to govern a college, and so, it was argued, the institution was subject to the will of the state. The courts of New Hampshire tested that proposition in 1819 after the legislature sought to restructure the trustees of Dartmouth College, claiming that the college was run by a "small self-perpetuating governing board [under] aristocratic rather than democratic principles."[12] Though New Hampshire's Supreme Court affirmed the state's right to revise Dartmouth's charter, the United States Supreme Court, in a majority opinion delivered by John Marshall, reversed the decision. Marshall wrote that "Dartmouth College was not a civil or public institution, nor was its property public. . . . [It] was indeed a private eleemosynary institution."[13] Marshall's opinion declared American colleges independent of state interference, characterizing the charter as a contract between the state and trustees that could not be arbitrarily altered by the state.

The paramount role of the college president prevailed up to and through the postrevolutionary period. Presidents such as Henry Dunster of colonial Harvard, Charles Elliot of 19th-century Harvard, John Henry Crowe of Hanover College in Indiana, Nathaniel Wayland of Brown, Nicholas Murray Butler of Columbia, and Robert Maynard Hutchins of Chicago are a few examples of great leaders in American higher education. They and many others like them gave voice to independent colleges and universities by clarifying their missions, building their curricula, constructing their edifices, and raising funds. Because most of the early colleges were small, presidents knew faculty personally and often taught the senior classes. The president controlled his institution with an iron hand, rebuffing challenges to his authority.

Trustees deferred to their president because they lacked either the training or the time to oversee the institution. Owing to his pervasive role and ultimate obligation to the trustees, the president could impose a governance system wherein the faculty was treated as a labor source. As independent colleges began to rely on presidential fund raising, presidents became more removed from daily operations. Thus, the governance of instruction and the faculty eroded further as bureaucracies supplanted the immediacy of presidential oversight. During much of the 19th century, faculties were exploited when colleges needed to balance the demands of students with operational costs. Rudolph cites poignant examples of faculty being paid a pittance or, in some cases, nothing at all.[14] The president and trustees of Yale, for instance, simultaneously reduced tuition and withheld pay to the faculty in 1827 with hopes of broadening the student body by diluting the representation of the privileged classes.[15] Faculty compensation in many independent colleges barely achieved the level of subsistence.

Post–Civil War

Classic independent colleges held on stubbornly until the mid 19th century. After the Civil War, competition from new land-grant colleges and independent colleges committed to technical, engineering, and scientific degrees forced these institutions to reevaluate their curricula to meet market demand. Purdue, which started as an independent college in 1869, Cornell in 1869, John Hopkins in 1867, and Lehigh in 1874 were a few of the new institutions promising educations to address the practical bent of young Americans seeking valuable skills in a more technical and professional labor market.

There was an obvious divergence between public and independent colleges' response to increased demand for such an education. State legislatures funding public colleges expected citizens to receive an immediate real return in the form of technical training. If state funds for public colleges failed to produce that return, dissatisfaction spread quickly through the electoral system, making the investment in public education a simultaneous investment in voter confidence. Independent colleges found their support in a much narrower realm, but one as demanding as state legislatures. Shrewd presidents of independent institutions began to recognize that the survival and growth of their institutions would depend on attracting funds from emerging national industries.[16] Wealthy industrialists used discretion when making gifts to colleges. The largest gifts went not to hatcheries for gentlemen, but to knowledge factories run by presidents with vision. Presidents of independent colleges sought to enroll the children of the new wealth so as to perpetuate the influx of their father's gifts, and also to ensure future gifts from the wealthy young students who would later become alumni.

It was not until the late 19th century and into the first decade of the 20th century that the powerful combination of philanthropy and foundations became a major force in financing independent colleges. The money literally exploded with the great industrialists' desire to avoid taxes while doing public good. Money came from the fortunes of John D. Rockefeller, Cornelius Vanderbilt, Asa Chandler, Andrew Carnegie, J. P. Morgan, Joseph Pulitzer, George Eastman, and Russell Sage, to name a few. To ease college dependence on student revenue, college presidents diverted their attention from the daily tribulations of the institution to woo rich donors and the staff of those wealthy foundations formed early in the 19th century. Indeed, as these independent colleges (especially those in the upper tier) built sizeable fortunes of their own, they no longer needed to grovel for students.

While changes in curricula from moral and orthodox to professional led to changes in the sources and amounts of gifts, alumni giving at independent colleges persisting in their religious bent led ironically to changes in the curricula. Industrialists with a rigid background in tenets of faith and discipline sought out colleges that would instill these same virtues in their children; however, as the children graduated, they saw promise in professional and technical careers. Students began to routinely expect more than classical training to prepare them for life. When the alma mater came calling for gifts from the second-generation industrial rich, the orthodox-gone-professional crowd stipulated that the gifts be used for curricular innovations.[17] The alumni at these colleges, not the presidents, became the source of curricular transformation from the classical to the career-oriented.

The change in curricula was accompanied by other significant changes for the president, as well as the faculty and students, of independent institutions. By the late 19th century, the faculty began to counterbalance presidential power with departmentalization, specialization, and tenure. Departments appeared as colleges grew larger and more complex, and presidents transferred authority to the departments in order to achieve efficient operations. The appearance of departments and career degrees coincided with a rise in the number of Ph.Ds, with field specializations becoming a requirement for faculty. Graduate students were now experts in areas in which the president was no longer conversant. Decisions about instruction, faculty hiring, and student admission began to fall to a specialized faculty. As faculty members gained esteem and value, presidents offered tenure as a way to retain them. Tenure simultaneously protected faculty from any arbitrary decisions made by the president and board of trustees. Departments, specialization, and tenure, while not affecting the ultimate power of the president, redressed the faculty's power, introducing faculty autonomy and academic freedom as significant hallmarks in American higher education.

The proliferation of duties continued beyond increased enrollments and competition for students, the prevalence of new wealth and presidential fund raising, and the specialization of faculty and departments and procedures. Before the Civil War, most colleges had only a president, a treasurer, and a librarian, but administrative expansion now exploded to include admissions officers, student relations officers, public relations officers, deans, registrars, vice presidents, and assistants to the president.[18] Each new administrative division within the institution increased its cost of operation, removed the administration from direct contact with faculty and students, and resulted in new divisions to better serve the administration.

It is important to note that while wealth and professionalism were enlarging the academic and administrative structures of the very best independent colleges, most independent colleges after the Civil War were small, hardscrabble places that were captives of remote neighborhood markets. These colleges, limited in their supply of students, were tuition driven and subject to the impoverished circumstance of the locals. With barely the means to enroll one or two hundred students and hire half a dozen professors, they lacked the resources to stay current with new branches of knowledge, and so they were removed still further from the mainstream of higher education.[19]

Between the Wars

After World War I, people began connecting a college degree with the idea of social standing and future income. Though some small colleges hung on to their spiritual or religious mission, focusing on exclusively classical or liberal arts training, higher education in the professions was becoming a necessity rather than a luxury. American corporations made the adjustment, offering careers, rather than mere hand and trade labor jobs, to qualified college graduates. White-collar managers, bureaucratic office workers, technicians, and scientists were replacing overalls and lunch pails.

Technical and scientific degrees were hard to come by, given a lack of resources for them. Mainstream colleges tried instead to provide an appropriate mix of professional and liberal arts courses to better prepare their graduates for careers in business, nursing, and education. The combination of specialty training with broad critical thinking and management skills was irresistible to large organizations; they recruited graduates between the wars as fast as colleges could certify them.

Now, colleges also began to offer social training—activities to help students learn the finer points of social interaction and teamwork. By the mid-1920s, athletic teams, Greek societies, and highly organized extracurricular activities were commonplace. Sports and social clubs provided an arena where ambitious young men could meet the "right" people, learning at the very least how to meld and work with strangers.

The security of the independent college's new standing as a place of social and professional development was bolstered in the 1920s and 1930s by a broadening of its accessibility.[20] A system of required elementary and secondary education extended the agrarian October-through-April school year to September through May. The pool of college applicants grew steadily as high school graduations became the norm rather than the exception.[21] The staunch rural ethic that one lived and worked on a farm and learned skills at the feet of one's parents was slowly shifting from reality to myth as the citizenry became more urbanized.

Ironically, the depression of the 1930s did not slow the progress of higher education. Rather, enrollments grew because the cost of attendance was lower and because employment was not a competing factor for students. The young were hungry for skills that would get them a secure job in a large company. By the start of World War II, one in six high school graduates were entering college, and one in twelve were graduating.[22]

The foundation for the huge expansion in college enrollments was laid in the two decades before America's entrance into World War II. Smaller colleges continued to struggle, but they, like their larger counterparts, were adapting to student and business demand for professional coursework. But as the depression wound down and the war geared up, colleges would make some patriotic changes, some playing major roles in training students for the war effort. Many would shorten the period required to fulfill degree requirements from four to two years to benefit government and armed services personnel. Streamlined in their ability to educate groups in abbreviated time periods, colleges would be ready to handle the influx of veterans to come.

Baby Boom, New Markets, and Uncertainty through the Present

The six decades since the end of World War II have been a roller coaster ride for higher education in general and small colleges in particular. The baby boom drove college enrollments to levels undreamed of before the war. Though enrollments during this period grew at independent colleges 2.8 times, enrollments at public colleges grew faster; 9.5 times the number of students who attended in 1950 were attending in 1990. Enrollments may have been up everywhere, but they were shifting. Before 1950, more than 50 percent of college students were enrolled in mostly small independent institutions. After 1950, shares steadily declined, reaching their nadir in 1991, with independent institutions enrolling 21.5 percent of the student market.[23] Obviously, students found federally subsidized public institutions more appealing, due in large part to their relative affordability. Not until the 1980s, when the federal government began providing grants and subsidizing loans regardless of whether students chose public or independent institutions, did the playing field level slightly.

Grants and loans did little to help independent colleges recover from the dismal forecasts and realities of the 1970s and 1980s, however. A sour economy, high inflation rate, and the stock market's low real growth rate compounded the relative drought in enrollments that followed the baby boom. Independent colleges staggered under the weight of rising energy prices, salary inflation, and endowments that had failed to keep pace with inflation. Although the number of colleges that closed their doors increased dramatically through the 1990s, total closings represented a small proportion of the total number of independent institutions. In 1994, for example, while 24 colleges closed during one of the worst years in the last 30 for independent college closings, 98.3 percent of them remained open.[24]

One propitious phase in America that kept independent colleges afloat was the return of adults, especially women, to college. Continuing education programs, offering professional degrees to women who had not worked outside the home, became the cash cow for colleges, ultimately subsidizing traditional undergraduate programs. The upward trend of female enrollees continues today, with women accounting for nearly 56 percent of all students in higher education. Expansion of services to nontraditional groups has helped keep many small independent colleges afloat for the last 20 years.

There was only one problem: continuing education and nontraditional populations tend to enroll on a part-time basis. It would generally take double the number of part-timers to compensate for the loss of traditional full-time students in the 1980s and 1990s. Coupled with credit-transferring part-timers from community and other colleges—a scenario that translates into shorter enrollments and fewer courses taken annually—the overall impact of the continuing education movement on the revenue of independent colleges has been small. Furthermore, the lower pricing of continuing education programs compared to traditional day programs has encouraged day students to take night classes—yet another hit to the flow of revenue. Colleges, forced to plug these leaks in revenue, have spent more money on advertising and recruiting to capture more of these nontraditional students. Part-time students, then, have been a mixed blessing through the 1980s and 1990s, with higher (but shorter) enrollments and increased (but quickly recycled) revenue.

Thanks in part to nontraditional students, the last half of the 20th century was a period of unprecedented growth for small independent colleges. Many of them have modified their admissions, registration, counseling, and payment process to efficiently accommodate part-time students, and, with the earlier help of baby boomers and more recent federal aid, they have survived.

Summary

The proliferation of independent colleges and universities in America has differed from English and European models in which large public institutions have been the norm until recently. The colonial period in this country set the stage for smaller private institutions. Run by trustees under authority granted by the state, these colleges received some tax support, but in the main were expected to survive on their own perspicacity. The diverse character of independent colleges and universities began in America because people with entrepreneurial vision had the opportunity to open them. Persisting to the present day with a sectarian flair for scriptural truth and a mission to provide young people with access to higher education, independent institutions have indeed followed the biblical command "multiply and prosper."

The postrevolutionary era began a shift in both the structure and mission of higher education, with state challenges to trustees' power and a general dissatisfaction with classical coursework. Independent colleges predominated until the appearance of land-grant colleges in the late 19th century. Presidential fund raising increased during the post–Civil War period, as college leaders tapped the new industrial wealth for support. While enrollments grew, college-educated individuals continued to represent a small portion of educated Americans. Wealth and power were still possible through hard work, unschooled intelligence, luck, and in some instances a ruthless streak. A college education remained a preserve of the rich until World War I, when professional degrees began to take on importance and education became a major player in the national economy.

Due to increasing enrollments in the 19th century, faculty powers had grown at first, then disseminated through various new administrative departments. Despite the growth, however, most colleges remained small, enrolling on average 243 students per institution in 1900. Between the World Wars, with the significant shift in academic mission from classical to professional, enrollments rose. By 1920, the average enrollment in independent colleges had grown to 543 students. Degrees took on new meaning, with independent colleges offering practical social and business skills, and by 1950, the average enrollment grew to over 1,000 students per institution.

Surviving through the baby boom and the enrollment let-down following it, the small independent college still exists, yet its financial condition remains tenuous. Of the 1,539 independent colleges in 1997, the average enrollment at 516 of them was 152 students. In 1998, 17 percent of the private sector enrolled fewer than 243 students, and 31 percent of them enrolled fewer than 543 students. Like their 19th-century predecessors, the modern small college lives today in penury, barely able to survive and lagging behind technological and academic advances—certainly still struggling to support the demands of students for posh living conditions.

While some independent colleges may rue their sensitivity to market demands, they have produced colleges able to respond to the marketplace with an agility not always evident in public universities and large independent colleges and universities. Small independent colleges have enlivened American higher education because they have responded to educational needs outside the mainstream of higher education. The medium through which diversity has flourished, small independent colleges have served students, beliefs, and aspirations that larger, more conventional colleges have ignored.

Robert Birnbaum contends that the diversity of American higher education in general differentiates it from the educational systems of other countries because that diversity has been essential to meeting societal needs.[25] Providing educational choice and access to all populations of students, and operating out of a freedom to promulgate missions of their choosing, American institutions offer a diverse experience unmatched abroad.[26] It is this gift of diversity that independent institutions have bestowed on America—a gift now threatened by the inherent financial weakness of a portion of the sector and the impact of market forces upon it.

Notes

1. "English and Scottish Education. Universities and Public Schools to the Time of Colet." (1907–21), *Cambridge History of English and American Literature*, vol. II, pp. 37–38.
2. E. D. Duryea, "Evolution of University Organization," in *Organization and Governance in Higher Education*, ed. Michael Peterson (Needham Heights, Mass.: Ginn Press, 1991), pp. 3–16; "English and Scottish Education," pp. 37–38.
3. Christopher Jencks and David Riesman, *The Academic Revolution* (Garden City, N.Y.: Anchor Books, 1969), p. 90.
4. Ibid., p. 257.
5. Ibid.

6. Ibid.

7. Frederick Rudolph, *The American College and University* (New York: Random House Vintage Books, 1962), p. 9.

8. Ibid., p. 12.

9. Jencks and Riesman, *The Academic Revolution,* p. 91.

10. Ibid.

11. Rudolph, *The American College and University,* p. 47.

12. Ibid., p. 208.

13. Ibid., p. 199.

14. Ibid.

15. Ibid.

16. Jencks and Riesman, *The Academic Revolution,* p. 259.

17. Ibid., pp. 260–61.

18. Rudolph, *The American College and University,* p. 434.

19. Jencks and Riesman, *The Academic Revolution,* p. 186.

20. Ibid., p. 94.

21. Ibid.

22. Ibid.

23. "Table 175: Total Full-Time Enrollment in Institutions of Higher Education and Degree-Granting Institutions by Attendance Status, Sex of Students, and Control of Institutions 1947 to 1997" (Washington, D.C.: U.S. Department of Education, National Center for Education Statistics, June 1999).

24. "Table 248: Institutions of Higher Education that Had Closed Their Doors by Control and Type, 1960–61 to 1997–98" (Washington, D.C.: U.S. Department of Education, National Center for Education Statistics, November 1999).

25. Robert Birnbaum, "Value of Different Kinds of Colleges," in *Foundations of American Higher Education*, ed. James L. Bess (Needham Heights, Mass.: Ginn Press, 1991), p. 111.

26. Ibid.

Challenges Facing Small Colleges

As evidence mounts that small colleges face unprecedented threats to their financial viability, fear of chronic financial distress grows. At the beginning of the 21st century, the state of the economy represented the most immediate threat to small colleges. Moody's Investor Service predicts that small colleges with moderate-sized investment portfolios could fall victim to the prolonged weakness in the economy that began in 2000.[1]

John Nelson, Moody's senior vice president, believes that small colleges with less than $20 million in revenue will be under the greatest pressure.[2] Gordon Winston, a Williams College economist, suggests that if these colleges do not have large endowment funds, they will barely survive a prolonged period of economic stagnation.[3] "Many schools are only three bad enrollment years away from bankruptcy," according to the president of a small college in the Philadelphia region. There are even rumblings that the private sector could find itself in a merger frenzy similar to that which swept community colleges and airlines in the last decade.[4]

These dire predictions come on the heels of one of the greatest periods of wealth building in the history of higher education. Gift revenue spurred by the bull market of the 1990s jumped 46 percent between 1991 and 1996, and endowment income grew by a spectacular 180 percent. Tuition and fees also turned in a strong collective performance, growing by 42 percent.[5] If the private sector enjoyed a golden age in the 1990s, why are some financial analysts and economists warning that all is not well today?

While the stock market and tuition increases made some institutions very wealthy, not all independent institutions benefited equally. For example, a study by KPMG and Prager, McCarthy, and Sealy of 41 institutions in the Philadelphia area during the period 1996–99 revealed that 22 percent were in deep financial distress during a time when the economy was most robust.[6] Survey data suggest that financial weakness was not isolated to the Philadelphia region. Thirty-three percent of independent colleges reported deficits for three of the five years between

1992 and 1996.[7] A report on higher education from Williams University confirms the suspicion that not all colleges prospered in the 1990s. Many independent colleges, unable to set aside funds to bolster reserves, remain vulnerable to economic shock.[8]

As the current stock market wipes out any gains of the late 1990s, the number of small colleges with strong reliance on tuition may be growing. If these conditions prevail, these institutions will discover that the assumptions underlying their financial structure and budgets are obsolete. They may have to reach deeper into the student's pocket to compensate for diminishing gifts and endowments, especially since the catastrophic events of September 11, 2001. Many small colleges that had tucked away savings or a reliable donor base to cushion effects of economic uncertainty may have discovered that their cushions have disappeared. A market crash of this magnitude wipes out the excess capital gains that many donors use as gifts to independent institutions. In addition, these donors may need to retain a larger proportion of their returns to supplement their own incomes or cover personal debt.

Even colleges with reliable endowment and gift income may find themselves hammered in the relentless bear market of the new century. "The market in 2001 is brutal," says William M. Rose, treasurer of Case Western Reserve University, where the endowment dropped about $115 million in value during 2001.[9] Beginning in September 2000, Standard & Poor's 500 index fell 25 percent by spring 2001. The NASDAQ index took a breathtaking 60.8 percent dive from its high.[10] "Gift income has dwindled, too. The year 2000 saw the smallest increase in gift giving since the recessionary 1970s, and market stress in 2001 caused donors to hold back amounts already pledged to small colleges.[11]

At an annual growth rate of 10 percent, it will take nearly 10 years for the NASDAQ to rebound to its highest price. According to Michael McPherson and Morton Schapiro, even investments indexed to the S&P 500 could lose some of their capacity to fund tuition discounts.[12] Investor analyst Barton Biggs of Morgan Stanley Dean Witter says: "Many institutional programs are going to have to recognize declines in their overall portfolios that are so large that some combination of return assumptions, contribution levels, and payouts will have to be revised downwards.[13] Portfolios that have 80–90 percent of their investments in equities and private venture capital, he believes, could see a substantial erosion of value. In other words, the little guy won't be the only one hurt by the stock market. Even big players who made large bets in the venture capital market could be hurt.

More than likely, however, the heaviest blows will strike small institutions with modest endowments. Sidney Evans Jr., vice president for business and finance at

Dillard University—where the endowment dropped from $53.3 to $51.8 million in January 2001—explains the predicament: "If Harvard loses 10 percent, its endowment is still the largest ever. If I lose 10 percent, that is $200,000 that can't go in my budget."[14] The loss of endowment income will hurt those institutions that relied on this income to fund their tuition discounts. This means that some portion of the tuition discounts will go unfunded or the discount will be reduced. Lost endowment revenue and a concomitant reduction in discounting capacity could put heavy pressure on the balance sheets of independent colleges that are heavily dependent on tuition.[15]

A weak economy and a declining stock market are only the beginning. The elimination of the estate tax—long an incentive for the wealthy to create foundations or give large portions of their estates to charity—creates more uncertainty. Although estate bequests only account for 5–6 percent of gifts, according to Sheldon Steinbach of the American Council of Education, any disincentive challenges fund-raising efforts.[16]

Other problems that began during the last decade continue to jeopardize the financial viability of small colleges, including moribund enrollment, spiking tuition, uncontrollable expenses, the high cost of technology, and tough competition.

Enrollment and Tuition

Enrollment growth from the late 1980s through the late 1990s indicates the instability of many independent institutions. While total enrollment grew only 1 percent annually throughout this period, IPEDS data show that 38 percent of independent colleges saw lower enrollment from 1988 to 1997; nearly 10 percent saw enrollment shrink more than 5 percent.[17] For small colleges living on the edge of financial disaster, a shrinking enrollment base is discouraging for the college and its benefactors. Thirty-five percent of small colleges depend on student enrollment to generate more than 60 percent of their revenue.[18] Twelve percent are practically commercial enterprises; they rely on student enrollment for more than 85 percent of their revenue.[19] If financial reserves dwindle, the relationship among tuition, expenses, and student ability to pay becomes crucial to these colleges' standing in a competitive higher education marketplace as well as to the future viability of their financial structure.

Maintaining that financial structure is difficult. Table 3.1 quantifies what the private sector has done to match revenue to expenses, showing the relationship of such efforts to the Consumer Price Index. The rate of growth for current revenue exceeded expenses for only the first five-year period, 1981–86. For the two remaining five-year periods, the rate of revenue growth fell behind the growth in expenses. In other words, independent colleges were beginning to lose some of the surplus revenue they needed to support expenses. The contribution of tuition and fees to total revenue expanded from 37.4 percent to 40.6 percent of revenue. In contrast, nontuition revenue's contribution to total revenue shrunk from 62.9 percent to 59.4 percent of revenue. The change in revenue shares put tremendous pressure on tuition and fees to keep pace with expenses, a challenge quantified in the ratio of expenses to inflation for the three five-year periods: 2.8, 2.3, and 2.3, respectively.

Table 3.1
Comparison of Rates of Growth, 1981–96

	Tuition and Fees Revenue	Tuition Share	Students	Nontuition Revenue	Nontuition Share	Current Revenue	Current Expenses	CPI
1981–86	65.9%	37.4%	2.4%	53.3%	62.9%	57.7%	57.4%	20.6%
1986–91	60.8%	38.7%	9.35%	49.9%	61.2%	54.7%	56.3%	24.3%
1991–96	41.8%	40.6%	5.3%	30.0%	59.4%	33.6%	35.2%	15.2%

Source: Digest of Education Statistics (Washington, D.C.: U. S. Department of Education, National Center for Education Statistics, 1999), tables 175, 334, 347, and 352; "Consumer Price Index: All Urban Consumers Services," Series CUSR0000SAS, 2001, 146.142.4.24/servlet/SurveyOutputServlet?/.

Tuition and fees clearly were the major impetus for revenue growth in each five-year period, outpacing nontuition revenue by 12.6 percent, 10.9 percent, and 11.7 percent, respectively. The rate of change in expenses was just too great, and nontuition sources and enrollment growth was too small. The push of tuition past inflation and personal income was inevitable. Table 3.2 shows the ratio of tuition to the CPI—3.2, 1.8, and 2.2—and the ratio of tuition to disposable income— 1.7, 1.4, and 1.6. Even during periods of relatively low inflation and a strong economy, tuition continues to have a major impact on families.

These ratios serve as rough quantifications of press and government complaints that independent colleges gouge students and parents. Tuition rates do relate to other revenue sources and to expenses. Other revenue sources grew more slowly between 1981 and 1996, and their share of total revenue declined relative to tuition.

Table 3.2
Comparison of Rates of Growth, Tuition Charges
to CPI and Tuition Charges to Disposable Income

	Tuition	CPI	Disposable Income	Tuition to CPI Ratio	Tuition to Disposable Income Ratio
1981–86	64.9%	20.6%	38.7%	3.2	1.7
1986–91	43.4%	24.3%	30.7%	1.8	1.4
1991–96	35.1%	15.2%	20.8%	2.2	1.6

Source: "Consumer Price Index: All Urban Consumers Services," Series CUSR0000SAS, 2001, 146.142.4.24/servlet/SurveyOutputServlet?/; "Personal Income and Its Disposition," Table 2.9M (Washington, D.C.: Bureau of Economic Statistics, 2001), bea.doc.gov/.

For revenue to match the inexorable increases in expenses, tuition would have had to increase faster than inflation so as to offset other revenue and keep revenue in stride with expenses. The tuition-pricing equation is simple: change in tuition is a result of balancing changes in enrollment, other revenue, and expenses. In most cases, when any of the three variables changes, price (or tuition) changes.

Sticker Price vs. Net Price

Tuition at independent colleges underwent a disturbing rate of change between 1982 and 1996 (tables 3.3, 3.4 next page). The net price—the posted charge net of restricted or unrestricted financial aid—leveled off, indicating larger discounts to the sticker price—the posted charge for tuition, fees, room, and board. The average sticker price moved in a positive, nearly linear direction over 14 years, a commentary on the general public's impression that tuition charges keep going up.

During the same 14-year period, the sticker price of an education at independent institutions steadily emptied bill payers' wallets (table 3.4). In 1982, the sticker price left the bill payer with 43 percent of his disposable income. By 1996, a typical bill payer considering an average independent college or university discovered that the sticker price would leave him with only 18 percent of his disposable income. In other words, those unfortunates who paid the sticker price

Table 3.3
Sticker Price vs. Net Price, 1982–1993

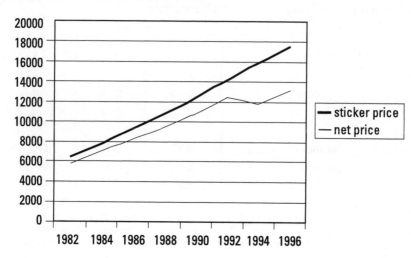

Table 3.4
Disposable Income Remaining after Sticker or Net Price

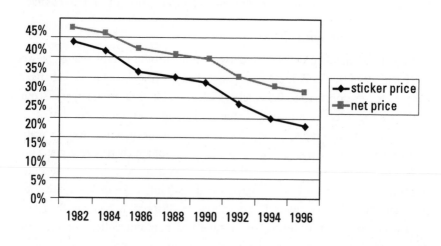

in 1996 were poorer afterward than those who paid the sticker price in 1981. The sticker price trend line is sharply negative, leaving the impression that at some point in the near future, an education at a independent college will absorb every last penny of the bill payer's disposable income.

Parents are indeed feeling the financial pinch of college tuition after the market crash of 2001, and especially after the terrorist attacks of September 11, 2001. Despite higher tuition discounts, parents will pause if not panic at the thought of a high sticker price combined with room, board, and supplies charges. Many parents have begun turning away from pricier independent institutions toward better bargains at public institutions.[20] Whether or not this trend continues, it is an ominous sign for independent institutions that they may have to compete with public universities with comparable academic reputations and lower sticker prices.

Despite the headlines' focus on "sticker shock," most people do not pay the posted price at independent colleges. The sticker price assumes that parents or students pay tuition from current income without financial aid or that they offset tuition charges with employer reimbursements or subsidized loans. Between 1988 and 1996, the proportion of disposable income remaining after deducting the sticker price fell 21 percent (table 3.4). During the same period, the proportion of disposable income remaining after net price fell 15 percent. However, parents and students have no financial aid information when beginning the college search. The sticker price is what narrows the education consumer's list of affordable colleges.

Independent institutions face an expensive credibility problem resulting from the gap between sticker price and net price. High sticker prices lead prospective bill payers to believe that colleges are growing richer from tuition, when in fact they are merely covering their losses. The higher sticker price signals higher quality to the purchaser, who then demands more, and more expensive, services. Instructional quality is not easily measured, but better dorms, workout gyms, brick walkways, and technology offer tangible signs of quality. Matching service value with price value forces colleges into a very expensive corner.[21]

Independent institutions also face the very real cost of net price. Those offering large unfunded discounts (the institution loses the cash represented by unfunded aid) are finding their revenue dwarfed by their expenses. These financially fragile institutions are most vulnerable to changes in competition, demographics, economic difficulty, and other factors that disrupt the influx of funds. So, while parents, students, and the media worry about increasing sticker prices, independent colleges watch with trepidation the rising discount on tuition.

Between 1990 and 1996, net price followed the same upward trend as sticker price. The bad news for many colleges is that the tuition discount (sticker price minus net price) increased an astronomical 255 percent during that period, from 9.8 percent to 25.20 percent of the sticker price.[22] This shift added to the financial pressure on independent colleges because the higher sticker prices are not yielding commensurate increases in net tuition revenue. Upper-tier colleges may have opted to increase their discounts substantially with negligible effect on their bottom lines. Small colleges, which lack the endowment resources of larger and wealthier colleges, have found that the tuition discounts essentially forced upon them by the market have taken an ever-increasing chunk of their net cash from tuition.

Fewer than 20 percent of full-time students pay the sticker price at independent colleges and universities (table 3.5). Some 65 percent to 95 percent of freshmen receive some form of financial aid.[23] Colleges typically do not award grants or subsidized loans to students whose attendance status falls below a government minimum or who earn more than is allowable under government standards. Part-time students—despite being the faster-growing segment of the college population—are less likely to receive aid than full-time students.

Table 3.5

Percentage of Students at Independent Institutions of Higher Education Receiving Financial Aid during the 1995–1996 Academic Year

	Grants	Loans	All Aid
Full-time students	71.9%	57.2%	80.4%
Part-time students	47.1%	28.9%	59.7%

Source: "Percentage of Undergraduates Receiving Loans, Grants, and Work Study by Type and Sector of Institution and Attendance Status: 1995-96," exhibit 1-6 in *Straight Talk about College Costs and Prices: Report of the National Commission on the Cost of Higher Education* (Phoenix, Ariz.: Oryx Press, 1998), p. 141.

Full-timer or part-timer, shopping for an education is a daunting task for the buyer—and the seller. After recovering from the shock of the sticker price, the consumer musters the determination to find a better deal. Despite the many available sources of information on independent colleges—from friends to books to the Internet—no single source can guarantee a final price. Consumers, misinformed by the press, prepare for price gouging, and when the search is over, they wonder if they really got the best deal. Colleges at the low end of the market may accept price negotiating as a normal way of doing business. These are the colleges that scramble through the summer and even early into the fall semester trying to fill their classrooms. They are also the colleges forced by price competition to give incoming freshmen the largest discounts (43 percent in 2001).[24] More selective independent colleges and universities, on the other hand, must find selling education a distasteful process. Price negotiations can quickly turn into the negotiation of academic standards, with colleges ending up feeling like used-car dealers rather than elite purveyors of a quality service.[25] Through pricing, discounting, and negotiating the cost of services, independent colleges and universities realize their place in a difficult marketplace.

Expenses

So far, we have considered how revenue flows and how tuition affects financial stability at independent institutions. Now we turn to expenses—how they are shaped and how they absorb revenue. Expenditures encompass the cost of producing the service a college offers to the market. They also determine the level to which tuition and other revenue sources must be matched in order to maintain financial stability.

Keeping pace with expenses has been a monumental challenge over the 11 years from 1985 to 1996 (table 3.6). In each year, regardless of the general pressure on prices, expenses have grown consistently faster than the rate of inflation. Even in 1996, when expenses only grew 4.49 percent, they were still 52.05 percent greater than the CPI. For half of the 11-year period, expenses rose at more than twice the CPI. With such an inordinate increase, expenses create tremendous pressure on prices and on the financial stability of an institution during times of financial and economic stress. From a labor-intensive service industry, to decision dynamics, to dilution of institutional goals, to preference for new products, several propositions have been advanced to answer the question: Why are colleges unable to rein in the cost of delivering their services?

The cost structures of service industries like higher education are governed primarily by labor costs. Labor—college instructors and researchers—characterizes production of services. Certain rules constrain the productive capacity of the labor cost structure. For example, the cost of teaching students is constrained by faculty-student ratio, instructional programs and policies, classroom size, distribution of classrooms by discipline, and mix of full-time and part-time faculty. Once an

Table 3.6
Comparison of Rates of Growth to Current Expenses and CPI,
Independent Colleges and Universities, 1985–1996

	Expenses	CPI	Expenses/CPI
1985	10.0%	3.9%	153.92
1986	9.9%	2.9%	222.49
1987	14.1%	2.2%	539.77
1988	6.6%	4.1%	61.83
1989	9.0%	4.7%	91.17
1990	8.8%	4.8%	70.81
1991	9.0%	5.4%	65.72
1992	8.3%	3.2%	159.32
1993	5.8%	3.1%	88.51
1994	6.2%	2.5%	147.98
1995	6.3%	3.0%	108.43
1996	4.5%	3.0%	52.05

Source: Digest of Education Statistics (Washington, D.C.: U. S. Department of Education, National Center for Education Statistics, 1999), table 352; "Consumer Price Index: All Urban Consumers Services," Series CUSR0000SAS, 2001, 146.142.4.24/servlet/SurveyOutputServlet?/.

institution sets the parameters, momentum and the high financial and political cost of change act to adjust them over time. As a result, colleges, like all labor-intensive industries, are unable to easily "substitute other inputs for labor in the face of the rising relative cost of their labor inputs."[26]

Labor's impact on independent colleges and universities is apparent in the proportion of total expenses devoted to compensation. In 1998–99, 56 percent of total expenses were devoted to wages and benefits.[27] This figure corresponds with earlier findings in 1974–75 that 58 percent of total expenses went to compensation. When viewed in terms of current expenses, total compensation (which typically encompasses the institution's operational costs) accounts for 73 percent of current expenses.[28]

Labor costs are problematic in higher education, where labor decisions are often made by those whose interests are not necessarily served by limiting the cost of labor. Academic excellence, prestige, and self-interest may influence a decision about expenditures because independent nonprofit institutions are not disciplined by profit motives to control costs. William Massy and Robert Zemsky posit that baseline cost decisions can be explained by a process they call the "academic ratchet and administrative lattice."[29]

The academic ratchet refers to a tendency to steer faculty work away from traditional instructional and institutional goals and toward the "specialized concerns of faculty research, publication, professional service, and personal pursuits."[30] Institutions have reassigned services like academic advisement from faculty to specialized counselors—a faculty-supported reassignment, fueled by the desire to pursue more appealing work. Massy suggests that as faculty gains are made, research time traded from instruction, specialization within the curriculum, and maintenance of departmental norms become the "new baseline" for departmental operations.[31]

The administrative lattice—akin to empire building of days past—describes the expansion of administrative responsibilities and positions within colleges. Transfer of responsibility for academic counseling from the faculty to administrators, for example, resulted in a 60 percent expansion of staff positions between 1975 and 1985.[32] Expert managers beget expert managers along with support services to execute their decisions. Other examples abound in marketing, admissions, institutional planning, finance, and academic administration as administrators expand the lattice of their responsibilities and staff to serve their institutional and self-interests. In addition, consensus, once reserved for the faculty, has spread to administrative units, a transfer that has had less-than-salutary effects on cost.[33] Consensus makes decisions cumbersome, contentious, and time-consuming. When one decision is reached, a forward momentum generates other costly decisions that cannot be reversed because so many parts of the institution have affirmed them. Moreover, consensus obscures responsibility and enhances aversion to change because the parties to the decision often have a vested interest in the status quo.

Another way to view the phenomenon of the lattice and the ratchet is through the lens of economics. Oliver Williams suggests that in the absence of measurable goals, opportunistic self-interest will govern decision making.[34] As decision making seeps to experts and specialized cadres, institutions lose the ability to establish goals without the review and approval of those experts. The experts gain power, independence, and the opportunity to exploit decisions to their advantage. When colleges and universities create a productive capacity based on the unmonitored self-interest and opportunism of faculty, costs necessarily rise because decisions stem not from institutional goals but from personal ones.

The lattice and ratchet phenomenon speaks to the challenge of institutions of higher education to monitor their internal activities. For example, categorizing the internal costs of producing services is a useful way to monitor and justify allocation decisions. But what if the functional accounting system used to report expenses blends the categories? Allocation decisions will remain obscure at best, and the blending of instructional and research salaries makes it nearly impossible to distinguish the actual costs of instruction from those of research. Another example is the administrative resistance to carefully assigning enrollments, classes, and expenses to specific departments, which makes it difficult to determine actual expenses from one department to the next. Finally, consider the administrative failure to match costs and revenue, making the true financial benefit of research virtually indiscernible.

When we rank-order growth and consider relative changes in the allocation of expenses for the major functions, we see what institutions did to deliver services and remain competitive between 1981 and 1996 (table 3.7). Financial aid expenses grew 363.4 percent, increasing from 6.6 percent to 11.4 percent of total expenses. Academic/student expenses grew 168.4 percent, increasing from 10.1 percent to 11.4 percent of total expenses. Instruction expenses grew 125.6 percent with no significant change in the percentage of total expenses. Institutional support, research, and noncore services grew, but their respective allocation shares decreased.

The big winners in terms of increased share of expenses were financial aid and academic/student services. In 1981, academic/student services were clearly considered more important than financial aid. At that time, colleges devoted the least amount to financial aid, but by 1996, financial aid services ranked fourth in total expense share, making financial aid services equal in importance to academic/student services. Instruction's share of expenses was unchanged. The losers over the 15-year period were institutional services, research, and noncore services. CPI ratios confirm that independent institutions believed it was important to bolster financial aid, the allotment of which grew at five times the CPI. The academic/student services allotment also outpaced the CPI. Instructional expenses matched inflation, while noncore services barely kept up.

From 1981 to 1996, independent institutions redirected resources in order to attract and retain students through improved student and academic services. They maintained instructional expenses but cut resources dedicated to noncore activities. One could insist that independent colleges are not mere pawns in the economy, reacting to their status as labor-intensive service providers and unable to adjust inputs to improve efficiency. But the data in table 3.7 imply that colleges knowingly reallocated funds, pumping substantial resources into areas they believed would enhance their product, advance their market image, and enlarge their consumer pool—in fact reacting to market demand.

Table 3.7
**Allocation of Expenses, Distribution of Revenue across
Expenses, and Growth of Current Expenses, 1981–96**

	Instruction	Research	Academic /Student[a]	Financial Aid	Institutional Support[b]	Noncore Activities[c]	Total Expenses
1981 Expenses							
Expenses (in thousands)	5,883	1,844	2,202	1,440	4,192	6,211	21,773
Expense Share	27.0%	8.5%	10.1%	6.6%	19.3%	28.5%	100.0%
1996 Expenses							
Expenses (in thousands)	19,157	5,442	8,113	8,110	12,852	17,278	70,951
Expense Share	27.0%	7.7%	11.4%	11.4%	18.1%	24.4%	100.0%
1981–96 Increments							
Expenses	13,273	3,597	5,911	6,670	8,659	11,067	49,178
Expense Share	26.9%	7.3%	12.0%	13.6%	17.6%	22.5%	100.0%
Revenue share	26.4%	7.1%	11.8%	13.3%	17.3%	22.0%	97.9%
Growth	125.6%	95.0%	168.4%	363.4%	106.6%	78.2%	125.9%
CPI ratio[d]	1.73	1.31	2.32	5.00	1.47	1.08	1.73

(a) Expenses for academic support and student services

(b) Expenses for institutional services plus plant

(c) Auxiliary, hospital, independent, and public services

(d) Rate of growth/CPI; CPI, 72.61% for the period

Source: *Digest of Education Statistics* (Washington, D.C.: U. S. Department of Education, National Center for Education Statistics, 1999), tables 334 and 347.

Technology

The investment of independent institutions in technology between 1957 and 1993 had a critical impact on their financial structure. Until the 1980s, higher education was reputed to be a labor-intensive industry. In 1980, independent colleges and universities began making substantial investments in technology, forming an expansive fissure between equipment purchases and buildings purchases. At the beginning of the period, the equipment to buildings investment ratio was 1.3 to 1. By 1993, it had exploded to 8 to 1.[35] As William Massy points out, colleges are shifting from labor-intensive to capital-intensive institutions; the current combination of labor and capital intensity is the worst of all possible scenarios.[36]

Labor intensity—given ineffective substitutes for the handicraft method of delivering instructional, research, and community services—results in a production function that cannot keep pace with production improvements in the broader economy, which in turn leads to a cost structure that outruns the rate of inflation. As higher education becomes more capital intensive owing to technology investments, Massy contends, colleges will see no short-term or medium-term productivity improvements because they are not prepared to make "paradigm shifts" in the way they deliver services.[37]

Table 3.8
Comparison Cost of Equipment/Student vs. Building/Student, 1975–1993

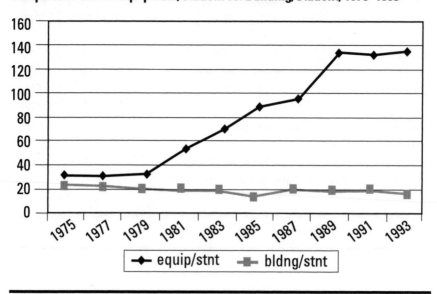

Furthermore, technology is not just a capital investment. With technology comes a large repair and replacement component. For example, colleges felt internal and external pressure to ensure that Y2K problems would not destabilize operations. They invested heavily in their repair and replacement components, significantly expanding the institutional services expense share (table 3.6) and pushing expenditures on equipment to a new level (table 3.8).

Competition

Pricing information, application services, aggressive marketing campaigns, and savvy parents and students have changed the independent education marketplace dramatically. Students no longer pay tuition; they are consumers of education. Given the general environment of consumerism, students want colleges to win them over. They want price discounts, flexible academic standards, and a broad range of extras, such as fitness centers, dorms wired for the highest level of technology, refrigerators, microwaves, and televisions, to name a few. They want satisfaction guarantees if the services are not up to par.[38] All this comes with a cost, which independent colleges often do not have the scale economies to accommodate. They still operate within the traditional model of a stand-alone institution anchored to a piece of real estate.

Enter the competition. While high-end sellers enjoy the excess demand for their programs and perks, the middle and low tiers of the market are finding competition sharp. High-tier colleges have students fighting to get in their doors, while middle-tier colleges are fighting over the best candidates. As a result, prospective students approach them with considerable market power. The National Center for Postsecondary Improvement suggests that these colleges are in the unenviable position of attracting both strong and mediocre students.[39] Their competitive potential may depend on the size of their endowments and the strength of their donor networks. If gifts or endowments are weak, these institutions may be unable to offer the hooks they need to snag their preferred students. The lower tier, or convenience colleges, survive on wit and nimbleness.[40] To these colleges, tuition discounting is negligible. According to Massy, they compete primarily through price and marginal cost.[41] They survive by building market share, which means either finding untapped markets—a rare occurrence—or luring students away from their competitors. These colleges survive from one registration period to the next.

There is some evidence that a new player in the market for independent education may be changing the rules within the lowest tier of the student market. For-profit colleges target continuing-education, nontraditional, and working students who have collectively been the cash cow of not-for-profit colleges. The dream of for-profit colleges like the University of Phoenix, DeVry Institute, Strayer Education, Quest, Corinthian, Career Education, and Argosy Education is to combine a credible, accredited brand name with a national reputation. They undermine the basic assumption within the convenience market that small colleges can offer a credible product to students locally without expending money on a brand name. In contrast, a not-for-profit college is probably unknown outside its geographic market area; the competition among these colleges might be hard-nosed, but their reputations were established locally and are valued locally. To the dismay of local colleges, students will likely respond favorably to the renowned status of the for-profit entities.

Robert Ruch describes the strategies for-profit colleges will use to attack the convenience market: a customer-service orientation, career-oriented curricula, a flexible academic calendar, reasonable prices, a tightly controlled cost structure, and rapid responses to changes in the market.[42] Though for-profits currently have a small market share, they appear to have the strategy, drive, and resources to upset at least a segment of the college market. In 1999, the number of bachelor's degrees in business at these colleges jumped 180 percent.[43] Even so, for-profit enrollments constitute a minor slice of the market. Their impact won't be appreciated for some time.

Internet colleges may begin to draw the part-time segment of the student market away from small colleges. Some are new for-profit ventures, and others are well-known independent universities with established reputations. They attract students who struggle to balance work and education or who need certification or ongoing job training. Online universities may free some students from the strictures of curricula and graduation requirements as they pick and choose among online courses offered by various institutions and combine them with traditional credits. A "degree-granting board" will be the only missing ingredient in the designer degree recipe.[44]

If students do take control of their educations by custom-designing personal degrees, the impact on fixed costs of higher education could be dramatic. Colleges would find it impractical to support courses, programs, requirements, or faculty that were not cost-effective. Some traditional colleges might turn into shells similar to World Wide Web sites that exist to construct designer degrees or certification programs. It is too soon to tell how online options might affect higher education, especially since many of the sites went down with the stock market.

Debt

Colleges have always been labor intensive, but they are becoming even more so as they attempt to meet rising student demand for modernized programs and personal services. Students want the most current technology in their classrooms and dormitories. They won't tolerate low-speed Internet connections, group showers, or inadequate electrical service. They want to cocoon themselves from daily pressures by playing the latest skateboard game on their computers in climate-controlled dormitories. Students want this home-away-from-home to include the same amenities parents made available before college: personal trainers, around-the-clock facilities, game rooms, and feedings on demand.

In many ways, student demand has contributed to a devaluing of the entire college experience. "Going away to college" used to be an initiation of sorts, a time in a young adult's life for beliefs and prejudices to be challenged by fellow scholars and for rewards to come in the form of intellectual esteem and respectable grades—not privacy, air conditioning, and high-speed Internet connections.

From six weeks at boot camp to a day at the spa, the feel of college has changed in response to student demand, and the public bond market reflects just that. In the early 1990s, colleges used most bond issues to refinance older bonds in order to take advantage of lower interest rates. By the mid-1990s, during a period of modest enrollment growth, colleges were putting 64 percent of tax-exempt bonds toward buildings and other capital projects to maintain their market positions. Having taken full advantage of the removal of caps on tax debt, colleges and universities now carry more than $100 billion in bond debt. In 2000, institutions of higher education added more than $15.5 billion in bond debt to their balance sheets. Public institutions can turn to legislatures to fund their capital projects, while independent colleges and universities hold most of this new debt.[45]

Only a fraction of *small* independent colleges hold public debt, however, for they are tuition-dependent. Without sufficient gift or endowment revenue to fund debt service, they must depend on revenue growth to cover debt payments. And revenue growth is a risky bet for small colleges; any downturn in enrollment threatens their financial stability. Further complicating the assumption of debt is the local bank, which tends to tolerate short-term financial instability but which will mercilessly call in debt during economic contraction. Many struggling colleges discovered that a few late payments can knock the charitable wind right out of the friendly neighborhood bank.

Small colleges that have substantial gift and endowment revenue—and even some supposedly rich colleges—may find themselves in "debt trouble," too, following a sharp downturn in the stock market or during a prolonged period of economic stagnation. Donors can become downright stingy, and endowments will cast off fewer dollars to cover debt. How the bursting of this century's economic bubble plays out in terms of debt management should be interesting. It would not be unreasonable to assume that small colleges with weak balance sheets will be hard-pressed to employ debt as a competitive tool, let alone make their debt payments on time.

According to Moody's senior vice president John Nelson, small colleges have no choice but to invest in themselves because their competitors are doing the same thing.[46] Colleges that persist with old wiring and group showers "can kiss off ten years from now. They aren't going to make it that long."[47] But while debt can provide leverage for change, it also carries large risks. Most small colleges fail because they cannot cover debt payments during times of financial crisis (see chapter 7).

Summary

Many institutions have coped successfully with the unprecedented challenges discussed in this chapter:

- declining endowment valuations
- shrinking individual gifts
- costs that outrun inflation
- tuition that absorbs a larger and larger proportion of bill payers' disposable income
- shrinking nontuition revenue and more pressure to match expenses with tuition
- the demand for sizeable tuition discounts to attract students
- the high cost of new technology
- new competition from brand name for-profits and Internet colleges

Through wit, good fortune, and Byzantine accounting systems, small independent colleges survived through the 1990s and projected a financial front capable of withstanding most forms of shock. But whether these institutions have the financial wherewithal to sustain themselves in the long run—especially as they meet the challenges of this century's roughening economic tide—is a matter of some debate.

Notes

1. Kit Lively, "For Private Colleges Without Large Endowments, Bearish Markets Bring Anxiety and Caution," *Chronicle of Higher Education*, April 20, 2001.
2. Quoted in Martin Van Der Werf, "More Colleges Are Seeing the Virtues of Merging," *Chronicle of Higher Education*, March 23, 2001, p. 4.
3. Quoted in ibid.
4. James O'Neil, "An Exacting Education in Economic Realities," *Philadelphia Inquirer*, January 28, 2001, pp. 1–7.
5. "Current Fund Revenue of Private Nonprofit Institutions of Higher Education by Source: 1980–81 to 1995–96," in *Digest of Education Statistics* (Washington, D.C.: U. S. Department of Education, National Center for Education Statistics, January 1999), table 334.
6. O'Neil, "An Exacting Education."
7. Sheet 0818020.wk1: Unrestricted and Restricted Fund Types: 1987–96, National Science Foundation WebCASPAR Database System, http://caspar/nsf.gov/, 2001.
8. John L. Pulley, "Researchers See a Widening Gap Between Rich and Poor Colleges," *Chronicle of Higher Education*, July 31, 2001.
9. Quoted in John L. Pulley and Anne-Marie Borrego, "Wealthiest Colleges Lost Billions in Endowment Value in Last Year," *Chronicle of Higher Education*, October 19, 2001, p. A24.
10. "S & P 500 Index: May 1999–May 2001"; "NASDAQ: May 1999–May 2001," *Commodity Systems, Inc.,* June 12, 2001, www.finance.yahoo.com.
11. Kit Lively, "Gifts to Education Hit Record $28 Billion in 2000, *Chronicle of Higher Education*, May 24, 2001, p. 1; Lively, "For Private Colleges Without Large Endowments, Bearish Markets Bring Anxiety and Caution."
12. Michael McPherson and Morton Owen Schapiro, "Preparing for Hard Times Shows Wisdom," *Chronicle of Higher Education*, April 20, 2001.
13. Barton M. Biggs, "Venture Debacle" *U. S. and the Americas Investment Perspectives* (Morgan Stanley Dean Witter), April 18, 2001, p. 5.
14. Quoted in Lively, "For Private Colleges Without Large Endowments," p. 5.
15. Ibid., p. 3.
16. Quoted in Sara Hebel, "Tax-Repeal Plan Could Cause Drop in Gifts," *Chronicle of Higher Education*, June 23, 2000, p. 2.
17. Sheet 10463025.wk1: Enrollment Level, 1988–97, National Science Foundation WebCASPAR Database System, http://caspar/nsf.gov/, 2001.
18. "Management Ratios FS 9899 Private Institutions Financial Statistics and Ratios" (Boulder, Colo.: John Minter Associates, Inc., 2001).
19. Ibid.
20. Elizabeth Bernstein and Sarah Collins, "Colleges for a New Era," *Wall Street Journal,* October 5, 2001, pp. W1, W10.

21. Lucie Lapovsky and Loren Loomis Hubbell, "An Uncertain Future," *Business Officer* 34, no. 8 (February 2001): 29.

22. *Digest of Education Statistics* (Washington, D.C.: U. S. Department of Education, National Center for Education Statistics, 1999), table 317.

23. Alan Reynolds, "The Real Cost of Higher Education, Who Should Pay It and How?" in *Straight Talk About College Costs and Prices: Report of the National Commission on the Cost of Higher Education* (Phoenix, Ariz.: Oryx Press, 1998), pp. 106–7.

24. Loren Loomis Hubbel and Lucie Lapovsky, "Tuition Discounting in Challenging Times," *Business Officer* 34, no. 8 (February 2002): p. 25.

25. David R. Riesman made this observation in *On Higher Education* (New Brunswick, N.J.: Transaction Publishers, 1998).

26. Malcolm Getz and John J. Siegfried, "Cost Inflation," in *Economic Challenges in Higher Education*, ed. Charles T. Clotfelter, Ronald G. Ehrenberg, Malcolm Getz, and John H. Siegfried (Chicago: University of Chicago Press, 1991), p. 265.

27. "Management Ratios FS 9899 Private Institutions Financial Statistics and Ratios."

28. Howard Bowen, "What Determines the Costs of Higher Education?" in *Finance in Higher Education,* ed. Larry L. Leslie and Richard E. Anderson (Needham Heights, Mass.: Ginn Press, 1990), p. 155.

29.   "Management Ratios FS 9899 Private Institutions Financial Statistics and Ratios."

30. Robert Zemsky, "The Lattice and the Ratchet," *Policy Perspectives* (Pew Higher Education Research Program) 2, no. 4 (June 1990): 1–8.

31. Ibid., p. 5.

32. William F. Massy "A New Look at the Academic Department," *Distillations* (Pew Higher Education Research Program)

33. Zemsky, "The Lattice and the Ratchet," p. 2.

34. Oliver E. Williamson, *Markets and Hierarchies* (New York: Free Press, 1975).

35. *Digest of Education Statistics* (Washington, D.C.: U. S. Department of Education, National Center for Education Statistics, 1998), table 359.

36. Massy, "Remarks on Restructuring Higher Education," p. 89.

37. Ibid.

38. David Riesman foresaw this trend in 1980 when he wrote about the rise of student consumerism and its implications for higher education. See Riesman, *On Higher Education.*

39. "In Search of Strategic Perspective: A Tool for Mapping the Market in Postsecondary Education," *Change,* November/December 1997, p. 26.

40. Ibid.

41. Massy, "Remarks on Restructuring Higher Education," p. 87.

42. Robert Ruch, *Higher Education, Inc.* (Baltimore, Md.: Johns Hopkins Press, 2001).

43. Katherine S. Mangan, "Business Enrollments Boom at For-Profit Colleges," *Chronicle of Higher Education,* October 10, 1999, p. 1.

44. John Seely Brown and Paul Duguid, "Universities in the Digital Age," in *The Mirage of Continuity* (Washington, D.C.: Council on Library and Information Resources and Association of American Universities, 1998), p. 59.

45. Martin Van Der Werf, "Colleges Turn to Debt to Finance Their Ambitions," *Chronicle of Higher Education*, March 19, 2001, p. 2.

46. Quoted in Martin Van Der Werf, "More Colleges Are Seeing the Virtues of Merging."

47. Van Der Werf, "Colleges Turn to Debt to Finance Their Ambitions," p. 3.

Economics of Small Colleges

Major benefactors distinguish the Harvards, Princetons, and Yales from the small independent colleges struggling to survive in their market. Indeed, it is great wealth that transformed many of today's prestigious independent institutions from their comparatively ragged financial beginnings. Though small colleges can be wealthy, their size, minimal government support, and dependence on students for revenue make them especially dependent upon the economics of the marketplace. They survive relative poverty not through the beneficence of a great benefactor, but through a steady flow of income from their students.

Small independent colleges operate in a very competitive environment where the effects of cost and price may profoundly impact their financial stability. If we intend to analyze their place in the market, their financial structure, and their financial distress, we must understand how these institutions operate as economic firms—a difficult task, because as Howard Bowen suggests, colleges do not participate in a "well functioning market."[1] Before we discuss an economic model of independent colleges, then, we must consider the circumstances that mitigate against a "well functioning" market. First, most college markets do not satisfy the conditions for perfect competition that underlie basic propositions about free markets. Second, externalities, or public benefits, distort the market decisions of students and colleges. Third, market imperfections prevent students and colleges from optimizing their economic decisions.

Market Conditions

The concept of the market begins with the assumption of perfect competition in which buyers and sellers enter the market with no impediments to their decisions. Under this assumption, their decisions yield a price that clears the market (all products offered on the market are purchased and there is no surplus or excess demand). Perfect competition in a market is governed by these conditions: product uniformity, small size and large numbers, resource mobility, and perfect knowledge.

- Product uniformity—Within a given marketplace, if the products offered to buyers are not uniform from firm to firm, then the firms are not competing on equal ground. For instance, the degrees offered by colleges vary in terms of major, coursework, and mode of instruction. These and other apparent differences may result in various market niches, each containing few competitors.

- Small size and large numbers—When many small firms exist in a market, there is no single firm large enough to dictate price. This condition also exists when several firms collude to set price. Within the private sector, there is evidence that the top segment has considerable influence over the price in its market. The Overlap Group, a collection of 23 prestigious independent institutions, collaborated in the awarding of financial aid to prospective students until 1991, when the U.S. Department of Justice claimed that such collaboration was in fact setting the market price for tuition in violation of antitrust laws. The Overlap Group reached an agreement with the Department of Justice to limit how they collaborate on admission or financial aid awards.[2]

- Resource mobility—A market can adapt to changes in demand and supply when there is the free movement of labor and firms. In the case of higher education, the free movement of faculty (labor) is constrained by tenure, which deters faculty members from seeking employment at another institution. The mobility of colleges themselves (firms) is constrained by accreditation, licensing requirements, and product indivisibility, all of which prevent colleges from entering different geographic markets.

- Perfect knowledge—This demanding condition assumes that both seller and buyer fully recognize all costs and consequences associated with their transaction. Students in the market to "buy a degree" often misunderstand the true costs and risks of their enrollment decisions, many simply not availing themselves of information about college prices and the future income of graduates.

Externalities

Externalities occur when the buyer (student) does not capture the full benefit of a product (college degree). A student loses part of the benefit of his or her degree and may consequently decide not to pursue it at a high cost, because the public receives a portion of its value. Externalities can include the following situations:

1. Graduates contribute to science through research and discovery. While the student may receive some immediate benefit through publication or some other form of recognition, scientific contributions, after some period of uncertainty, ultimately benefit society.

2. Fewer graduates than nongraduates participate in violent crime, and while the immediate benefit to the graduate is obvious, the benefit to society is also significant.

3. Graduates tend to perceive people, regardless of their individual differences, more rationally and fairly than do nongraduates. While such an approach benefits the graduate directly, society also enjoys the harmony of it. A more open, less stereotypical citizenry contributes in turn to the efficiency of economic and political decision making.

4. Graduates produce goods and services rather than depending on transfer payments from the government. Beyond the immediate benefit to the graduate lie lower welfare costs for society.

5. The increased salaries and buying power of graduates contribute broadly to economic activity.[3]

Externalities pose a problem because a private individual may not want to pay top dollar for a degree, given the apparent public benefits associated with it. Several tuition-reducing solutions have been employed to reduce the impact of externalities, including subsidies to public institutions, tax incentives for donations, direct grants to students, and grants and tax-free bonds to colleges and universities for their capital expenditures. Not all tuition reductions represent attempts to lessen the impact of externalities. Some colleges use tuition discounts to improve their competitive positions, picking and choosing students who will contribute to the prestige of the institution.

Market Imperfections

Market imperfections in higher education cause students and colleges to make suboptimal decisions about enrollment or instructional offerings. David Mundel claims that three significant market imperfections exist in higher education.[4]

Capital imperfections occur when students do not enroll because they cannot afford the cost of borrowing, because financial markets refuse to make loans, or because of the "investment risk" involved in degree purchases. Financial institutions are reluctant to extend student loans because the intangibility of a degree makes it so difficult to collateralize and because students may make career choices that reduce their potential to pay off a loan. Government has resolved part of the impasse between banks and students by underwriting losses, but students face another capital imperfection: investment risk (for which no risk insurance exists). Students invest in a long-term degree program without a guarantee of the outcome. Will the student complete the work and receive the degree? Can students predict future income, assuming the awarding of the degree but given uncertainties in the job market? This last imperfection is most burdensome to the poor, who may have to carry relatively large loan balances.

Not-for-profit status. Most independent colleges are not-for-profit, meaning that they do not maximize profits. As such, they do not have the incentive to respond quickly to changes in demand, nor do they need to contain costs in order to yield a profit. Not-for-profits find, however, that they lack the for-profit sector's iron discipline of a single goal. Colleges do not have a clear-cut definition of the goals that they maximize or the relative importance of those goals. Resource allocation decisions meant to maximize a core value become forums for conflict, often leading to a loss of direction on the purpose of the decision. Michael D. Cohen and James G. March describe this situation as organized anarchy, where goals are ambiguous and decisions are the product of chance events.[5]

While not-for-profits benefit from their tax-free status, they also find that it constrains capital formation. When they need to add capital, they do not have access to equity markets to fund new investments. Rather, they have to turn to the donor market, which can severely restrict how money is used and how much money can be raised. Operating outside the equity market is another reason why not-for-profits have not been forced to set priorities on their goals or performance.

Oligopolistic markets exist when a few firms control pricing within the market. The Seven Sisters in the oil market are one example. In higher education, the Overlap Group represented a potential oligopoly. Oligopolistic markets rise when barriers to entry (new firms find it difficult to enter the market to offer goods or services) are created by economies of scale, control of critical factors of production, advertising, or collusion.

Studies suggest that independent colleges require 2,000 students in order to reach the lower end of the *economy of scale* among independent colleges.[6] New nonprofit entrants into the market either would require sufficient capital on hand to cover the time needed to enroll 2,000 students; or they would have to build a large enough donor base to make up the difference between tuition and costs; or they would need to borrow the funds if trustees were willing to personally guarantee a loan. The challenge of the first two options and the extreme unlikelihood of the third help to explain why new colleges struggle for so long to achieve financial stability.

Colleges control the *factors of production* in several ways. First, they pay top dollar for the best instructors, or they use tenure to make it too costly for instructors to move to another institution. Second, they uphold their reputations of academic quality by enrolling the best students, thereby fostering a scholarly community. Evidence exists that the best prospective students choose colleges that enroll the best students so that they can participate in the intellectual ferment.[7] Third, independent colleges respond competitively in their market by controlling prices or containing costs in response to state regulations that limit the entry of colleges into existing markets (states argue that such regulations prevent the dilution of their educational investment).

Advertising supports oligopolies by allowing a college to portray its degree as dramatically different from the same degree offered by another college. Through admissions literature and media advertising campaigns, an independent college will try to convey that its degree or college experience is so superior that students can purchase it from only one college or find it in only one segment of the market.

When colleges within a segment conduct meetings about standards and pricing, they risk landing on the slippery slope of *collusion to establish an oligopolistic market,* as in the Overlap Group's understanding. Of course, not all segments of the higher education market are oligopolistic. The National Center for Postsecondary Improvement suggests that the market for independent colleges and universities can be divided into three competitive segments:

- a brand-name segment with excess demand, in which highly selective colleges (brand names) compete nationally by offering a medallion education;

- a convenience segment with excess supply, in which colleges use price to compete fiercely for students; and

- a middle group that tries to attract both the best students and those students seeking a good education at the best price.[8]

It is within the first segment—where the Overlap Group operated—that excess demand exists. Oligopolies seem to be constrained by the strong competition in the convenience and middle segments.

Economic Model of Small Colleges

Given the preceding reservations about the marketplace, an economic model can be presented that can inform us about the economic condition of small colleges as well as offer insight into their allocation decisions, financial stability, and financial strategies. The model is based on the precepts of David Hopkins and William Massy and of Gordon Winston.[9] We will consider small independent colleges in a five-piece economic framework: goal optimization, production functions, market structure, financial constraint, and financial equilibrium.

Goal Optimization

The not-for-profit status of a college does not negate the production of excess revenue, or profit. Rather, these colleges cannot distribute their profits for personal gain. Personal inurement, transfer of excess funds for personal use, and self-dealing through contracts to family members or hidden business associates are prohibited. Tax penalties apply to not-for-profits that attempt to pass their profits to individuals within the organization. Unlike publicly owned companies, not-for-profits do not have a duty to maximize profit; however, they may optimize some other set of values. Howard Bowen contends that colleges maximize revenue and spend all of it on academic excellence, prestige, and influence—maximizing cumulatively toward "ever increasing expenditures."[10]

While the Bowen model is appealing, the Hopkins and Massy model provides a richer explanation of the economic operation of higher education institutions. Their model is based upon the proposition that colleges maximize a set of core values, which the board members, as trustees of financial assets held for the public good, will achieve desirable social goals.[11] Though independent colleges do not answer directly to the government, as nonprofit corporations they are sanctioned by government, and the institution benefits from avoiding taxes—subject to the condition that it produces valuable public benefits without simultaneously rendering private benefits to the trustees or key members of the institution. Hopkins and Massy postulate that independent institutions seek a set of goals to maximize these core values, construed as a set of activities, stocks, or prices.[12]

An *activity* refers to some action over time, usually described in physical or behavioral terms, which may be tangible or intangible. Tangible activities may include students, credit hours, degrees, skills, research articles, or faculty. Intangible activities may include student academic potential, class performance, quality of research, faculty effort, or quality of library resources.[13]

Stock variables may be delineated physically or behaviorally, and while activities occur through time and may be characterized as "flows," stocks are fixed in time. Stocks typically include items from a balance sheet, such as cash, receivables, investments (endowments), debt, and net worth, but they can also include the number, capability, and quality of human capital employed by the institution. The value of stocks is that they may be turned into activities, and, the reverse being true, that activities can rebuild stocks. An important decision boards must make is the "spending-savings" question. They must decide how much stock to turn into activities. For example, boards must determine an acceptable endowment payout rate to be used for current operations (activities). They must also determine how surplus revenue will be used: to expand the endowment fund, build cash, construct buildings, or buy equipment, for example.[14]

Price assigns monetary values to those inputs (labor, materials, and capital) and outputs (degrees, athletic events, continuing education credit, etc.) of the institution that are subject to market forces. Price like everything else in the economic model is very complex. For instance, many institutions discount price (tuition) to gain control over the "quality and quantity of admissions."[15] (This latter aspect of the model will become important later on.) However, some institutions discount price not to gain control over quality and quantity but to match real price levels for their segment of the market. Many small colleges fall into this category.

This economic model posits that allocating activities and stocks and setting prices involve decisions by a board of trustees to maximize a core value. For example, the board may choose to maximize the core value of teaching by adding star instructors, students from the top of their high school classes, and research media to the library. The board also may choose to improve laboratory technology by expanding the endowment fund so that it supplies 35 percent of total revenue instead of 30 percent.

Maximizing the core values of a college is subject to production, market, and financial constraints. These constraints force the board and president to adapt their decisions to limits imposed by the organizational choices, the position of the college in the market, and the scale of financial resources available to the college. The characteristics of students, faculty, instructional methods, and facilities tend to be givens that inhibit the board's capacity to reallocate resources, change priorities, or go in new directions.

Production Function

A college must offer products or services that will maximize its value. Production functions in higher education defy easy depiction because (1) colleges are multiproduct firms, (2) the technology used to produce, for example, an educated student is not understood, and (3) production methods vary across instructional programs, within instructional programs, and between instruction and research. Finally, there is a confounding aspect of instruction: the student is both an input and an output in terms of the intellectual capabilities he or she contributes (the input of instruction) to learning (the output of the instruction).

A separate production function, implicit or explicit, exists for each output placed on the market—for degrees, certification programs, research, community service, and acquisition of gifts. Activities and stocks are associated with both the inputs and the outputs of the production function. For instance, separate production functions would specify the inputs and outputs for each degree program by major in the institution. And even then, the list of functions may not be sufficiently exhaustive to cover all the products and methods of production for instructional programs.

Market Structure

The market is the arbiter of the value of the products, services, and prices through the interplay of demand, supply, and the set of institutions competing within a particular market. A separate demand and supply function exists for each product offered on the market and for each market segment. These functions are predicated on the structure of the market (set of competing colleges and the degree of control those institutions have over price), the appeal of the products offered, the price of the products, and the alternatives available to the purchaser (students, donor, granting agency, or corporation). Furthermore, the market for instruction is not the same as the market for research, donors, or hospital services, and each of these products and services is subject to its own demand and supply relationships.

Since most small colleges operate primarily in the student market for instructional services, it will be useful to consider that particular market. The old assumption was that the student market was homogeneous; that is, every college had an equal chance of enrolling a prospective student. The prevailing assumption today is that the student market is fragmented in terms of the capacity of a set of institutions to control demand. Institutions like the Overlap Group, which can determine price and limit admissions, are at the top of the market. Institutions with excess capacity and those that offer small discounts, if any, on tuition participate in the convenience or bottom end of the market. Their students need a degree, may be older, and do not want to leave home. Market structure (the set of competitive colleges), the degree of control the institutions have over price, the relative appeal of the degrees, and their payoff to the student all affect student demand, admission spaces, price elasticity, the production function, and financial resources.

For instance, in the brand-name segment of colleges, we can presume that the number of admission slots will be limited; price will be relatively more inelastic; production functions will include large inputs of quality; tuition dependency will be low, with gift and endowment income contributing a greater proportion to revenue; and research will constitute a relatively large portion of total expenses. In contrast, colleges in the convenience segment might be expected to have excess classroom space, enabling student enrollment to enter right up through the start of classes; the production function will have a small investment in quality; price will be relatively less inelastic, perhaps even elastic; and research expenses may be negligible.

It may be that many colleges in the convenience segment are small and struggling to survive financially, while colleges in the brand-name segment are large and financially stable.

Financial Constraint

Colleges deal perpetually with financial constraint—with revenue, expenses, excess revenue, or deficits. The upper boundaries of revenue constrain expense boundaries, assuming that the institution intends to yield zero net profit (the not-for-profit constraint). Of course, the zero net profit is not a condition that must be met each year, but large and continuing profits do require decisions to be made about pricing and allocation of revenue toward expenses or the expansion of financial reserves. Likewise requiring attention are deficits continuing over several years—a troubling trend because of the implication that stock resources (balance sheet items such as cash and endowments) are being depleted to keep the doors of the institution open. The limits on how long an institution can continue to run deficits are cash position, endowment and gift restrictions that limit their conversion, and the capacity of other assets (receivables, plant, and equipment) to be collateralized.

Financial Equilibrium

Independent institutions maximize their core values, according to the Hopkins and Massy economic model, only when they reach a state of long-range financial equilibrium—when revenue and expenses and long-term growth rates for such are in balance. Financial equilibrium occurs when the underlying economic forces of demand, supply, prices, and production sustain long-run financial equilibrium. Reaching and maintaining equilibrium are accomplished through careful monitoring of key factors, such as rates of growth and contributions to revenue or expenses. The importance of a set of key factors—such as tuition, endowment pay-out, gifts, compensation, equipment and building maintenance, student services, and administration—are subject to the financial structure of an institution. Long-run financial equilibrium is the *sine qua non* of independent colleges in general, and small independent colleges in particular.

Due to their sheer size, large colleges tend to achieve and maintain financial equilibrium more readily than do smaller colleges. As such, they can compensate for any imprecision of allocation decisions made by presidents and faculty far removed from the large departments and programs they oversee. In contrast, small colleges have maintained (sometimes just barely) their financial equilibrium in the *absence* of sufficient reserves through superior management control; presidents and faculty of smaller institutions have the agility to respond and improvise more quickly in the face of economic uncertainty.

Economic Model

The preceding economic maximization model for independent institutions of higher education can be generalized through the following relationships:

maximize $V(X,S,P)$ subject to the following constraints:
$$F^k (X,S) = 0 \quad (k = 1, 2, ...m)$$
$$D^k (X,S,P) = 0 \quad (k = 1, 2, ... n)$$
$$R(X,S,P) - C(X,S,P) = 0$$

where

V = values to maximized
X = activities (tangible and intangible)
S = stocks
P = price
F = production function; $F = 0$, the elements stand in relation to each other

D = demand function; D = 0, the elements stand in relation to each other

R = revenue

C = cost

R - C = 0; revenue minus costs over the long term equal zero

k = there are k production and demand functions

long-run financial equilibrium, subject to:

$$(R_g (X_{gw,} S_{gw,} P_{gw}))_t = (C_g (X_{gw,} S_{gw,} P_{gw}))_t$$

where

R_g = rate of growth for revenue

C_g = rate of growth for expenses

$X_{gw,} S_{gw,} P_{gw}$ = rate of growth and weighted value for X,S, and P1

t = time period (1,2,n)

Winston Variation

Gordon Winston sheds light on how the market for higher education is shaped by a college's nonprofit status, its method of production, and its relative position in the market. As nonprofit entities, independent institutions cannot appropriate excess revenue (profits) for personal benefits. Because no payoff exists for having profits as a goal, Winston suggests that independent institutions turn to maximizing academic quality as their primary goal. Academic excellence as a goal, "often defined relative to other institutions . . . has a positional aspect." In other words, the academic quality of any institution, be it demarcated externally or internally, is defined relative to others. How do colleges achieve academic excellence? According to Winston, they buy it on the market using tuition discounts to attract top-quality students.[16]

The best students are valuable inputs to instruction and to the academic reputation of the institution. Students add a synergism to instruction, with the quality of instruction presumed to advance given the quality of the students involved. Recall that the best new students seek colleges that enroll the best students. The top new students, because they represent an important asset to colleges seeking to maintain or advance their quality rankings, can actually sell their services to the highest bidder; colleges will vary discounts based on relative differences in academic quality among students.[17]

According to Winston, a defining economic characteristic of colleges is that they set prices lower than the cost of production, thus creating substantial subsidies to the cost of education. Independent nonprofit colleges can offer subsidies to the extent that revenue from sales (of degree programs) is supplemented by donations (gifts and endowment funds built from gifts). Donations provide the wealth needed to create subsidies and to determine relative position in the market.[18]

Winston offers evidence for two levels of subsidies upon which donated wealth has an influence: (1) the tuition subsidies already discussed and (2) a general education subsidy. According to Winston, the tuition discount is relatively small when compared to the general subsidy, the general subsidy being the difference between the total cost of production and the sticker. The ratio of the average general subsidy to the average tuition discount is about 3 to 1.[19]

Table 4.1
Cost, Prices, Subsidies, and SAT Scores: 1995

Decile	Students	Average Student Subsidy	Average Costs	Net Price	Price/Cost Ratio	% Applicant Accepted
1	3,300	22,800	28,500	5,700	20.1%	67.1%
2	3,800	11,100	14,900	3,800	25.4%	78.6%
3	4,300	9,300	12,300	3,000	24.4%	81.6%
4	4,500	8,200	11,000	2,800	25.6%	85.1%
5	3,700	7,300	9,900	2,600	25.6%	84.9%
6	3,900	6,500	9,400	2,900	30.8%	87.1%
7	3,500	5,800	8,700	2,900	33.1%	86.9%
8	3,500	5,100	8,400	3,300	39.5%	88.6%
9	2,900	4,100	8,700	4,600	52.5%	87.1%
10	1,600	1,800	7,900	6,100	77.4%	84.7%

Source: Gordon C. Winston, "Subsidies, Hierarchy, and Peers: The Awkward Economics of Higher Education," *Journal of Economic Perspectives* 13, no. 1 (winter 1999): 19, 28.

Table 4.1 includes student enrollment, general subsidy, average cost per institution (the economic cost comprising general educational expenditures, plus capital expenditures), cost ratio, and acceptance rates. The cost ratio is the ratio of the average cost of education compared to net price. Table 4.1 clearly illustrates a vertical ranking based on the cost ratio. An increase in subsidies appears to be closely associated with an increase in the percentage of applicants accepted. This relationship between the size of the subsidy and the acceptance rate supports the contention that wealthier institutions can use their subsidies to create excess demand. They therefore have greater control over the characteristics of applying students.[20]

The general subsidy is valuable to the extent that a wealthy institution creates a product attractive to students seeking academic excellence. The wealth must be invested in a prestigious faculty, state-of-the-art technology, pleasant surroundings, the latest in student services, and a quality student body.[21] As colleges descend the subsidy scale, where donated wealth diminishes to the point where it virtually disappears, they enter a highly charged marketplace where they find themselves competing frantically for students—as convenience colleges providing immediate services and facing excess demand.

Another notable relationship in table 4.1 is that the smallest subsidies are associated with the smallest colleges. This relationship suggests that size (number of students) may have an independent effect on the wealth of an independent college. Small colleges may not be operating at an economy of scale that permits them to accumulate wealth. In addition, donors may perceive them to be inefficient due to their size, choosing not to assist them because of a belief that gifts may not be used efficiently.

Winston's proposition says simply that the relative shares of tuition and donated wealth determine an independent college's capacity to subsidize its costs, which in turn determines whether the college has excess demand for its product. In other words, colleges that can create oligarchies will have a stronger place in the market than those that cannot.

The Winston relationship can be stated in a simple algebraic form, which can then be substituted in the financial constraint (revenue minus cost equals zero in the long run for a nonprofit organization) and in the long-run financial equilibrium (revenue and costs are balanced in the long run) of Hopkins and Massy.

The following four equations express Winston and Hopkins and Massy propositions. The first equation is Winston's subsidy relationship, which is then substituted in the financial constraint model of Hopkins and Massy (the second expression). The third equation weights the tuition and donated wealth factors to indicate their relative shares in the revenue mix. The fourth equation, the relative impact model, restates the weighted constraint equation so that donated wealth, tuition, and cost are a set of proportions relative to revenue. The relative impact model delineates that changes in the proportion of donated wealth directly influences the scale of the subsidy. The fourth equation modifies the relative impact model to conform with the long-run equilibrium model of Hopkins and Massy, resulting in a balanced relationship between the weights and growth rates of revenue and expense components. The relative impact model and long-run equilibrium model will be used in later chapters to frame the assessment of the financial structure of independent colleges and universities in general, and small independent colleges in particular.

Restatement of Financial Constraint Model in Terms of Subsidy

subsidy = (cost-tuition) = donated wealth

financial constraint = ((cost-tuition)-donated wealth) = 0

weighted constraint = ((cost-((tuition/revenue) revenue))-((donated wealth/revenue) revenue))

relative impact model = donated wealth/revenue = ((cost/revenue)-(tuition/revenue))

equilibrium model = $(d/r)gwt = ((c/r)gwt-(t/r)gwt)$

d = donated revenue,

c = cost,

t = tuition,

r = revenue,

g = rate of growth over time (t),

w = weighted to revenue,

t = time = (1,2,. . . n)

Economy of Scale

Economy of scale describes an organization's capacity to provide its services at a minimum unit cost or, more precisely, "marginal cost or average cost per student." The resulting number is usually viewed as a summary figure denoting how cost-effective an organization is at providing services or goods.

Although economy of scale is an abstraction, its value is determined by the conditions that define the organization. For example, many small colleges need every smidgen of revenue to survive, so courses—often called independent studies—frequently are offered at well-below-average class size. The instructor is paid a pittance of the usual adjunct rate, perhaps no more than 10 percent per student. But the pay is so low that incentives for instructors to meet regularly with students or to provide sufficient hours of instruction disappear. Financially weak colleges find the arrangement worthwhile because instructors are paid below the tuition rates. If colleges offer higher pay rates to increase hours of instruction, the new pay may act as a perverse incentive that yields more courses and no improvement in time spent with students. The result of trying to do right by the student is to reduce net income flow to the college, a powerful disincentive to an impoverished college.

As independent courses proliferate, the value of the degree deteriorates. Students pass through some colleges with a high percentage of courses taught as independent studies. Credit for such may have less to do with knowledge gained than with ticket punches accumulated to meet credit requirements. At this point, inefficient scale becomes truly destructive to the small college. The value of the student's education declines because graduates do not have the skills purported to accompany the degree. Employers become disenchanted with the college's graduates in general. Word spreads first among graduates that their investment holds little value, then among potential students, and the college's applicant pool shrinks. The college must turn to the least-qualified applicants and produce more unqualified graduates. Falling enrollments lead to higher tuition rates, one more disincentive to potential enrollees.

Inefficient scale of operations can slowly but surely grind away the capacity of a small college to offer a credible product. Regularly scheduled, publicly monitored classes must be regarded not just as a cost-efficient goal, but as necessary discipline for both students and instructors if small colleges and their graduates are to survive their respective marketplaces.

Summary

Although economics can be a dreary science, it does provide insight into decisions made in response to forces that shape a market, particularly a highly complex market like higher education. Small colleges can have a vibrant economic life if they understand the markets in which they operate. Those markets can be just as complex as those for large prestigious institutions. Student market segments, grants and gifts markets, labor, supply, and capital markets all have a powerful influence on a college's fundamental decisions. Markets have a direct effect on faculty quality and work loads, staffing, student services, tuition pricing, admissions requirements, degrees, facilities, alumni wealth, and other decision areas. The board and president, if they want to foster a vibrant institution, must have a well-honed appreciation of all the markets that drive operations and decisions.

Notes

1. Howard Bowen, "What Determines the Costs of Higher Education," in *ASHE Reader on Finance in Higher Education*, ed. Larry L. Leslie and Richard E. Anderson (Needham Heights, Mass: Ginn Press, 1990), p. 253.

2. Scott Jaschik, "Ivy League Agrees to End Collaboration on Financial Aid, " *Chronicle of Higher Education*, May 29, 1991.

3. Kenneth A. Feldman and Theodore M. Newcomb, *The Impact of College on Students*, vol. 1 (San Francisco: Jossey-Bass, 1976); Alexander Astin, *What Matters in College?* (San Francisco: Jossey-Bass, 1993); David Mundel, "Whose Education Should Society Support?" in *Does College Matter?*, ed. Lewis C. Solmon and Paul J. Taubman (New York: Academic Press, 1973).

4. Mundel, "Whose Education Should Society Support?" pp. 313–14.

5. Michael D. Cohen and James G. March, *Leadership and Ambiguity: The American College President* (New York: McGraw-Hill, 1974).

6. Malcolm Getz and John J. Siegfried, "Costs and Productivity in American Colleges and Universities," in *Economic Challenges in Higher Education*, ed. Charles T. Clotfelter, Ronald G. Ehrenberg, Malcolm Getz, and John J. Siegfried (Chicago: University of Chicago Press, 1991).

7. Astin, *What Matters in College?*, pp. 189, 384–85, 409–10.

8. "In Search of Strategic Perspective: A Tool for Mapping the Market in Postsecondary Education," *Change* 29, no. 6 (November/December 1997): 23–39.

9. David S. P. Hopkins and William F. Massy, *Planning Models for Colleges and Universities* (Stanford, Calif.: Stanford University Press, 1981); Gordon C. Winston, "Subsidies, Hierarchy. and Peers: The Awkward Economics of Higher Education," *Journal of Economic Perspectives* 13, no. 1 (winter 1999): 13–36.

10. Howard R. Bowen, *The Costs of Higher Education* (San Francisco: Jossey-Bass, 1981), pp. 19–20.

11. Hopkins and Massy, *Planning Models for Colleges and Universities*, p. 80.

12. Ibid., pp. 8, 83.

13. Ibid., pp. 75, 76.

14. Ibid., pp. 76, 77.

15. Ibid., p. 17.

16. Winston, "Subsidies, Hierarchy and Peers," p. 17.

17. Astin, *What Matters in College?*

18. Winston, "Subsidies, Hierarchy and Peers," pp. 16–21.

19. Ibid., p. 20.

20. Ibid., p. 23.

21. Ibid., p. 21.

Financial Structure of Small Colleges

Financial resources enable colleges to fulfill their missions. A sound financial structure provides resources for instruction, research, public service, and the other services that we expect an institution to provide. Stewardship of college finances—the protection of current and future resources for the benefit of students—is one of the chief responsibilities of presidents and boards of trustees. This chapter considers the financial essentials of small colleges, specifically the components of financial structure, financial performance measures, and strategic allocation decisions.

Few studies address how colleges in general finance themselves through financial structure, let alone how small colleges do so. Presuming net income as an adequate indicator of finance practices, studies have focused on the only information available—revenue, expenses, and net income flow from operations. A sustained period of negative net income suggests the depletion of financial resources, and positive net income suggests the expansion of financial resources. But the net income presumption is not always valid. Colleges with strong endowments, for example, can endure long periods of negative net income, preserving financial resources even during periods of economic expansion. Moreover, positive net income does not necessarily indicate financial strength. Receivables rather than cash may constitute net income, and a large portion of receivables may be uncollectible. Many colleges operating on the brink of financial distress use receivables as a form of financial aid— a risky tactic if students neglect their bills.

Colleges with financial systems weighted heavily toward net income are vulnerable to changes in the student market. Leaders who build financial systems with a diversified mix of financial components reinforce their colleges against the vicissitudes of the market and the economy. These enviable colleges have a strong flow of net income from gifts, which results in large transfers into the endowment fund and cash reserves that grow without reliance on short-term borrowing. They build market power by using their strong financial position to buy the best students. Less sophisticated colleges, on the other hand, do not have sufficient financial resources to build market power. As a result, they are like small businesses taking whatever the market gives them. Price is determined by external factors, not by internal financial reserves. These colleges operate with negligible or negative net income, and they fund current operations through short- and long-term debt.

A college's president and chief financial officer must mix and weight net income, cash, receivables, payables, debt, endowments, fixed assets, and net assets—the components of financial structure—such that they are convertible assets to current operations. Wealth is created from net income, endowments, gifts, or debt. Short-term assets such as cash or receivables usually flow directly from net income. Payment of short-term liabilities such as payables, accruals, and short-term notes usually depends on cash from students paying their bills (receivables) and on the cash flow as students register. If students are slow to pay or if they do not pay, then the college may have to convert long-term assets (endowments or buildings used as collateral) to cash or make short-term loans.

The conversion rate of a fixed asset depends on the asset, its residual values, and its use. Buildings, given their flexible design, and chairs and desks, given their standard design, may be useful for decades if not centuries. Computers and electrical equipment, however, may have much shorter utility spans due to the rapid obsolescence of technology. Depreciation measures the conversion of assets into current consumption. Though accounting standards require that colleges record depreciation, its impact on financial structure may not be taken seriously.[1] As a result, some colleges fail to build sufficient reserves to replenish existing assets and improve productive capacity, and they end up offering inferior educational services on the market.

Endowment conversion is constrained by a payout rate that follows the "prudent stewards rule," which charges the board with preserving the value of the endowment.[2] Given that constraint, endowments are typically converted for use either to support scholarships for students or to provide a general subsidy for operations. Though a college's capacity to subsidize a student's education is critical to its standing, tuition discounts during a bidding war can quickly eviscerate endowments or force the college into unfunded scholarships so that an endowment cannot offset the growing gap between tuition and net price. Growing an endowment depends on good fortune in investment choice—and presents quite a challenge to the small college that has an endowment but receives no additional gifts to expand it.

Because colleges cannot create wealth by selling new equity, new wealth will have to come from debt for those institutions that cannot generate adequate wealth from net income, gifts, or investments. Weak or negative net income combined with assets that have little residual value (depreciated assets or small endowments) translate into low credit ratings for the college and higher interest payments on the debt. The college with the capacity to generate positive flow from net income and assets that have sufficient or excess residual value will borrow with less risk and pay lower interest rates.

Elements of a Financial Structure

The financial structure's capacity to subsidize prices, boost production, and respond to economic change will determine whether a college survives or succumbs to market forces. The financial structure has three primary divisions that together represent how income is produced, stored, and used: income production accounts, working capital accounts, and permanent capital accounts (table 5.1 next page).

Income Production

Income production for small colleges denotes the stream of revenue and expenses from the production and sale of educational services and products. Revenue accounts include tuition and fees, government contracts, grants, gifts, auxiliary services, and interest income. Expense accounts include instruction, research, public service, student services, academic administration, scholarships, plant operations, institutional services, and auxiliary services. Institutional services encompass business office operations, telephones, administrative computing, insurance, and nondepreciable building and equipment projects. Auxiliary services refer to expenses associated with dormitories, bookstores, health services, and any other services funded through student fees.

Revenue accounts. Student revenue (tuition, fees, dormitory charges, and bookstore sales) is the principal revenue source at most small colleges, whose survival demands that in lieu of other revenue sources, student revenue be generated to build financial reserves. Gift and grant income contributions to operations are insignificant at these heavily student-revenue dependent colleges, and their endowment fund returns are too small to keep pace with inflation, building upkeep, or the cost of new equipment. Record keeping and auditing costs associated with federal grant requirements sometimes exceed the tuition revenue they generate. Like investors who place all their investments in a single market sector and watch them go south when that sector is out of favor, colleges that rely heavily on tuition revenue will watch such revenue evaporate in response to changing market demands.

Table 5.1
Chart of Accounts

The standard accounting classification used in higher education classifies expenses in terms of function and object accounts. Function accounts pool expenses around a common activity—for example, instruction and research. Object accounts include the usual accounting categories: salary, benefits, operations, etc. Account categories and descriptions are listed below.

INCOME PRODUCTION ACCOUNTS
Revenue Accounts
1. **Tuition and Fees**

    Includes continuing education fees, conferences, and seminars
2. **Government Appropriations**

    Includes federal, state, and local appropriations
3. **Government Grants and Contracts**

    Includes federal, state, or local government grants or contracts
4. **Private Gifts, Grants, and Contracts**

    Includes contributions
5. **Investment Returns**

    Includes investment income, interest, dividends, rents, and royalties; and gains and losses (realized and unrealized). May include student loan interest and irrevocable trust distributions
6. **Educational Sales and Services**

    Includes sales incidental to instruction, research, or public services. Examples: film rentals, university presses, or dairies
7. **Auxiliary Sales and Services**

    Includes sales from services to students, faculty, or staff. Fees charged are directly related to cost. Examples: health services, residence halls, intercollegiate athletics, and college stores
8. **Hospitals**
9. **Independent Operations**

    Includes operations independent of core mission. Example: revenue from federally funded research and development centers
10. **Other Revenue**

    Includes all other revenue. Examples: gains on sale of plant assets, actuarial gains, or unusual and nonrecurring items.

Expenditures: Functions

1. **Instruction**

   Includes credit and noncredit courses but excludes administration

2. **Research**

   Includes research commissioned by an agency external to the college or separately budgeted within the institution. Also covers institutes, research centers, and individual and project research

3. **Public Service**

   Includes noninstructional services beneficial to noninstitutional groups

4. **Academic Support**

   Supports the core missions of instruction, research, or public service. Examples: libraries, academic development or computing, administration, or any medical clinics supporting instruction

5. **Student Services**

   Includes admissions, registrar, or services contributing to students' emotional or physical well-being or cultural or social development outside of instruction. Examples: guidance counseling, financial aid, student records, intramural athletics, and student health services (if not an auxiliary enterprise)

6. **Institutional Support**

   Involves daily operational support. Examples: executive direction, legal or fiscal operations, administrative computing, and marketing

7. **Scholarships and Fellowships**

   Includes payments made for services not part of the institution. Does not include direct scholarship expenses reported net of tuition and fees

8. **Operation and Maintenance of Plant**

   Includes services for buildings, grounds, property insurance, utilities, etc.

9. **Hospital Expenses**

   Reported if hospital revenue

10. **Independent Operations**

    Includes expenses unrelated to primary mission of the institution but that contribute indirectly to it. Example: federally funded research and development centers

11. **Auxiliary Operations**

    Reported if auxiliary revenue

Object Accounts
1. **Salary**
2. **Benefits**
3. **Operations and Maintenance of the Plant**
4. **Depreciation**
5. **Interest**
6. **Other**

Changes in Net Assets
1. **Actuarial Gains or Losses**
   Any adjustments reported for funds held in trust
2. **Sale of Plant Assets: Gains or Losses**
3. **Other Gains or Losses**
4. **Discontinued Operations**
5. **Extraordinary Gains or Losses**
6. **Changes in Accounting Principles**
7. **Net of Revenue and Expenses**
8. **Total Change in Net Assets**

Working Capital
1. **Cash (asset)**
   Includes cash, certificates of deposit, treasury bills, etc.
2. **Receivables Net of Allowance for Uncollectible Amounts (asset)**
   Includes student billings, auxiliary enterprises, hospitals, government appropriations, interest receivables, and contribution receivables
3. **Inventories, Prepaid Expenses, and Deferred Charges (asset)**
   Includes inventories from bookstores or food service and any advance payments for services not yet received
4. **Accounts Payable, Accruals, and Deferred Revenue (liability)**
   Deferred revenue usually refers to tuition received in advance of instruction
5. **Postretirement and Postemployment Obligations (liability)**
6. **Government Grants Refundable Under Student Loans (liability)**

Permanent Capital

1. **Amounts Held for Construction (asset)**
2. **Long-Term Investments (asset)**
3. **Plant, Property, and Equipment - Net of Depreciation (asset)**
4. **Annuity and Life Income (liability)**

   Beneficiary interests from annuities, trusts, etc. held by the institution
5. **Bonds, Notes, Capital Leases, and Long-Term Debt (liability)**
6. **Other Liabilities**
7. **Net Assets**

   a. Unrestricted (Undesignated and Designated)

   Net assets with no restriction and quasi-endowments funds

   b. Unrestricted (Net Investment in Plant)

   c. Permanently Restricted

   Net assets with permanent donor or grantor restrictions

Definitions are taken from IPEDS (Integrated Postsecondary Education Data System), the U.S. Department of Education's reporting system for higher education. IPEDS definitions conform to accounting standards mutually established by FASB (Financial Accounting Standards Board) and NACUBO (National Association of College and University Business Officers).

Small colleges with strong income flows from donors and endowments are very fortunate. These build their financial reserves (endowment funds) to secure their place in the market and for the future. Financial risk for them involves errors that deplete resources over the long term, thereby reducing the stature of the college.

Expense accounts. Instructional services form the core of expenses at most small colleges, with research services playing a lesser role. During the first decade of the 21st century, as baby boomers retire to be replaced by a much smaller pool of qualified instructors and administrators, compensation will likely grow at a fast pace. Colleges that struggle with the cost of supply and demand will feel tremendous pressure to hire the best instructors while remaining price-competitive and offering large tuition discounts.

During the last decade of the 20th century, the largest growth in expenditures occurred in the area of financial aid services, which rose by more than 360 percent while instructional services increased only 125 percent during the same period.[3] Small colleges cannot ignore the impact of financial aid on student decisions and must increase their financial aid packages if they want to retain their mobile piece of the student market. *Business Officer* reports that tuition discounts on average now cover 25 percent of tuition costs, which is equivalent to giving away one year of a four-year degree.[4] The impact of such largesse on colleges' financial performance could be ruinous.

Small tuition-dependent colleges seeking long-term financial stability must figure out how to increase the flow of funds from operations to financial reserves. These colleges operate much like businesses that generate revenue primarily through sales to clients—they can fall into sustained periods of operational deficits if unforeseen events affect client demand. Thirty percent of colleges with fewer than 2,000 students reported deficits for five of the nine years between 1988 and 1997. When operational deficits become the norm, financial resources are sapped to fund instructional programs and student services. The college on a perpetual downward spiral becomes unattractive to potential students and easy prey for competitors.

Working Capital

Working capital includes assets and liabilities generated from income production. It exists because of accrual accounting. Receivables, inventory, accounts payable, accruals, and unearned revenue represent accounting devices used to match revenue and expenses to current operations. If the college has already produced the revenue but not received the cash, then receivables are booked. If courses have been taught but faculty not paid, then payroll accruals are booked.

Cash and short-term investments should be the most important components of working capital. These two accounts provide immediate reserves to pay outstanding bills, cover the payroll, and respond to opportunities or unexpected events. If cash and short-term investments fall short, the college must resort to short-term debt to cover bills and payroll. Cash shortages are the primary cause of sleepless nights for the chief financial officers of many small colleges.

Permanent Capital

Permanent capital includes net revenue retained from income production, permanent assets, liabilities, and net assets. Assets include plant, equipment, land, and investments; liabilities include long-term debt such as loans, mortgages, and bonds. Permanent capital represents the stored wealth of the institution and as such provides the fundamental support for income production over the long term. The rate of conversion of this wealth into current operations may be conceived as the depreciation rate on fixed assets and the payout rate on endowments, but the payout rate must not deplete the fund. Given the board of trustees' duty as stewards of the long-term assets of the institution, the board must carefully protect those resources so that future generations of students can enjoy a higher education. Complex algorithms may govern payout rates, but the general rule of preservation is fairly simple: the endowment payout should be less than the rate of inflation, or around 5 percent of the market value of the endowment fund.

Permanent assets will have short life spans if not rejuvenated with new funds. Net assets must grow fast enough for the college to invest in production and thereby match current demands of the market and the competition. Permanent capital can grow through funds from operations, investment growth, new asset gifts, or debt. When endowments and donations are modest, colleges must rely on either net income from operations or on debt to fund internal investments. Many small colleges may use net income to stoke minor capital projects such as painting buildings, renovating offices, or purchasing computers. Major projects must then be funded judiciously by debt so that the college is not overwhelmed by debt service as it works to maintain productive capacity.

Capital investments with life spans of only a few years make heavy demands on the capital reserves and net income of small colleges. Outmoded hardware, software, and instructional programs must be brought up to speed if colleges intend to maintain student interest as well as an efficient flow of information. The big problem, of course, is how to continuously fund the investments that will provide for appealing programs and new computers and telecommunications equipment. Unfortunately, a little obsolescence goes a long way in dulling the competitive edge. Colleges large and small ought to look to depreciation as an indicator of competitive weakness. More than a simple accounting exercise, depreciation reflects the condition of a college's fixed assets. As depreciation increases relative to plant assets, the college loses its ability to reinvest in itself.

The board and president must balance income production, working capital, and permanent capital in a way that affords the college flexibility to respond to change, improve services, and maintain stability in times of crisis. Revenue flows must be strong enough to sustain core services while producing sufficient excess revenue (net income) to bolster financial reserves in the form of investments. Net income must therefore generate enough cash for the college to support short-term reserves and make capital investments. As the Hopkins and Massy planning models suggests, managers of a college's financial structure must have as their goal an equilibrium state wherein revenue is balanced with expense growth, and financial resources expand.

Measurements of Financial Structure

Measurements of financial structure delineate how a college finances itself. Does it do so primarily through operations, cash reserves, endowment, or debt? Market, reputation, and financial capacity constrain the construction of financial structure from one college to another. If a college's student market consists of low- to middle-income students, that college will find it difficult to raise prices rapidly in response to inflationary or technological change. Colleges reputed to be great centers of learning are particularly attractive to donors, and their alumni (the former student market) are likely to have the means to provide substantial gifts. Existing financial resources may impose the greatest constraint on a college, with wealthy colleges thriving and penurious colleges sinking in a sea of rapidly changing market demands.

To ascertain financial structure, one can measure the relative weights of the revenue, expense, asset, liability, and net asset accounts. For example, tuition and fees could be divided by total revenue, instructional expenses divided by total expenses, cash divided by total working capital assets, or investments divided by assets. One could also compare the components to show how funds flow and how financial reserves (endowments, buildings, and equipment) are converted to use. A variety of financial ratios provide insight into the internal relationships among different parts of the financial structure and the relative capacity of the financial structure to withstand unexpected events. Data used to compute relative weights of accounts, growth rates of accounts, change in dollars over time, and standard financial ratios that provide comparative benchmarks can be found in colleges' annual audits.

Relative Weights

Relative weights are simple computations that provide information on revenue sources and on allocations for expense, working capital, and permanent capital accounts. Performed over time, these weightings reflect changes in allocations and help to minimize distortion when large dollar changes have occurred. The relative weight of revenue (or expense) accounts can be figured by dividing the relevant account by total revenue. Weights for working capital and permanent capital are figured by separating assets and liabilities. The weight for a working capital asset (or a working capital liability, permanent capital asset, or permanent capital liability) is the relevant account divided by total working capital assets.

Rate of Growth

To compute the rate of growth, divide the current value for an account by its value during an earlier period. For example, if gifts totaled $2 million during the year 2000 and $1 million during 1996, the rate of growth is 100 percent, or $2 million divided by $1 million. A compounded rate of change would yield the account's annual growth rate. Rates of growth can be used to compare and track changes among the interactive parts of the financial structure. It is important, for example, that revenue growth match or exceed expense growth. (When expenses outpace revenue, net income eventually turns negative despite any surplus produced by operations.) A combination of growth rates and relative weights can identify strengths, weaknesses, or impending problems within the financial structure's various accounts.

Dollar Tracking

Dollar tracking can pinpoint the underlying distribution of the flow of new revenue through expenses and net income. What proportion of new revenue goes to instruction, student services, administration, or compensation, for instance? Because budgets tend to be constructed incrementally, with new monies being haphazardly added rather than strategically integrated, it is especially important to highlight budgetary changes. Following money through the financial structure will enable financial leaders to test the assumption that incremental changes to the budget make sense.

Tracking the flow of dollars from net income to working and permanent capital accounts will indicate whether operations yield commensurate increases in cash, or whether net income is being absorbed by receivables, or whether cash is being bolstered through short-term loans or long-term debt that has not yet been dispersed for capital projects. Small colleges must be familiar with the flow of dollars through their financial structures. What are the sources of new dollars for fixed assets and investments, for example? Are the dollars coming from net income? Restricted gifts? Increases in the market value of investments? Debt? Dollar tracking, weights, and growth rates are simple measures that can help small colleges embolden their financial wherewithal.

Financial Ratios

Credit-rating agencies, government agencies, auditors, and consulting firms developed financial ratios to determine if the financial condition of a college is adequate to support its mission and its long-term debt obligations.[5] Ratios and trend analysis are often combined to see whether a college is maintaining, building, or depleting its financial reserves.

Moody's Investor Service, the leading credit-rating agency in higher education, began using ratios in the early part of the 20th century to rate the ability of companies selling public debt to meet their debt service obligations. Moody's has applied its experience to higher education when colleges and universities entered the public debt market. The National Center for Higher Education Management Systems (NCHEMS, a U.S. Department of Education Center) tested financial ratios in the late 1970s to find measures that could identify financially weak colleges. Although these tests were never completed, NCHEMS did identify several ratios that were linked to financial risk in independent colleges and universities. For example, they found that colleges with higher interest expenses, higher rates of tuition dependence, and smaller reserves faced greater financial risk.[6] Two national firms, KPMG and Prager, McCarthy & Sealy, have also formulated ratios to measure the financial viability of higher education institutions. They base their ratios on field experience analyzing the finances of colleges and universities and on their work with ED on financial assessment ratios. ED used the assessment ratios to ascertain whether colleges receiving federally sponsored financial aid funds were financially viable. NACUBO had KPMG and Prager apply their ratios to independent institutions so that the private sector would have the means to assess its finances.

The Moody's, NCHEMS, and KPMG and Prager ratios will be used here to follow the flow of funds within the financial structure. Small colleges can use the ratios to gain insight into the factors that shape their financial structures. Tables 5.2–5.6 illustrate several ratios, categorized to monitor income production, working capital, and permanent capital (see Appendix B for additional ratios).

Table 5.2
Ratios for Monitoring Income Production: Operations

Annual operating margin[7]	adjusted total unrestricted revenue* — total unrestricted operating expenses ÷ adjusted total unrestricted revenue *Limit gains and losses to 4.5 percent of last year's cash and investments less net assets released from construction acquisition of fixed assets.
Debt service coverage[8] A ratios of less than $2.08 is a concern to credit rating agencies.[9]	operating surplus (deficit) + interest and depreciation ÷ principal and interest payments
Risk ratio[10]	interest expense ÷ total expenditures
Revenue flexibility ratio[11]	total unrestricted revenue ÷ total revenue
Expenditure flexibility ratio[12]	full-time faculty + operations and maintenance of plant ÷ total expenditures
Revenue source risk[13] Measures tuition dependence	tuition and fee income ÷ total revenue

Table 5.3
Ratios for Monitoring Working Capital

Operating cash[14] Measures cash reserves; the trend should increase.	$$\frac{\text{net cash}}{\text{unrestricted revenue less gains and losses}}$$
Current ratio[15] Measures capacity to meet short-term debt; satisfactory level is 2:1.[16]	$$\frac{\text{current assets}}{\text{current liabilities}}$$
Available funds ratio[17] The most conservative measure of liquidity; .75 or above is satisfactory.[18]	$$\frac{\text{cash and short-term investments}}{\text{current liabilities}}$$

Table 5.4
Ratios for Monitoring Permanent Capital

Return on net assets[19] Measures change in an institution's wealth; the numerator drives the change.	$$\frac{\text{change in net assets}}{\text{total net assets*}}$$ * Sum of net assets beginning and end of year, divided by two
Unrestricted financial resources to direct debt[20] A ratio of greater than 1 indicates financial assets are retained; a ratio of less than 1 indicates a lower return or investments that are less than physical assets.	$$\frac{\text{unrestricted net assets — net investment in plant}}{\text{direct debt}}$$
Change in composition ratio Identifies *which* is growing faster, financial assets or plant.	$$\frac{\text{change in financial assets}}{\text{change in physical assets}}$$

Table 5.5
Ratios for Monitoring Permanent Capital: Debt Management

Expendable financial resource to direct debt[21] Unrestricted and restricted net assets minus property plus long-term debt. A ratio below 1 is less able to respond to adverse conditions (KMPG, 22).	$$\frac{\text{total unrestricted and temporarily restricted net assets} - \text{net investment in plant}}{\text{direct debt}}$$
Leverage ratio[22] A ratio of less than 2:1 implies that during short-term economic adversity, the institution would have difficulty making loan repayments.	$$\frac{\text{total available net assets}}{\text{direct debt}}$$

Table 5.6
Ratios for Monitoring Permanent Capital: Plant Management

Plant coverage	$$\frac{\text{plant expenses}}{\text{fixed assets}}$$
Depreciation	$$\frac{\text{depreciation expense}}{\text{fixed assets}}$$

Allocation Decisions

A college can also mine its financial structure to discover how it deploys resources to strengthen market position or how it builds wealth. Michael S. McPherson and his colleagues contend that institutions share four basic objectives directed toward achieving academic excellence. How each college achieves these objectives varies according to its wealth-building and resource allocation practices:

- Institutions seeking to *maintain or improve* educational quality prefer larger endowments.

- Institutions seeking to *build financially viable enrollment bases* and institutions seeking to *increase the number of select students* prefer lower tuition to higher tuition and higher to lower quality of educational instruction.

- Institutions that *recruit a broad socioeconomic population* of students prefer larger to smaller spending weights and growth rates on financial aid.

- Institutions that want to *improve prestige and reputation* prefer larger to smaller spending weights and growth rates on instruction and research.[23]

The McPherson study found that as wealth increased at independent colleges (in the form of government appropriations, grants, endowments, and gifts), financial aid increased faster and tuition increases were smaller.[31] Federal financial aid had a comparable wealth effect on tuition.[24] In addition, increases in endowment wealth led to positive changes in instructional spending.[25]

While most colleges strive for academic excellence, small colleges battling to survive from day to day and from registration to registration may have a more prosaic goal: financial stability. They have different objectives and allocation preferences.

- Institutions that want to *increase enrollment* prefer lower vs. higher rates of increase in sticker price and are indifferent to student quality.

- Institutions that want to *control costs* prefer part-time faculty, lower rates of growth in expense components, relatively low weights for institutional financial aid, and greater rates of growth in administration.

- Institutions that want to *build short-term financial stability* prefer increased cash and net working capital and reduced debt vs. expanded endowment funds.

- Institutions that want to *improve their reputation* prefer permanent assets vs. endowment assets, or instruction over research. [26]

Price Elasticity

Financial structure should provide enough information to compute a simple price elasticity measure for each college. Price elasticity suggests the relative degree of control institutions have in the market—in particular, their ability to change price without adversely affecting revenue. Gordon C. Winston's model suggests that price should be less elastic for independent institutions with greater wealth because they control the selection of students by creating excess demand.[27] The corollary of this proposition is that price is more elastic for independent institutions with less wealth. Therefore, it should be expected that for institutions with very low tuition dependency, price would be less elastic, and price for institutions with high tuition dependency would be more elastic.

Summary

This chapter has provided the components and means of measuring the financial structure of small independent colleges. Each division of financial structure—income production, working capital, and permanent capital—is built around a set of accounting categories, such as revenue, expenses, assets, and liabilities. The means to measure the financial structure—weights, rates of growth, dollar tracking and financial ratios—ascertain resource allocation and wealth within and between financial structures. The financial structure can be further explored for information on how small colleges deploy their financial resources to strengthen financial stability, and price elasticity can be used to assess the relative power of small colleges within their markets.

Notes

1. Financial Accounting Standards Board, "Statement of Financial Accounting Standards No. 93: Recognition of Depreciation by Not-for-Profit Organizations," August 1986, no. 047.
2. William S. Reed, *Financial Responsibilities of Governing Boards.* (Washington, D.C.: Association of Governing Boards of Universities and Colleges and National Association of College and University Business Officers, 2001), p. 3.

3. "Sheet 08180820.wk1: Unrestricted and Restricted Fund Types, 1987–96," National Science Foundation WebCASPAR Database System, 2001, http://caspar/nsf.gov/.

4. Lucie Lapovsky and Loren Loomis Hubbell, "An Uncertain Future," *Business Officer*, February 2001, p. 39.

5. Kent John Chatobar, "Financial Ratio Analysis Comes to Nonprofits," *Journal of Higher Education*, March/April 1989, pp. 188–89.

6. Douglas J. Collier and Cathleen Patrick, "A Multivariate Approach to the Analysis of Institutional Financial Condition," unpublished report (Boulder, Colo.: NCHEMS, 1976), p. 63.

7. John Nelson, *Private Colleges and Universities Outlook 2001/02 and Medians* (New York: Moody's Investors Service, 2001), p. 13.

8. Ronald E. Salluzzo and Philip Tahey, Frederic J. Prager, and Christopher J. Cowen, *Ratio Analysis in Higher Education*, 4th ed. (New York: KPMG LLP and Prager,McCarthy & Sealy, LLC, 1999), p. 69.

9. Nelson, *Private Colleges and Universities Outlook,* pp. 11, 13.

10. Collier and Patrick, "A Multivariate Approach to the Analysis of Institutional Financial Condition," p. 21.

11. Ibid., p. 23.

12. Ibid.

13. Ibid., p. 15.

14. Salluzzo et al., *Ratio Analysis in Higher Education*, p. 41.

15. J. Fred Weston and Eugene F. Brigham, *Managerial Finance*, 7th ed. (Hillsdale, N.J.: Dryden Press, 1981), p. 149.

16. Chatobar, "Financial Ratio Analysis Comes to Nonprofits," p. 193.

17. Ibid., p. 194.

18. Ibid., p. 195.

19. Nelson, *Private Colleges and Universities Outlook,* p. 14.

20. Ibid., pp. 10, 12.

21. Ibid., p. 12.

22. Ibid.

23. Michael S. McPherson, Morton Owen Schapiro, and Gordon C. Winston, eds., *Paying the Piper* (Ann Arbor: University of Michigan Press, 1994), pp. 241–42.

24. Ibid., p. 247.

25. Ibid., p. 248.

26. Michael K. Townsley, "Brinkmanship, Planning, Smoke, and Mirrors," *Planning for Higher Education* 19 (summer 1991): 27.

27. Gordon C. Winston, "Subsidies, Hierarchy and Peers: The Awkward Economics of Higher Education," *Journal of Economic Perspectives* 13, no. 1 (Winter 1999): 13–36.

Chapter

6

Identifying Financial Distress in Small Colleges

Chronic financial distress is not a temporary lapse into deficit, but a pervasive condition. Considerable evidence suggests that many colleges operate in chronic financial distress. During a five-year period in the 1990s—one of the strongest growth periods in America's history—33 percent of independent colleges reported deficits for three of the five years (see chapter 1). In colleges that struggle daily with financial distress, boards and administrators spend most of their time seeking cash to keep the doors open. Planning focuses on finding the money to pay faculty and vendors, not on improving the instructional program or responding to changes in the marketplace. Colleges in chronic financial distress survive from registration to registration, on donor gifts as they trickle in, and from one bridge loan to the next. The long-term view does not exist for them.

No matter how redeeming a college and its mission may be, certain events combined with a severely weakened financial structure can push it over the brink. A college that has relied on short-term bridge loans, for example, would almost certainly be forced to close if banks refused to provide further funding. A college in this situation probably would be forced to apply all excess operating income to short- and long-term debt reduction. Credit analysis would eventually indicate the hopelessness of its financial condition, donors would shun the college, and the bank would decide to cut its losses.

Financial distress can be defined using the composite financial index™ (CFI), developed by KPMG and Prager, McCarthy, and Sealy to assess the financial viability of independent colleges. This model employs financial ratios, which are converted to strength factors, weighted, and summed to produce an index score that measures financial condition.

The CFI assigns scores to 10 levels of progressively stronger financial conditions and then combines the scoring system with broad financial strategies. A college with a low CFI, for example, might be advised to assess its survivability, while a financially flexible college with a high CFI might be advised to experiment with ways to build a more robust financial structure. CFI offers a powerful tool for financial strategy because the index score measures financial condition and the components of the ratios suggest where colleges need to focus their attention.

Using the Consolidated Financial Index

The CFI model is built on simplicity and easy access to data. It focuses on a set of core ratios that represent important aspects of financial risk that should be monitored consistently:

- operations (primary reserve ratio)

- long-term debt (viability ratio)

- short-term results (net income ratio)

- the ability to increase wealth (net asset return)

The resulting score dilutes weakness in one ratio with strength from another.[1]

The CFI is computed using a four-step process. After the value of each ratio is calculated, it is converted to a strength factor that compares individual ratio values with corresponding threshold points on the CFI scoring scale (table 6.1). The strength factor is then weighted for the relative importance of that factor in the final CFI score. The weighting factors are normalized for retained wealth rather than for income from current operations.

A college's financial health is ascertained by comparing the CFI score to the CFI performance chart (table 6.1). The scores overlap because the index is not intended to represent financial health as a precise point on a chart, but rather as a range for a particular level of health. Given the CFI score, the range also suggests action the institution ought to consider.

Core Ratios and Computations

Primary Reserve Ratio

The primary reserve ratio measures the financial strength of an institution, indicating the surplus resources it could use for debt without recourse to additional net income (net asset) support from operations (table 6.2). Preferably, the ratio would increase

Table 6.1
Consolidated Financial Index Scoring Scale

Scale Level	CFI Scoring Range	Action
One	-1 to 1	Assess viability to survive
Two	0 to 2	Re-engineer the institution
Three	1 to 3	
Four	2 to 4	Direct resources toward transformation
Five	3 to 5	
Six	4 to 6	Focus resources to compete in future state
Seven	5 to 7	
Eight	6 to 8	Experiment with new initiatives
Nine	7 to 9	New initiatives/achieve a robust mission
Ten	>9	Deploy resources to achieve a robust mission

Source: Ronald E. Salluzzo, Philip Tahey, Frederic J. Prager, and Christopher J. Cowen, *Ratio Analysis in Higher Education*, 4th ed. (New York: KPMG LLP and Prager, McCarthy & Sealy, LLC, 1999), p. 24.

at the same rate as growth in expenses. If the ratio increases more slowly than expenses, expendable net assets will represent a shrinking margin of protection during adversity. A declining primary reserve ratio indicates a weakening financial condition. A ratio of .4 indicates that the institution has five months of reserves (40 percent of 12 months), which suggests cash flow for short-term cash needs, reasonable levels of cash for facilities maintenance, and reserves for unanticipated events. When the ratio is below .15, the institution probably uses short-term borrowing for cash and struggles to find reserves for reinvestment.[2]

Net Income Ratio

Net income ratio indicates whether operations produced a surplus or a deficit. This ratio has a direct bearing on the other three (primary reserve, return on net assets, and viability). Given the impact of depreciation, net income ratio should fall within or above 2–4 percent. Large deficits over a period of years signal the need for the institution's board and management to focus on restructuring the institution's income and expense streams. A deficit in a single year is not cause for concern if the institution is financially strong, understands the reasons for the deficit, and has a plan to remedy the situation. There are two computational forms of this ratio. The first—excess (deficiency) of unrestricted operating revenue over operating expenses (table 6.3)—is used when operating activities are separated from nonoperating activities. The second form—change in unrestricted net assets (table 6.4)—is used when operating activities are not disaggregated.[3]

Table 6.2
Primary Reserve Ratio

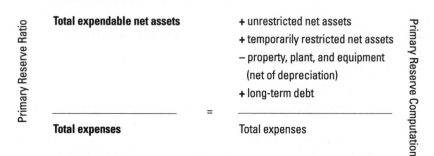

Primary Reserve Ratio	Total expendable net assets		+ unrestricted net assets + temporarily restricted net assets − property, plant, and equipment (net of depreciation) + long-term debt	Primary Reserve Computation
	Total expenses	=	Total expenses	

Source: Salluzzo et al., *Ratio Analysis in Higher Education*, p. 14.

Table 6.3
Net Income Ratio, Form 1: Excess (Deficiency)
of Unrestricted Operating Revenue over Operating Expenses

Net Income Ratio—Form 1	Excess (deficiency) of unrestricted operating revenue after unrestricted operating expenses		Excess (deficiency) of unrestricted operating revenue unrestricted operating expenses	Operating Activities Computation
	Total unrestricted operating income	=	Total unrestricted revenues and gains (losses) + Net assets released from restrictions	

Source: Salluzzo et al., *Ratio Analysis in Higher Education*, p. 16.

Table 6.4
Net Income Ratio, Form 2: Change in Unrestricted Net Assets

Net Income Ratio—Form 2	Change in unrestricted net assets	Change in unrestricted net assets		Change in Unrestricted Net Assets Computation
	_____	=	_____	
	Total unrestricted income	Total unrestricted revenues and gains (losses)		
		+ Net assets released from restrictions		
		+ Unrestricted investment return, excess		
		of spending rate		

Source: Salluzzo et al., Ratio Analysis in Higher Education, p. 17.

Return on Net Assets Ratio

Return on net assets ratio shows whether the institution is increasing its wealth (table 6.5). This trend is the best indicator of long-term changes in wealth. Owing to the volatility of the underlying asset returns (for example, endowment funds), KPMG and Prager recommend that a real rate of return (discounted for inflation) is in the range of 3–4 percent.[4] The degree of volatility in the underlying assets depends on the mix of endowment-to-plant assets. When liquid assets are turned into plant assets, the presumption is that the institution is adding to its productive capacity. Changes in plant assets may temporarily depress returns either until production expands to offset the loss of investable wealth or until donations are received to offset the investment in plant.

KPMG and Prager note that the return on net assets ratio may be calculated by removing permanently restricted net assets from the numerator and denominator, leaving assets that are under the direct control of the institution.[5] Those are the assets that the board can redeploy toward investments or production.

Viability Ratio

Viability ratio, according to KPMG and Prager, is "one of the most basic determinants of clear financial health: the availability of expendable net assets to cover debt should the institution need to settle its obligations as of the balance sheet date" (table 6.6).[6] From their review of financial statements, KPMG and Prager delineate the preferable range for this ratio as between 1.25 and 2.00 and higher. The viability ratio is an institution's safety net in the event of extraordinarily adverse conditions.

Table 6.5
Return on Net Assets Ratio

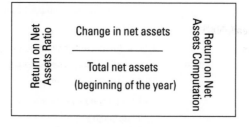

Source: Salluzzo et al., Ratio Analysis in Higher Education, p. 21.

When the ratio falls below 1:1 (expendable net assets match long-term debt), external agencies may see the institution as a credit risk and deny it capital. KPMG and Prager note that institutions may survive for long periods with a high level of debt leverage, but they lose their flexibility to raise capital, resulting in severe pressure to borrow for short-term cash needs to respond to changes in the market.[7]

Core Ratios: Strength and Weighting

The next steps in computing the CFI score involve converting ratio values into strength factors and weighting those factors. Strength factor conversion is carried out by dividing one of the ratios—primary reserve, net income, return on net assets, or viability—by its respective strength factor (table 6.7). The threshold for a strength factor is set to position a ratio relative to a CFI score of 1. For example, to perform the strength factor conversion for an institution with a primary reserve ratio of .5, divide .5 by .133 (its strength factor) to get 3.76.

After strength factors for each ratio are computed, they are weighted toward a "normalized" institution, one biased more toward retained wealth and less toward income generated from current operations.[8] This weighting scheme fits Gordon C. Winston's proposition that retained wealth gives institutions greater control over prices, improves their position in the market, enhances their ability to subsidize the total cost of education, and affords them the flexibility to make changes in the production of services.[9] The weights offset any inherent bias in the value of any one ratio.

Strength is weighted by multiplying the strength factor times the weight. The weights are taken from column 3 or 4 of table 6.7, depending on whether the

Table 6.6
Viability Ratio

Source: Salluzzo et al., *Ratio Analysis in Higher Education*, p. 22.

Viability Ratio			Viability Computation
Total expendable **net assets**		Unrestricted net assets + Temporarily restricted net assets − Property, plant, and equipment (net of depreciation) + Long-term debt	
———————	=	———————————————	
Long-term debt		(denominator) Long-term debt	

Source: Salluzzo et al., *Ratio Analysis in Higher Education*, p. 22.

Table 6.7
Strength Factors and Weights for CFI Scoring Ratio

Ratio	Strength Factor at Scale = 1	Weight With Long-term Debt	Weight Without Long-term Debt
Primary reserve	.133	35%	55%
Net income Operations model	.7%	10%	15%
Net income Change in unrestricted net model	1.3%	10%	15%
Return on net assets	2.0%	20%	30%
Viability	.417%	36%	

Source: Salluzzo et al., *Ratio Analysis in Higher Education*, p. 28.

institution has long-term debt. Continuing the example of the college with a strength factor conversion of 3.76 and assuming long-term debt, multiply 3.76 by the weight 35 percent (from column 2) for primary reserve weighting of 1.32. Assuming no debt, the weighting would be 2.07 (3.76 x 55% = 2.07). The strength and weighting factors for the net income ratios will depend on which form of the net income ratio is used (refer to the definitions of ratios earlier in this chapter).

Next, the CFI score is computed by summing the ratios after strength factor conversion and weighting, and then rounding. For example, if primary reserve is 1.32, net income is .05, return on net assets is .60, and viability ratio is 1.20, then the CFI score is 3.17. The scoring scale in table 6.5 suggests that this institution, which has a score of 3, should seriously consider reengineering itself.

Moderate financial distress under CFI is defined here as any institution with a score of greater than 1 but less than 3. Severe financial distress under the CFI scoring system is defined here as any institution whose score, averaged over a three-year period, is less than 1. Institutions meeting that criterion barely have working capital to cover short-term cash needs and may be surviving on borrowed funds.

Chapter 7 illustrates through four case histories the power of financial distress to force small colleges to close their doors. Their financial problems could have been detected earlier if the measures cited here had been used. Detecting financial distress early grants a college an important gift—time to build a viable strategy.

Notes

1. Ronald E. Salluzzo, Philip Tahey, Frederic J. Prager, and Christopher J. Cowen, *Ratio Analysis in Higher Education, 4th ed.* (New York: KPMG LLP and Prager, McCarthy & Sealy, LLC, 1999), pp. 10–11).
2. Ibid., pp. 11, 14.
3. Ibid., pp. 14, 15.
4. Ibid., pp. 16, 17.
5. Ibid., p. 21.
6. Ibid.
7. Ibid., p. 22.
8. Ibid., p. 28.
9. Gordon C. Winston, "Subsidies, Hierarchy and Peers: The Awkward Economics of Higher Education," *Journal of Economic Perspectives* 13, no. 1 (winter 1999): 13–36.

Why Small Colleges Fail: Four Cautionary Tales

Failure may come in many shapes, but as far as sizes go, it is the small college that struggles to stay open. Seventy-one percent of the colleges that closed between 1988 and 1997 enrolled fewer than 1,100 students. Despite larger beginnings, these colleges shrunk dramatically before they passed through the crucible of failure. With an average enrollment of 566 students, they were in a size category all their own. Four "micro" colleges that closed during the 1990s offer instructive illustrations of why small colleges fail. The common themes: too much debt, too little cash, and too little skepticism by boards and presidents.[1]

Upsala College

Upsala College was formed to serve New Jersey's Swedish Lutherans. Indeed, until the college's last days, students from Sweden traveled there to pursue college degrees. In the late 1960s, however, a denominational change removed the firm church underpinning from Upsala, leaving it to its own devices to fill a void left by the dwindling enrollment of middle-class Swedish Lutheran suburbanites. Upsala was left with an inner-city campus in East Orange, next to Newark, and no good ideas about how to generate revenue from a market of students with relatively little money and weak academic skills. As the college scrambled to boost enrollments, it saw a rise in the number of African American students (from 18 percent of total enrollment in 1976 to 47 percent in 1994), but few of them could afford an Upsala education.[2] When government aid did not cover the full cost of tuition, these students were not making up the difference. Increased enrollment may have indicated higher revenue, but it did not guarantee cash.

Enrollment peaked in 1984 at 1,822 students but shrunk thereafter for several reasons.[3] The college instituted new admission standards, reducing the size of the freshman class and requiring that returning students pay tuition and fees prior to reenrollment. What followed was an academic and financial disaster. More students were on academic probation, and payment defaults climbed alarmingly.[4] As enrollment declined, Upsala's operating deficit ballooned.

Hoping to reverse the situation, Upsala hired a consulting firm to recruit students. And recruit it did: From a low point of 1,138 students in 1990, enrollments climbed quickly to 1,556 students.[5] Once again, however, many of the new enrollees did not have the financial wherewithal to pay for their classes or the academic ability to do their work. Federal financial aid made up some of the difference between what students owed and what courses cost, but the rest was spread out over payment plans. By the early 1990s, nearly 50 percent of the accumulated operating deficit was due to uncollectible tuition accounts, a situation that was exacerbated by Upsala's irregular billing practices.[7]

Without cash, Upsala could not pay its bills; the college's bill paying cycle was twice as long as the industry's averages.[7] The endowment fund was depleted to meet operational expenses while accounting legerdemain obscured the fund's erosion. Through fund accounting, the college could project the appearance of a stable endowment fund by treating the transfer of endowment funds either as a receivable or as a loan to fund current operations. The endowment fund would continue to show an acceptable balance, but there would be no reality behind the number.

In midcrisis, Upsala's president decided that any external sign of this financial quandary would engulf the college in rumors, pushing it deeper into financial distress. The chimera of enrollment growth was allowed to perpetuate the delusion that just a few more students would resolve the financial strain. Despite their lack of preparation to study and to pay bills, each new student helped to hide the reality that many of them would not even complete one course.

The college was becoming a Potemkin village. Four new vice presidents had joined Upsala's administration during the early 1990s to help ease the financial crisis. At that time, the vice president of finance warned that the college would have to close unless drastic measures were taken. He was promptly fired. The new chief financial officer indicated that the college would need a substantial cash infusion to survive. The board agreed but established no targets.

The college did sell some property, two sister colleges loaned funds, and East Orange—a city that could ill afford being bilked for its generosity—guaranteed a $4 million bond.[9] But Upsala applied the money to capital projects, not to its ever-present and mounting cash deficit. The drumbeat of impending doom continued into the mid-1990s, when the U.S. Department of Education determined that the college was no longer able to meet its financial obligations. Upsala would have to provide a letter of credit for $1.5 million to continue to receive federal financial aid support. But bankers would not provide the letter. So, in 1994, the Commission on Higher Education of the Middle States Association of Colleges and Schools ruled that accreditation would be discontinued on December 31 of that year.[10]

The Upsala College community was stunned. Many people had been lulled into believing that growing enrollment and the new loans meant that "the college was turning the corner." A glimmer of hope appeared in the form of a South Korean industrialist who pledged $12 million to the college. It never materialized because the South Korean government required that such a large gift be devoted to a charitable organization at home.[11]

Ultimately, Upsala failed because it had not figured out how to accommodate itself to the loss of its original, financially reliable student market. This problem was severely complicated by a delusional enrollment strategy, failure in the leadership of Upsala's president and board, and an ineptly run financial office. In particular, the Upsala situation illustrates the consequences of a board's neglect of its role and responsibilities. The board might have been better served if it had taken a hard-nosed approach to the financial and market conditions facing the college. Although financial measures—ratio, trend analysis, and CFI scoring—might not have prevented the downfall of Upsala, at least they would have provided a realistic base from which to judge the future. Many boards make the mistake of granting the administration a charity assumption, assuming that since the operation is a charity and not a real business the college does not have to be held to rigorous standards. Board members who see their role as an honorary, community-service function abdicate oversight of the college to the administration. They willingly adhere to the belief that only administrators understand the inherent complexity of higher education.

As a result, these boards do not conduct thorough reviews of financial reports and documents. The college's financial condition and annual audit are presented to the board in a perfunctory report from the chief financial officer or the president. The audit management letter may be omitted from the audit review, leaving the board in the dark about problems in the financial office. The board may never see the auditors or have a chance to question them. The board's detachment from financial realities can be particularly damaging during a crisis, as administrators submit inadvisable plans for board approval without inviting board members' analysis of assumptions, prospects, or actions. This situation is even more shocking because most college board members come from business, where they would never give employees the leeway that they grant to college administrators. When the board finally voted to close Upsala College, it brought in a retired accountant to oversee the closure. To his horror, he found that financial records were out of date, inaccurate, or had not been kept at all.[12] One can only surmise how a board could allow this situation to occur.

Bradford College

Bradford College originally was a small finishing school for fashionable young women in the Boston area. Its mission was abandoned as more and more women sought professional lives of their own rather than becoming handmaidens to their husbands' careers. In response, Bradford developed an alternative niche in the 1980s—an "applied liberal arts" curriculum that integrated training for a specific career with the classic disciplines. As appeal for a liberal arts education grew, so did competition among colleges offering similar degrees. Bradford compensated for drops in enrollments by adding new majors, eventually offering nearly 40 majors despite having only 35 faculty members.[13] Bradford's marketing strategy was simple, albeit indiscriminate. The college trolled for and reeled in any student it could find. Typical of many small colleges, enrollment numbers were not known until August 1.

In 1989, a new president came on board. An executive director of Oxfam America, he was a money-raising whirlwind who increased Bradford's endowment fund from $7 million in 1989 to more than $23 million in 1998. In keeping with the tendency of small colleges in chronic financial distress to misapply endowment funds, Bradford put a substantial portion of its $23 million into building renovations. Enrollments did not increase as a result, and by 1997, deficits remained unchanged at more than $5 million. That year, the college hired George Dehne, a noted marketing specialist in higher education, to help develop an effective marketing strategy. He recommended that Bradford "define its specialties, concentrate on them, and get rid of everything else."[14] This is a prescription that few college presidents or boards want to hear.

In 1998, the president proposed a drastic move: Bradford should borrow $17.9 million to build a new dormitory. The dorm would attract a new cadre of students, pushing enrollments from 550 to 775 students, reducing the unfunded tuition discount (which was running at 30.3 percent), and pulling the college out of its financial misery.[15] One board member resigned rather than support such a wishful project, which he predicted would fail. The rest of the board bowed to the president's wishes. Their unwillingness to take a tough stance meant that students would be given short shrift.

Table 7.1
Summary of Bradford College's Finances and Enrollment

	1998	1997
Enrollment	494	586
Tuition discount	18.6%	48.0%
Net income	$13,000	$361,000
Cumulative net income since 1988	$13,000	–$3.4 million
Net assets/total assets	—	56.0%

Source: "Sheet 08180820.wk1, Unrestricted and Restricted Fund Types: 1987–96," "Sheet 10463025.wk 1, Enrollment Level 1988–1997," NSF WebCASPAR Database System, http://caspar/nsf.gov.

Table 7.1 shows what happened at Bradford between 1988 and 1997, two years before its collapse. In 1988, net income contributed only $13,000 toward the college's financial reserves. Obviously, such lackluster performance could not sustain the college. Apparently, the college invested considerable effort in increasing its enrollment, which grew 19 percent by 1997. Growth came at a high price; tuition discounting rose from 18.6 percent of tuition during this period. Larger discounts would have diminished cash needed for operations and cut funds to support inflationary increases in expenses. The good news was that net income for 1997 was $361,000. However, a cumulative deficit of $3.4 million remained. In 1999, the chickens came home to roost.

According to the *Chronicle of Higher Education*, projections unraveled in the fall of 1998. Only 175 students enrolled, and unfunded financial aid "skyrocketed" from 30.3 percent of tuition to 48.2 percent. On top of this, the Asian market collapsed along with its local currencies. This situation caused problems for Bradford when Asian students could not afford to return. The college's deficit for 1998 and 1999 was $6.1 million out of a total budget of $14 million.[16] Recognizing that the bell was tolling, Bradford hired a new president who immediately set about cutting the deadwood from the curriculum. Despite the board's willingness to focus on fund raising to cover deficits, no one would give money in the amounts needed to ensure the college's survival. In September 1999, with only 497 students enrolled and unfunded financial aid at 60 percent of tuition and fees, Bradford was practically giving education away. The end came swiftly, with the board voting to close in November 1999. The class of 2000 was Bradford's last.

Why did Bradford fail? It was too small, and it had no financial reserves to counterbalance its size. Competition ate away mercilessly at its student market, forcing enrollment of every willing body. The coup de grace was the president's decision to use endowment for construction, driving the college into the ground. In summary, by the time Bradford's leadership recognized and accepted the college's woeful condition, it was too late to take further reasonable action.

Trinity College

Trinity College, an innovative school near Burlington, Vermont, is the third sad refrain in our repertoire of small-college tales. Trinity was a women's college that admitted men who were at least 22. It was the first college in the region to offer night, weekend, and continuing education classes. But beyond its small size, Trinity was handicapped because the campus was set far from populated areas, which are few and far between in Vermont. As competitors with nontraditional programs of their own entered the market, Trinity's cash cow jumped over the fence.

Between 1990 and 1999, enrollment in continuing education dropped 29 percent, from 673 to 304 students. During the same period, enrollment in the traditional women's program fell from 411 to 264 students. The loss of undergraduate students was buffered by 416 incoming graduate students, but the graduate enrollment shift was not large enough to completely offset the loss of revenue from low enrollment in the traditional and continuing education programs. Although Trinity enrolled 147 new students for the 1998–99 academic year, it was discounting tuitions 45 percent—a larger discount than the college could afford. Still worse, despite their hugely discounted educations, many students found they did not like Trinity, and they left before finishing their coursework, adding insult to a $2.7 million cumulative-operating-deficit injury.[17]

In July 1999, the board announced that Trinity would close at the end of the academic year. But, alas, good fortune befell the college in November, when it leased a freshman dormitory to a health care facility. Giving it the old college try, Trinity stayed open, culling 20 out of its 30 majors, cutting expenses beyond the 10 faculty members released in May 1999. Committees worked to polish the college's image, strengthen finances, improve technology, and discover new money-making ventures. The admissions office, which had been closed for six months, reopened. Unfortunately, as one board member said, as agile as Trinity was, its competitors were more so.[18]

The college had already lost valuable recruiting time. Of the 120 new students Trinity had hoped to enroll, only half actually did, and 15 of those were lost to attrition.[19] No college would take Trinity up on its offer to merge. Size, excessive discounting, mounting deficits, a huge debt load, and confusion over closing announcements had finally and completely doomed the college.

There are two important lessons to be learned from Trinity's experience. First, a college should never announce closing plans if there is a chance it will remain open. The momentum of closure may be impossible to interrupt, let alone reverse. Second, when a college loses most of its students, it will hold little or no merger value in the marketplace. Without enrollments to offer a potential merge partner, colleges have only a campus to sell, and in most cases, the buildings on the land are worthless.

Spring Garden College

Spring Garden College had a long and hallowed history as one of the first technology colleges in the nation. Originally located in central Philadelphia, it moved in 1905 to Chestnut Hill, an affluent suburb. There the college prospered and slowly grew for nearly 80 years. In 1971, its enrollment experienced a growth spurt, bringing the number of students to 1,051. The following year, however, enrollment slipped more than 30 percent.[20] Not until 1978 did enrollment exceed the 1971 level. That period of low enrollment had a devastating effect on fund balances, and Spring Garden's deficit grew to $1.1 million.[21]

Hoping for a turnaround, the college moved in 1983 to a 33-acre Victorian campus within a few blocks of the recently closed Pennsylvania School for the Deaf. But unanticipated increases in plant maintenance and a larger debt load pushed the college closer to financial calamity. Volatile enrollments were another issue. Spring Garden reached its peak enrollment of 1,667 in 1985, when its fund deficit was at a seven-year low.[22] By 1989, however, enrollment had fallen back to 1,084 students, and the fund deficit had risen to $3.8 million.[23] At the end of the 1989–90 academic year, the college was so poor that it had to defer its summer payroll until September. Like the other financially desperate examples described earlier, Spring Garden frantically sought ways to salvage its financial structure.

More than 30 staff members were released, and a fund-raising campaign was begun to offset the deficit.[24]

Despite two years of respite, by 1992 enrollment had collapsed to 681 students. A final rescue effort—selling the campus to another college and then leasing it back—failed. Spring Garden—burdened by a weak financial structure and mired in high expenses following the ill-advised move to the new campus—closed its doors in 1992 after 141 years of service.

Lessons Learned

These four examples suggest that there is more to failure than high debt and low cash. Upsala, Bradford, Trinity, and Spring Garden, were small colleges. Lacking adequate financial reserves and enrollment levels, they could not compensate for their relatively insignificant positions in the education marketplace. Three of the colleges—Upsala, Bradford, and Spring Garden—were too weak to service the debt they undertook.

To bolster enrollment levels, Bradford, Upsala, and Trinity discounted tuition excessively. The most egregious example is Bradford. The year it closed, net price fell to 3 percent of tuition. Apparently, Bradford's leaders had predicted that short-term spikes in enrollment and revenue would translate into cash gains. But unfunded financial aid only translates into a *loss* of cash. The difference between sticker price and net price—the amount of the tuition discount—is lost. Unfortunately for these colleges, in times of crisis, cash is king. When a college does not have money to pay bills, debt load, tuition discounting, revenue, and expenditure balances take a back seat to making the next payroll, or paying vendors, or paying the bank. Employees and vendors can be put off for a while, but when a college can't pay the bankers, the game is over.

Bradford also borrowed huge sums to finance a dormitory and fuel a pipe dream. Without enrollments and reserves to fall back on, the college collapsed under its own weight. When Bradford closed, its cumulative operating deficit for the previous nine years was $3.8 million. Deficits were reported for six of those years, and net assets/total assets had declined 30 percent. The college had violated nearly every rule of prudent financial management. Excessively high debt loads and continuing deficits are ready signs of financial problems.

Trinity may be the most unfortunate example, because it was not burdened by debt or by bad decisions. Its discounting policy was a vain attempt to match the prices offered by its competitors, mainly public institutions. Ultimately, the college was struck down by a market (traditional-aged women) that was no longer interested in attending an isolated rural women's college. Perseverance, diligence, and faith in mission were not enough to make up for size, lack of resources, and geographic location.

Leaders at all four colleges failed or were unable to address the loss of equilibrium between revenue and expenses early enough. These colleges were in financial distress long before they closed their doors, having accumulated deficits that amounted to a sizeable portion of their annual incomes. But the ambiguities of leadership had paralyzed decision making until it was too late. Once these colleges entered financial crisis, they had lost a precious commodity—time. In a state of crisis, there is no time to judiciously prune programs, conduct another fund-raising program, build a strategic competitive plan, or formulate an effective marketing program.

Problems with marketing and competition put the first nails in the college coffins. Recall that Upsala lost its original student market and was never able to figure out how to deliver services effectively to another market of low-income students. Bradford tried to offer too many programs within its market, thereby diluting its image and mission. To project a competitive reputation, small colleges must focus on what they do best. They must keep in touch with their students and remain vigilant about what the big college down the street and the small competitor across town are doing to secure enrollments. Trinity and Bradford saw competition chew away significant portions of their markets; Trinity lost its continuing education cash cow to bigger and stronger players. When students shopped for an education, they looked to colleges with broader reputations, better services, and up-to-date facilities. Swift evaluation of trends and a competitive strategy are crucial weapons a small college can use against larger colleges prepared to trump it.

When the end came, it was swift. Most of these colleges were able to subsist from year to year on small gifts or loans. Although tuition dependency supposedly signals financial risk, the emergency transfusions of gifts to Bradford and Trinity lowered their tuition dependency rate well below the high-risk level of 60 percent. However, the gifts never produced surplus income that could be translated into endowments. Despite the donors' generosity, these colleges could never gain traction; deficit financing continued to absorb every new dollar. Donors either grew tired of throwing good money after bad or could not afford to keep contributing to these colleges. Banks would no longer lend to them. So when the gifts stopped or the loans were due and not paid, the colleges closed their doors.

Who should have evaluated the trends for these micro colleges? Who should have made or at least overseen marketing decisions? Just who *was* calling the shots when mistakes were made about tuition discounting, or debt management, or capital expenditures? The presidents of these colleges served them poorly, either misunderstanding financial dynamics in general or ignoring the potential financial implications of their individual actions in the hope that their colleges would somehow squeak by. Board members deferred to presidential pipe dreams, perhaps not demanding enough evidence or information to justify critical financial decisions. And faculty members, left to fend for themselves as forgotten players in the game of rebuild vs. collapse, probably resisted change and passively or actively played a part in their college's demise.

Were there obvious signals of impending doom? Leading up to their demise, these colleges reported rising debt loads, continuing deficits, shrinking net assets, falling enrollment, investments converted to fixed assets, and dwindling amounts of cash. These conditions are major factors in both the CFI scoring system and the Moody's and NCHEM ratios of credit worthiness. If the president and the board had tracked financial trends using these ratios, it would have been apparent that financial and marketing strategies, instead of improving their financial condition, were making it markedly worse. Having this knowledge, they could have improved their chances by targeting the ratio factors to improve their financial condition. Moreover, attention to financial performance could have given them more time to look at reasonable alternatives to a precipitous closing. Alternatives evaporate as a college's fortunes decline because potential suitors will prefer the carrion to the cost of buying a half-dead corpse.

As John Nelson, senior vice president at Moody's Investor Services, suggests, "Small colleges have the best chance of surviving when the president understands finances and works well with the chief financial officer, and when the board takes a critical role in decisions."[25] Small colleges need decisive, creative, inspirational leaders. The shrewd president of a small college will design a financially viable course and demonstrate it to the board, the faculty, the students, and the larger marketplace. Find a president with perspective and foresight and join him or her with a board that refuses to humor the administration, and you will have created true leadership.

Upsala, Bradford, Trinity, and Spring Garden reached the end because they lost their markets, made bad decisions, and were no longer economically viable. The sad and demoralizing prospect of closing should not become an excuse for preserving the inept or the inefficient. The discipline of the market is a better incentive for allocating resources in higher education. These four colleges are like many that seem to stumble from one catastrophe to another. Barely able to sustain the resources to stay open, they are hard pressed to deliver an education that prepares their students for the labor force.

Notes

1. "In the Matter of Upsala College," Student Financial Assistance Proceeding: Compliance and Enforcement Division, Office of Postsecondary Education, U.S. Department of Education, May 17, 1994, docket no. 93-148-St, www.ed-cha.org/cases.
2. "Sheet 10463025.wk 1, Enrollment Level 1988–1997," National Science Foundation WebCASPAR database system, caspar.nsf.gov/.
3. Joyce Mercer, "Death Throes at Upsala," *Chronicle of Higher Education,* April 24, 1995.
4. Ibid.
5. NSF WebCaspar Database System; http:// caspar/nsf.gov/.
6. Ibid.
7. Ed, "In the Matter of Upsala College."
9. Mercer, "Death Throes at Upsala."
10. ED, "In the Matter of Upsala College."
11. Mercer, "Death Throes at Upsala."
12. Ibid.
13. Martin Van Der Werf, "The Death of a Small College," *Chronicle of Higher Education*, May 12, 2000.
14. Ibid.
15. Ibid.; "Sheet 08180820.wk1 Unrestricted and Restricted Fund Types: 1987–96," NSF WebCASPAR Database System, http://caspar/nsf.gov.
16. Van Der Werf, "Death of a Small College."
17. Martin Van Der Werf, "Vermont's Trinity College Survives a Scare, but Its Future Remains Uncertain," *Chronicle of Higher Education*, May 12, 2000.
18. Ibid.
19. Ibid.
20. "Sheet 15565881 wk.1: Opening Fall Enrollment: 1967 to 1997," NSF WebCASPAR Database System, 2001, http://caspar/nsf.gov/.
21. "Sheet 08073296 wk.1: Spring Garden College Unrestricted and Restricted Fund Types: 1975 to 1991," NSF WebCASPAR Database System, 2001, http://caspar/nsf.gov/.
22. "Sheet 15565881 wk.1: Opening Fall Enrollment: 1967 to 1997."
23. "Sheet 08073296 wk.1: Spring Garden College Unrestricted and Restricted Fund Types: 1975 to 1991."
24. "Spring Garden College Fails to Meet Payroll," *Chronicle of Higher Education,* June 6, 1992.
25. John Nelson, interview by author, August 7, 2001.

Financial State of Small Colleges

The future of small colleges depends on how well they manage their financial structures. We have not systematically studied small colleges to determine their overall financial condition, so we can only conclude from anecdotal and fragmentary evidence that it is quite precarious. This chapter demonstrates and comments on the financial condition of particular sets of small colleges during the academic years 1996, 1997, 1998, and 2000. First we will define the entire data set, then the nonfinancial characteristics of the institutions within it, and finally the financial structure of the smaller members of the cohort.

Data Set

Longitudinal comparisons are not easy. Data errors make it hard to determine whether missing data indicate a zero value or an oversight, whether suspicious entries are anomalous or incorrectly categorized. Further complicating longitudinal comparisons is the lack of generally accepted accounting practices (GAAP). Some colleges still do not depreciate plant or buildings according to GAAP rules, for example, which leads to distorted relative asset values. Finally, IPEDS, which compiles large volumes of information into reports for the U.S. Department of Education, has undergone disruptive accounting and formatting changes and sometimes fails to record data on its financial databases.

Included in our data set are independent colleges classified by the Carnegie system as institutions that grant bachelor's, master's, or doctorate degrees and those with reported enrollment, revenue, and expense data for each of the four years 1996, 1997, 1998, and 2000. Specialized independent colleges—theological, business, art, music, or tribal—are excluded. Our criteria yield 825 independent institutions out of an original data population of 1,064 independent institutions. (In several instances, data reported by an institution for a variable were excluded if the value was a significant outlier—an indication of the data error.)

The 825 colleges were subdivided into six enrollment categories. Though this study focuses on small colleges with fewer than 3,000 students, larger institutions are included to serve as reference points.

Category I   500 or fewer students
Category II   501 to 1,000 students
Category III   1,001 to 2,000 students
Category IV   2,001 to 3,000 students
Category V   3,001 to 5,000 students
Category VI   more than 5,000 students

Independent institutions are moving targets (table 8.1). Over the four-year period, institutions have migrated between enrollment categories as they have grown or shrunk. Nevertheless, the 825 institutions in the cohort have remained intact for the four years.

Table 8.1
Number of Independent Colleges Included in the Data Set
by Year from 1997–2000

Category	Enrollment	1997	1998	1999	2000
I	Less than 500	40	77	30	36
II	501 to 1,000	150	172	143	140
III	1,001 to 2,000	282	278	290	280
IV	2,001 to 3,000	144	115	149	147
V	3,001 to 5,000	85	74	89	98
VI	Greater than 5,000	124	109	125	124
	Total	825	825	825	825

Source: "Financial Trend Data CD Fiscal 1997 to 2000: Private Colleges and Universities, IPEDS, College Board Institutional Characteristics" (Florence, Oreg.: John Minter Associates, 2002).

Institutional Characteristics

The average weighted enrollment was 326 students for Category I colleges, 750 students for Category II colleges, 1,470 students for Category III colleges, and 2,443 students for Category IV colleges. Enrollment for the first two categories is well below the nominal enrollment of 1,100 students for optimum scale economies for four-year colleges.[1] Nearly 90 percent of the colleges in Categories I and II grant bachelor's degrees. Sixty-six percent of Category III colleges are four-year colleges with near-optimum enrollment. Category IV is within the range of optimum economy of scale for all four-year colleges; however, only 43 percent of colleges in this category are four-year institutions.

Obviously, the proportion of undergraduate students reflects the mission of the college. The smallest set of colleges (Categories I, II, and III) report that 90 percent or more of their students are undergraduates. The proportion of undergraduates trails off to 84 percent for Category IV and to 74 percent for Category V. The largest institutions report only 64 percent of their students as undergraduates.

A striking feature of the four categories with the fewest students is that all but Category IV colleges report enrollment declines from 1997 to 2000. Enrollment fell 9 percent at Category I colleges, 2.4 percent at Category II colleges, and .2 percent at Category III colleges, while enrollments grew 1.2 percent at category IV colleges. Growth is apparent among the remaining categories as well: Category V saw enrollment increase 4.9 percent, and Category VI saw a modest growth of 1.1 percent. Enrollment trends put tremendous pressure on tuition dependent colleges to find alternative sources of funding. It will be interesting to see in the next section how these colleges have resolved this conundrum.

Beyond enrollment comparisons, we must consider academic quality, student retention, graduation rates, student faculty loads, and doctoral faculty—all of which play major roles in maintaining a college's desirable image to students, grant agencies, and donors.

Quality indicators move in tandem with institutional size. The percentile ranking of colleges with students scoring at the 75th percentile for the SAT is lowest for the first two categories, with respective rankings of 35 percent and 34 percent. The rankings then rise above 40 percent for the next three categories, with the sixth category having the highest percentile ranking of 58 percent. Students with better SAT scores tend to choose larger colleges.

Retention figures indicate not only a freshman's willingness to return as a sophomore despite the emotional and maturational bumps inherent in the first year of college, but the likelihood that he or she will persist in the long haul to graduation. Colleges with low retention rates have to expend scarce funds to find replacement students. Net flow of income falls as upper-level class sizes shrink. Dormitories are not filled, food service operates at less than capacity, the bookstore sells fewer books, and scale economies are lost in administrative and student services.

Colleges with fewer than 1,000 students face the greatest struggle retaining their students; retention rates range from a low of 69 percent for Categories I and

Table 8.2
Weighted Averages for Key Institutional Characteristics, 1997–2000

Enrollment Categories

(I)	Less than 500
(II)	501 to 1,000
(III)	1,001 to 2,000
(IV)	2,001 to 3,000
(V)	3,001 to 5,000
(VI)	More than 5,000

	I	II	III	IV	V	VI
Enrollment	326	750	1,470	2,443	3,803	10,253
Undergraduate percent	94%	94%	90%	84%	74%	64%
Selectivity percentile	35%	34%	43%	47%	44%	58%
Retention rates	69%	69%	77%	79%	80%	85%
Graduation rates	46%	46%	60%	63%	60%	67%
Doctoral faculty percent	59%	58%	67%	64%	66%	63%
Student faculty load	14:1	18:1	20:1	23:1	29:1	36:1

Source: "Financial Trend Data CD Fiscal 1997 to 2000: Private Colleges and Universities, IPEDS, College Board Institutional Characteristics"

II colleges, 76 percent for Category III colleges, 79 percent for Category IV colleges, 80 percent for Category V colleges, to a high of 85 percent for Category VI colleges.

Graduation rates, like retention rates, measure persistence, but they also suggest how well a college moves its students toward the goal of a college degree. High graduation rates build the alumni base and therefore the gift base. Satisfied students advertise well to potential enrollees and employers. The productive capacity of the institution with high graduation rates probably has been fully and optimally utilized and managed.

The IPEDS graduation measure is the percentage of students who graduate after six years. As with retention rates, the lowest graduation rates after six years can be found at the smallest colleges: Categories I and II struggle with 46 percent graduation rates. The rate rises to 60 percent for Category III colleges and 63 percent for Category IV colleges, slips to 60 percent for Category V colleges, and rebounds to 67 percent for colleges with more than 5,000 students.

The *proportion of doctoral faculty to undergraduate faculty* is inverse. Doctoral faculty seems key in the productive structure of institutions with graduate programs.

An interesting contrast exists between Categories II and III; though colleges in both categories are small relative to their larger sisters, 58 percent of full-time faculty members at Category II colleges hold doctorates, while 67 percent of faculty members at Category III colleges hold doctorates. Category III has the highest proportion of doctorates of all categories, though the exact reason is unclear. Perhaps a difference in the missions of colleges across the categories could explain it. Recall that 85 percent of Category II colleges grant bachelors degrees, while only 66 percent of Category III institutions grant such degrees.

Student faculty loads at small colleges are ideal, indicating a more intimate, scholarly environment. These colleges lose out on the financial advantages of larger class sizes, however. Unfortunately, the same quality that makes small colleges appealing also adversely impacts income flow, with smaller classes generating significantly less net revenue than larger classes at larger institutions.

Colleges with fewer than 500 students demonstrate a 14 to 1 student to faculty load. The ratio jumps slightly to 18 to 1 for colleges with between 501 and 1,000 students; 20 to 1 for colleges with between 1,001 and 2,000 students; and 23 to 1 for colleges with between 2,001 and 3,000 students. The load factor jumps sizably to 29 to 1 for colleges with between 3,001 and 5,000 students—and 36 to 1 for the largest colleges enrolling more than 5,000 students.

Table 8.2 clearly shows that colleges with fewer than 1,000 students differ greatly from colleges with more than 1,000 students in terms of their selectivity, retention, graduation, doctoral faculty, and student-faculty measures. The next major division in the characteristics of colleges occurs when colleges enroll more than 5,000 students. From this information we can surmise the obvious: that institutional mission and size dramatically affect the characteristics of the institution, for better or worse.

Financial Structure

Table 8.3 offers an important insight into the financial structure of independent institutions. Tuition dependency (tuition and fees as a percentage of total revenue) is not associated with small size as would be expected. In reality, tuition dependency is lowest—35 percent, 39 percent, and 42 percent, respectively—for the smallest institutions (Categories I, II, and III), and it rises to 49 percent and 52 percent for the larger institutions (Categories IV and V), then drops to 46 percent for the largest institutions. This phenomenon is interesting, given that enrollments on average declined for institutions with fewer than 2,000 and grew at the larger institutions.

How do the smallest colleges resolve this problem? Investment returns and auxiliary services are not the answer. Investment returns are not significantly higher for Category I or II institutions, and the contribution of auxiliary revenue to total revenue for the first two categories is comparable to that of the other categories. The data suggest that small colleges offset reductions in tuition and fee contribution to total revenue through grants and gifts. The grants in our set of colleges were probably applied not toward research, but rather (like gifts) toward operational support or plant maintenance. (It is difficult to sort out the use of grants given how data are reported.)

Access to grant and gift income in the 1990s helped small colleges climb out of declining enrollments during one of the richest stock market booms in the 20th century. Foundations and individual donors were flush with money and looking for a charitable cause that would benefit from significant gifts. The problem is that the stock market has weakened since 2000, and 2002 cannot yet promise a turnaround. Continued market stagnation could see a serious and continued loss of funds in institutional coffers, in which case all but the smallest colleges (Categories I and II) could find themselves in serious trouble.

Table 8.3
Weighted Averages for Major Revenue Sources, 1997–2000

Enrollment Categories
(Revenue Source as Percentage of Revenue)

(I)	Less than 500
(II)	501 to 1,000
(III)	1,001 to 2,000
(IV)	2,001 to 3,000
(V)	3,001 to 5,000
(VI)	More than 5,000

	I	II	III	IV	V	VI
Tuition	35%	39%	42%	49%	52%	46%
Grants	10%	8%	5%	4%	5%	7%
Gifts	29%	22%	17%	14%	13%	9%
Investment Return	10%	11%	16%	15%	14%	15%
Auxiliaries	13%	15%	15%	14%	12%	10%

Source: "Financial Trend Data CD Fiscal 1997 to 2000: Private Colleges and Universities, IPEDS, College Board Institutional Characteristics"

Table 8.4 displays the compounded rate of change for revenue and expenses over the four years under consideration. If expense growth rates outpace revenue growth rates, the dollar value of expenses will eventually outgrow revenue, resulting in future deficits. For example, if revenue were to grow 1 percent compounded annually, $100,000 of revenue in 1997 would grow to $103,030 in 2000. If expenses were to grow 4 percent compounded annually, $95,000 would grow to $112,486 in 2000. A positive net income of $5,000 in 1997 would turn into a net loss of $9,456 in 2000. We could see this scenario arise due to a dramatic drop in grant or gift revenue owing to a stock market slide.

The net difference in growth rates for total revenue and total expenses is positive in all colleges except for those in Category II. The net growth rate for Category III is substantially higher relative to its neighbors, reflecting negative growth in total expenses. The category with the largest institutions differs massively in its growth rates, which probably reflects the inordinate size of their investment portfolios. Except for Category II colleges, then, revenue is growing so quickly that no dynamic exists to suggest that expenses will cross revenue in the near future. The scale of the negative difference in growth rates for Category II colleges could spell trouble.

When the focus shifts to operating margins, the picture is not so rosy for small colleges. Operating revenues and expenses refer to the flow of income from tuition and fees, auxiliaries, instruction, research, educational support, institutional expenses, financial aid, the plant, and auxiliary services. Investment returns are excluded, as are revenue and expenses from hospitals and independent operations. A look at the operating margin represents the best available picture of net income generated by the primary missions of the institution, whether education or research.

The compound rate of growth for operating income refers to the speed of change over time. For example, a 5 percent compound rate for the operating margin means that a margin of $100,000 in 1997 would have grown to $115,763 in 2000. Table 8.4 shows negative growth rates for colleges in every category except the category with the largest colleges. The three categories with the smallest enrollments have relatively large, and in several cases very large, negative growth rates. The magnitude of negative growth is greatest for the category with the very smallest colleges.

How do colleges manage this problem *when*, not *if*, investment returns or gift and grant revenue fall dramatically after a stock market crash? Some colleges will rely on net assets or turn to their huge investment portfolios. But many colleges with enrollments below 1,001 may not have as rich an option. For this group, the relationship of investment to expenses before the stock market crash of 2000 and 2001 is only 1.2 to 1 and 1.7 to 1, respectively. Any serious degradation in their

Table 8.4
Weighted Averages for Revenue and Expense, and Operating Margin Compound Rates of Change, 1997–2000

Enrollment Categories

(I)	Less than 500
(II)	501 to 1,000
(III)	1,001 to 2,000
(IV)	2,001 to 3,000
(V)	3,001 to 5,000
(VI)	More than 5,000

	I	II	III	IV	V	VI
Total revenue*	3.73%	2.56%	5.34%	5.55%	5.99%	12.52%
Total expenses*	2.08%	6.40%	-.54%	4.78%	4.00%	.72%
Net difference	1.65%	-3.84%	5.88%	.77%	1.99%	11.80%
Operating margin**	-11.2%	-6.34%	-8.62%	-5.27%	-4.09%	1.66%
Net assets (000)	$2,238	$1,665	$8,338	$15,266	$16,809	$53,538
Total investments (000)	$10,558	$24,376	$75,437	$98,591	$112,289	$655,110
Total net as percent of revenue	16%	20%	26%	27%	27%	29%
Institutions with negative net slopes***	15%	21%	23%	25%	26%	24%

* Compound rates of change for 1997–2000

** Operating margin growth rate excludes investment returns from revenue, and hospitals and independent operations from revenue and expenses; change is a compound rate of change.

*** Institutions with a negative slope of total net income for four years

Source: "Financial Trend Data CD Fiscal 1997 to 2000: Private Colleges and Universities, IPEDS, College Board Institutional Characteristics"

investment pool could quickly see these colleges eating their net assets for survival. The third category could find itself in a similar fix, as the negative growth rates for its operating margin are out-of-scale.

Small colleges did quite well, however, during the last four years of the 20th century. Total net income ranged from 16 percent to 29 percent as a percentage of revenue for the four years. Despite disappointing declines in revenue among smaller colleges, revenue from grants, gifts, and investment revenue more than make up the loss. The major issue facing the independent institutions in this study is whether growth dynamic built into the financial structure results in expenses outpacing revenue during periods of falling revenue, and whether nontuition and fee forms of revenue can sustain their rates of growth over the long term.

A fairly sizeable number of institutions had negative slopes for their net income—though not necessarily deficits—during the late 1990s. As with tuition dependency—and contrary to the assumption that small colleges encounter greater financial difficulties than large colleges—small colleges have the lowest percentage, with 15 percent of colleges having negative slopes for their net income. This percentage rises above 21 percent for colleges with enrollments between 501 and 1,000 and climbs well above that level to 26 percent for institutions with between 3,001 and 5,000 students. The percentage is slightly lower, at 26 percent for institutions with more than 5,000 students.

There are several possible explanations for this anomaly. Perhaps presidents and boards of small independent colleges manage their relatively meager resources more prudently because they have little slack in the system to overcome errors and bad times. In contrast, large, wealthy independent colleges and universities enjoy considerable slack and can afford to let net income slide without adversely affecting the institution.

Table 8.5
Institutions Facing Financial Challenges – Year 2000

	<500	Enrollment Groups 501 to 1,000	1,001 to 2,000	2,001 to 3,000	3,001 to 5,000	>5,000	Total
Total Institutions	36	140	280	147	98	124	825
Financial Challenged	8	33	43	13	12	19	128
Percentage	22%	24%	15%	9%	12%	15%	16%

Financial Challenges

Colleges or universities falling below three criteria—Moody's median for total resources per student, Moody's median for the operating margin ratio, and declining enrollment for the year—were judged to be financial distressed. The two Moody ratios were used because their research suggests that these ratios are significantly correlated with below-standard financial performance. Declining enrollments is the third criteria because enrollments generate a significant proportion of revenue for most institutions. Sixteen percent of all private institutions were classified as financial distressed, and the largest proportion of financially distressed colleges were those with fewer than 1,001 students. The next highest proportion of financially distressed institutions—15 percent—were colleges or universities with more than 5,000 students. The lowest percentage—9 percent—were those institutions enrolling between 2,000 and 3,001 students.

According to these criteria, the weakest colleges are the smallest colleges. How does this square with an earlier finding that fewer small colleges reported a negative slope for total net income? Total net income counts total capital gains or losses, but the Moody's ratio for operating income only counts 4.5 percent of total investment value. Their ratio attempts to smooth large jumps in capital valuation by standardizing the return. This suggests that the true financial condition of some institutions was masked by extraordinary gains in investment value through the late 1990s. The implication is that by mid-2002, many small private institutions, in particular small colleges, could find themselves squeezed by the market crashes of 2001 and a stagnant economy. These institutions could discover that 2002 is the beginning of an unrelenting financial crisis based on unrealistic expectations of huge returns from tiny endowments to cover an ever-widening gap between income and expenditures.

Summary

Colleges with enrollments below 1,001 differ significantly from other independent institutions of higher education. The characteristics of these institutions and their financial structure set them apart, with differences evident but not as pronounced for colleges with enrollments between 1,001 and 2,000. Institutions of this size produced large treasure chests over the four-year period 1997–2000, as did their bigger sisters, providing them with reserves in the face of unexpected economic events.

Note

1. Malcolm Getz and John J. Siegfried, "Costs and Productivity in American Colleges and Universities," in *Economic Challenges in Higher Education*, ed. Charles T. Clotfelter, Ronald G. Ehrenberg, Malcolm Getz, and John J. Siegfried (Chicago: University of Chicago Press, 1991), p. 355.

Chapter 9

Planning and Leadership:
Tools for Pulling Back from the Brink

For the typical small college president, financial strategy is not part of the lexicon of leadership and management. These presidents tend small crises by the hour and dedicate most of their professional lives to enrollment budgets, new instructional programs, faculty hiring, and donor wooing. They work with scant financial reserves, and—thanks to a lack of accountability standards for administrators and faculty members— they generally work alone. Although they have little if any time to map a strategic course for their institutions, if they want to avoid reaching the precipice of collapse, they must do so. As George Keller warns, "Presidents who do not look ahead, who do not plan, become prisoners of external forces and surprises most often unpleasant."[1]

Pulling back from the brink of failure—or, ideally, avoiding it altogether—is a three-part proposition that involves committing to strategic change; focusing on sound leadership and management practices; and asserting the board's role in financial oversight.

Committing to Strategic Change

Replacing Incrementalism with Strategy

A strategic plan delineates a destination, a single travel route, checkpoints, and an estimated arrival time. As simple as it sounds, developing and implementing a strategic plan is fraught with difficulties for many small colleges. Small-college leadership feels constrained by their inability to predict the future and by the challenge of coordinating and monitoring several divisions toward shared goals.[2] Yet, despite the inevitable dissension and roadblocks, a small college president *can* resolve financial problems strategically.

In the absence of a strategic plan, most colleges tend toward incrementalism, a process whereby small decisions nudge an organization toward some undefined future point. Given the lack of oversight and restraint associated with incrementalism, the small private college finds itself vulnerable to countless self-interests. Such an approach results in insignificant and uncoordinated growth. A financially distressed college depletes its scarce resources, along with the energies of its department heads, during vain attempts to synchronize and monitor divergent incrementalist strategies. Multiple small-scale decisions—most apparent during budget planning—grow from nubs into twisted tentacles that choke future action by the whole system.[3]

As mediator for budget negotiations, the president forges a multitude of small deals among various departments. But these small compromises may haunt the president later. Without an overarching strategy to direct a budget, bundles of small favors explode into potholes of money that can confuse the course of an already wayward institution. Like a traveler in a foreign land with only a street map, the imperiled college without a strategy has no concept of its ultimate destination, or of how it will get there, or how long it will take. Without a larger view, the traveler shuffles through numerous tolls trying to find her way, only to end up where she started—like the college, facing a long journey with a nearly empty pocket and a small-scale map.

Strategic Advantages of Small Colleges

Strategic planning demands a huge shift in perspective and requires significant resources. One irony in higher education is that those institutions with highly refined strategic planning processes are the ones that need it least. Wealthy private institutions have the resources to invest in strategic planning and to build intricate economic models that guide budgetary decisions. Small college presidents struggle not only with a lack of financial resources, but with a real or perceived lack of time, skill, and support. In lieu of strategy and elaborate planning models, presidents of small colleges "live by their wits . . . improvising, groping in the darkness, grappling in the confusion and blood of [everyday existence]."[4]

The small college can compensate for its size, however, by basing strategy on common sense, hard work, and rigorous testing and monitoring methods. Small college presidents should not consider themselves victims of circumstance. On the contrary, the wit, wisdom, and farsightedness of an involved president affords the small college an agility not shared by large, wealthy colleges.[5] In most cases, small college presidents have board members who live nearby and visit the campus regularly, and they often know virtually every member of the faculty, staff, and student body. With the levers of power and community close at hand, the president can efficiently gain consensus for action when challenges or opportunities arise.

Small colleges also have the advantage of less complex decision-making processes that do not jam nearly as easily as do those at larger colleges. Faculty members at many small colleges do not enjoy the immediate protection of tenure and tend to adjust readily to new standards. The small college president has a great deal of direct power over his or her institution—much more so than the president of a large college, where faculty members wield considerable influence and where presidential authority must be shared in order to manage a huge collective body of administrators, faculty members, and students.

Though one may accurately view shared power at a small college as more perfunctory than real, the small college president does share leadership with the chief academic officer and the chief financial officer. He or she works closely with them to solve problems, implement solutions, and scan the market for new opportunities.

Adopting a Market-Driven Approach

Colleges must look to the legitimate demands of the marketplace as they strive to boost market share. Potential students want quality education. They depend on their colleges to know the labor market and to offer relevant training. And potential employees want job security. Anyone seeking employment at a small private college will look first at its history and reputation, and then try to determine its current financial state and how attuned it is to the student market. With mutually supportive financial and market strategies in place, the college doors will stay wide open, indefinitely.

Robert Lenington suggests that a strategic plan be "market-oriented and . . . contain alternatives to a market position that goes awry."[6] According to George Dehne and the Noel Levitz Group, a college must know itself and its competitors.[7] Drawing on student interviews and surveys, state planning offices, the Internet, and the National Center for Education Statistics, colleges must extricate the dynamics of student choice—the differences in prices, programs, services, or other institutional characteristics that drive a student to a given college (or its competitor). Before crafting market and pricing strategies, the college must comprehensively collect and evaluate data on itself as well as its competitors, on current enrollees as well as "traitors."

Student demographics and economic conditions will change, and so too will colleges' internal and external market research and subsequent market goals. As markets and economies shift, college missions may be rewritten. And after the missions are rewritten, the market will undoubtedly shift again. The college that wants to survive 30 more years of change would do well to remain attentive and flexible to student demands, and open to alternative market strategies.

Building Board Commitment

A commitment to strategic change begins with the board, who must fully grasp the institution's present financial straits before approving a corrective plan. The president should oversee data collection and analysis, driven by a set of diagnostic financial questions (see chapter 10). Presented during "blackboard" sessions with key leaders, this identification and discussion of strengths, weakness, opportunities, and threats will steer the debate over the college's financial condition and will shape the goals, actions, deadlines, and performance benchmarks of the financial strategy. The board needs data on:

- financial trends in cash, revenue, expenses, net assets, debt, auxiliary net income, and cost per student;

- marketing trends in yield rates for admissions, matriculants, and enrollments;

- academic programs and enrollments by program, graduation rates, and attrition rates;

- student services programs and students served;

- personnel, i.e., employees by category, cost per employee, and trends; and

- assets, i.e., fixed assets, assets per student, and deferred maintenance.

They also must understand internal and external strengths, weaknesses, and threats: Where does the college excel, and where does it fall short? What internal or external marketing opportunities and threats can the college anticipate in the areas of finance, academics, and student services?

The board should also meet privately with the auditors of the college to gain a slightly different perspective, informed directly through audit work with the college and indirectly through work with other colleges that have undergone sweeping financial change.[8]

The Process of Planning for Change

Given the board's blessing, the president can rally the chief academic officer and chief financial officer in a shared commitment to develop a cohesive strategy for the good of the institution. Forsaking daily operations, the president must concentrate with his or her team on long-term operations. An outside consultant can help to streamline the process and keep the president's involvement manageable; if resources are not available to hire a consultant, the president might consider a special fund-raising campaign for this purpose.

The president should launch the planning process with an announcement to the college community. He or she must convince students, faculty members, and administrators that despite a miserable financial past, and despite the growing pains ahead, their college's future is certain. The president must justify the need for a financial strategy, describing the remedial process coherently and often in meetings with every segment of the college. Because the president's leadership underpins everything, he or she must be everywhere, reassuring everyone, to prepare the college for the winds of change.[9]

Once intent for the plan has been conveyed, debated, and championed, the real process of strategic planning begins. This process involves creating joint planning committees and task forces; establishing goals, objectives, and options; and developing implementation schedules, performance benchmarks, and monitoring schedules.

Planning Participants

Development of the strategic plan should take place within a joint planning committee headed by the president. This committee must maintain familiarity with, as well as ultimate control over, the strategic plan's progress. Other joint planning committee participants should include the chief academic and financial officers, academic department heads, and influential faculty members.

The president trusts each hand-picked member of the joint planning committee to reasonably debate the college's strategic direction. Senior Vice President John Stevens of Kaludis, a leading strategic planning firm, points out that nothing would be more dispiriting than to have a workable strategy deemed worthless by a few major players who missed out on their fair share in its development. [10] Beyond serving as an aid to participatory governance, the joint planning group will eventually spur the formation of task forces whose members will construct the specific targets, plans, and monitoring systems necessary to the larger strategic plan. Task forces shape the specifics of the larger strategy. Members meet regularly to devise, debate, and revise their piece of the plan. Each task force has a leader assigned by and accountable to the president. The greater the president's involvement—he or she should appear at as many task force meetings as possible—the greater the esteem and enthusiasm of task force members as they influence necessary program cuts and identify areas of opportunity.

Other Elements of a Plan

Planning task forces are charged with developing action plans, implementation schedules, benchmarks, and performance monitoring schedules for the president and key leaders to review and approve before the documents are blended into a formal task force report.

Action plans lay out precisely what, when, and by whom steps will be taken to achieve an objective through changes in staffing, policies, procedures, benchmarks, and monitoring schedules. An action plan may be the most important part of the strategic plan, and as such should be carefully drafted and critically reviewed. A slapdash plan of action, void of precision and purpose, will render the college just as lost as it was prior to its strategic awakening.

Performance benchmarks must be relevant to the strategic goals and measured against other (preferably competing) colleges. Benchmarks are targets the college tries to either match or exceed, depending on its current condition. Examples of benchmarks include admissions yields, enrollment growth rates, class sizes, student-teacher ratios, assets per student, net income, receivables, financial reserves, and debt targets. Monitoring reports will compare actual performance to established benchmarks and identify any variances. If performance falls substantially below a benchmark, the college must identify the cause and adjust operations.

The *monitoring schedule* should allow for progress checks of the strategic plan every quarter and before every board meeting. According to George Crouch of Georgetown College, colleges must also revisit strategic goals annually, revising them in accordance with current market conditions. [13] All reviews should be conducted in formal meetings; written reports will likely be set aside and ignored.

The *implementation schedule* will contain a timeline for seven critical events. The president must ensure that they proceed on schedule. Critical implementation events include:

- Meetings with departments and offices responsible for carrying out the strategic plan

- Implementation of major changes in the organization

- Meetings with departments and offices affected by such changes

- Production of policies and documents supporting the strategic plan

- Establishment of data systems to support changes in the organization and produce performance reports

- Purchase of supplies or equipment

- Training schedules for employees whose duties have changed

The Final Plan

After the compilation of goals, objectives, action plans, benchmarks, monitoring schedules, and the implementation plan, the entire strategic plan document goes to the board for review. The president reserves discretionary authority to revise each piece, in keeping with the timeframe and scope of the goals and objectives, and subject again to board review and approval. Following the final plan's approval, the president introduces major goals and objectives to offices and departments. He or she then designates responsibilities and encourages the accountability of each staff and faculty member in the implementation of the final strategic plan. The president may need to meet individually with key players to help them prepare their own objectives, plans, and monitoring systems.

Some Cautionary Notes

Remember that the strategic plan is *not:*

- A knee-jerk reaction to current events. Planning without discipline and risking without care pushed Bradford College over the brink (see chapter 8). From the brash to the timid, examples of thoughtless yet destructive actions abound. Risk-averse administrators—the norm in higher education—implement minor changes to instructional programs, student services, or admissions and ultimately contribute nothing to service improvement or to revenue. Strategy and reason must supplant impulsivity and fear.

- A perfunctory exercise. College leaders cannot approach strategic planning as a way to placate the board or an excuse to meet annually for coffee and donuts. The successful strategic plan has substance and is implemented by strong leaders who see to it that updates and meetings are taken quite seriously.

- A wish list. Strategic planning must not be confused with personal needs. The planning committee will reject staff and faculty wish lists for computers, desks, chairs, lights, buildings, new faculty, new staff, benefits, and the kitchen sink before such ridiculous examples of self-interest reach the chief financial officer. Scarce resources, time, and money should under no circumstances be devoted to spending that has no relation to institutional goals.

- Just another appointment on the president's calendar. The president must delegate the mundane as well as some of the critical daily processes he or she used to tend to. If appointed managers cannot handle the fog of daily battles for the president, management training should be introduced as a component of the strategic plan. The president who resists delegating authority out of ignorance or mistrust will be spread too thin to maintain strategic planning as a priority.

- An isolated financial strategy. Financial strategy must be integrated with the larger strategic plan. The chief financial officer must participate fully in all aspects of planning. The confidentiality of budgets, heretofore restricted to the president and chief financial officer, may need to be compromised in order to facilitate the melding of financial strategy with other strategic components. Key leaders must understand the link between financial resources and strategy, with the former perceived not merely as the forte of academicians and admission officers but as an indispensable thread in the strategic safety net.

- A straitjacket. Strategy provides a context for presidents to balance opportunities with risks and college goals with student needs. Strategy need not constrict in order to direct. Rather, strategy should allow the small college to mobilize quickly and opportunistically, anchored only by expressed goals and guidelines.

Leadership and Management

Implementing and managing a strategic plan that brings financial stability to a small college requires the right leadership. The bad news is that leadership and management skills in higher education are lacking. Leaders are not effectively delegating, supervising, evaluating, analyzing, reporting, or making decisions. "Management" implies informed, interdepartmental decision making and regular

Table 9.1
Ten Ways to Avoid Strategic Planning Mistakes

1. **Do the data.** Regardless of the demand involved, good data collection is a prerequisite for good strategy.
2. **Involve critical segments of the college.** Instruction, student services, and finance departments must interact.
3. **Be realistic about goals.** A poor or invisible college cannot become a Cinderella overnight. (It just might need a rich prince to transform it.)
4. **Find alternatives and test them.** Explore way beyond the obvious, resisting the urge to implement the first plan that comes to mind.
5. **Make managers accountable for carrying out the plan.** Passing the buck will impoverish the strategy.
6. **Measure performance.** Establish criteria for measuring performance in all departments. Back this up with a timetable.
7. **Monitor progress.** Assume nothing. Establish formal monitoring systems.
8. **Review and revise regularly.** Annual strategic review meetings should be supplemented as necessary throughout the year.
9. **Support the plan with policies and procedures.** A toothless plan is a worthless plan.
10. **Include options in the plan.** Allow for the unexpected by keeping viable alternatives.

monitoring of progress toward defined goals. Unfortunately, decisions tend not to be informed by objectively analyzed data, nor made uniformly across departments, nor evaluated continually against a backdrop of clear directives.

Why does this situation persist in higher education? The truth is that bureaucratic office holders tend to supplant managers. Administrators and presidents are adept not at managing, but at retaining power and control. In stark contrast to a conventional management approach that subordinates self-interest to the larger organization, a Machiavellian approach presides, and self-willed decisions trump institutional goals.[14] Departmental interdependence takes a back seat to self-preservation. Once ventured down, this path leads to nefarious behavior, with faculty members and administrators exhausting their psychic and professional energies trying to outmaneuver each other.

The good news is that there is a better road, albeit a less-traveled one. Beyond the administration that alternatively bickers and slinks in order to preserve itself is a president with the capacity and willingness to lead. He or she is charged with strategic oversight—with demanding accountability, breaking through collegial stalemates, and, in the words of George Keller, getting the "right things…done," keeping "spirits from flagging," and "wav[ing] the flag for all to see."[15]

What Makes a Leader?

Peter Drucker, who was instrumental in describing modern management theory and who writes with a large business perspective, can find no substitute for leadership at the institution that plans to embrace change.[16] The president's leadership underpins everything as he or she prepares the college community for the strategic revolution and the future of the college. Resistance to the new approach will undoubtedly surface, with some influential members of the institution working at cross purposes with the leadership. But the president—invested with the confidence of the board, key members of the administration, and the college community—must authoritatively push the strategic plan ahead, noting, rather than entertaining, dissension.

According to James L. Fisher, a 30-year leadership veteran and a noted author on the American college presidency, the president must keep the true state of the institution free from presumptions and clichés as well as controversy.[17] The president must be immune to the siren song of a smug or passive status quo and impervious to the jostling of powerful interest groups—not mediator or ticket-taker but the epitome of impartiality. Forsaking the comfort of routine and ordinary progress, the successful president will "hold out visions of potentialities and worthy objectives that motivate others to perform beyond the ordinary."[18] The college that embraces strategy but whose leader indulges mediocrity or conflict will find that its plans are for naught.

Great colleges, on the other hand, are run by great presidents.[19] A great leader knows the college, what its weaknesses are, what makes it work, who within its walls impedes change, and who inspires it. He or she maintains communication with subordinates, drawing on them for information and assistance. This leader deduces as well as intuits what needs improvement and wins swift approval for strategic patchwork and overhauls alike. While influencing necessary changes, the president delegates and demands accountability, yet gets his or her own hands dirty in the demanding work of setting policies, reviewing programs, controlling budgets, and monitoring performance.[20]

The president must enjoy ultimate authority, but the work of strategy cannot succeed without a supportive partnership between the president and board of directors. The board, after all, appoints the president, concocting either a recipe for failure in its choice of a passive president content with mere survival or an incompetent president who drives the college over a cliff, or a recipe for excellence with a powerful president who can actually lead. (See chapter 7, "Why Small Colleges Fail: Four Cautionary Tales" and chapter 12, "Small College Turnarounds: How They Did It," to see the powerful impact of the president on the success of a college.) Board members must "give [the] president adequate authority and staff, and their own support in the difficult task of encouraging constructive change— realizing that periods of change are also periods of unusual tension."[21] The small college with a progressive board and a dispassionate president will likely fulfill Fisher's proposition that leadership can propel a college to its highest potential.[22]

Add financial savvy to the mix and you have a small private college that just might see the next century. According to John Nelson, senior vice president at Moody's Investor Services, "Small colleges have the best chance of surviving [when] the president understands finances, works well with the chief financial officer, and [when] the board takes a critical role in [financial] decisions."[23] Ruth Cowan believes that financial paralysis can be overcome through sustained internal work. The college that waits for economies to stabilize and markets to cooperate won't build strength. Rather, when the president, board, key financial leaders, and the college community come to believe they can change their college's destiny from the inside out, and when they begin to act accordingly, financial mobility returns.[24]

Shared Leadership

Michael Cohen and James March equate the ambiguities of shared, or collegial, leadership with organized anarchy.[25] Professionals make decisions without presidential approval, and the consequences are either mismanaged or left unmanaged in the absence of central control and accountability standards. The most a president of a small college can do, then, is ride the issue carousel, and hope to glimpse the brass rings of presidential power and strategic financial success. Victor J. Baldridge and his colleagues compare shared governance to a political system, wherein a cycle of chaos, inactivity, conflict, and negotiation follows every decision posed to a disjointed interest group.[26] A president operating within a political ring can only hope that every wrestling match ends in a truce. In any case, shared governance equates to fragmented governance in which the formal authority of the small college president is indistinguishable from the professional authority of faculty members and administrators.

No wonder presidents find themselves hemmed in on all sides. Having little influence over tenured faculty, departmental budgets, or such basic college policies as the student-faculty ratio, presidents experiment with manipulation and bargaining to juice up the collective decision-making apparatus. But once self-interested parties have supplanted leadership, no brand of exploitation will keep mediocrity—the sum and average of multiple self-interests—from becoming the norm and the devastating goal for a leaderless institution. As George Keller notes, "every society and every major organization with a society must have a single authority, someone . . . authorized to initiate, plan, decide, manage, monitor, and punish its membership. *Leadership is imperative.*"[27]

Management-Style Leadership

According to Robert Lenington, organizational structures within higher education, from the autocratic to the diffuse, suffer from "lack of professional management and good business practice."[28] Too often, chief executive officers equivocate when it comes to delegating work. In the absence of clear directives, the person assigned a task may not know he has a job to do or may not understand the level of responsibility, the order or method of operations, the timeline, or the reporting practices. A vague leadership style may successfully keep people off balance, but it accomplishes little in the long run, and it conveys a lack of both knowledge and responsibility on the part of the president.

Most college leaders have not worked within a management framework, and they are not trained in management practices.[29] Management is almost scorned in higher education, for it interferes with the anarchic and political tactics, ranging from the passive to the cutthroat, that typically abound there. An administrator lacking in management skills but well versed in avoidance might adopt the role of the kid in the back of the classroom. He averts his eyes when called upon if he doesn't know the answer, or if he doesn't want to go where the "right" answer might take him. Amiability and invisibility are key in his response to a system in which job survival depends less on achievements (one person's progress is another person's setback) than on avoiding retribution.

But neither ambiguous nor Machiavellian tactics will pass muster in the 21st century. Presidents must become familiar with management practices. Management, in its most basic form, equates to self-discipline—a way for bureaucratic offices to achieve responsibility, accountability, and control within and over themselves. Authority can be a positive force if it is evenhandedly delegated to achieve compliance and productivity

Five basic management approaches would help college leaders minimize conflict and contribute to smoother operations, coordination and control, delegation of authority, unity of command, simplicity, and esprit de corps.

Coordination and Control

All participants in a given task should understand why a task has been assigned, to what extent they are accountable for its success or failure, how performance will be measured and coordinated, who is in charge, and to whom (and by whom) findings will be reported. The president can communicate his or her command of important processes and activities through regular staff meetings and performance evaluations. Ripe for coordination and control are the flow of work and students though admissions, registration, and payment processes; and the scheduling of classes, which requires that various offices work together to coordinate the availability of classrooms, parking, supplies, staff, and instructors.

Delegation of Authority

The president who fails to delegate will drown in detail while constricting the ability of others to learn both people- and stress-management skills. The last thing a president facing strategic change needs is a desk cluttered with memos from subordinates who don't have the knowledge, confidence, or desire to handle even the most trivial of dilemmas.

Unity of Command

The president must definitively empower one office, one committee, one person to see every task to its end. This practice will prevent confusion and conflict, duplication of work, and the failure to complete tasks.

Simplicity

From the course catalog, to accounting office protocols, to the layout of the library, college campuses are in need of simplification. Managers should translate goals, policies, procedures, and orders into forms digestible by staff and students. All will celebrate the reduction of superfluous costs and lengthy waits associated with unnecessarily tedious processes.

Esprit de Corps

Presidents would do well to herald any significant changes with a few symbolic adjustments. Whether in the form of painted classrooms, tidied grounds, small awards, or prompt payment of employees, small efforts signify a leadership's intent to see progress through. Ruth Cowan offers several pertinent suggestions to small college presidents:

1. Conduct frequent face-to-face meetings.
2. Acknowledge individual accomplishments, no matter how trivial.
3. Reestablish rituals and organize celebrations.
4. Invite prominent people to the campus so they can witness the changes taking place.
5. Take visible risks, such as raising salaries, even if only slightly.[30]

Scott Miller, president of Wesley College, advises new presidents and presidents facing new challenges to "make a splash"—to employ charisma, originality, and goodwill as they strive to better manage their institutions.[31] Leaders with confidence and vitality will elicit the same from their staff and students.

The Board's Oversight Responsibility

Governing boards have significant financial oversight responsibilities that are a key element to a college's financial health. As stewards of institutional assets, they must "maintain equity between generations"[32] so that the strength of financial and physical assets carries from current to future students. If these assets cannot support future generations, then the board must consider transferring them to an institution that can fulfill its mission. Board members must insist on frequent financial updates from the president and key leaders as they endeavor to monitor strategic planning closely and interactively. Keeping abreast of economic and legal currents, board members are also responsible for risk management to shelter the institution's physical assets from catastrophic financial losses and ensure that actions taken on behalf of the college—whether by a board member, administrator, faculty member, or staff member—abide by contract terms and state laws.

Audits, conflict of interest policies, and reviews of financial transactions are three means by which the board ensures that appropriate financial controls are in place. The board should hire a disinterested certified public accounting firm to conduct an annual audit of the college's financial condition and management practices. To ensure that audit findings are not filtered through self-interested administrators, the board must contract directly with the audit firm and demand that audit findings be prepared for the private consideration of board members.

The board must prevent conflicts of interests—or even the appearance of conflict—involving the college and board members, administrators, their family members, and their private businesses. Board members and administrators should at the very least identify business transactions that currently or potentially constitute conflicts of interest, or self-dealing. Self-dealing can be limited through a policy that defines the conditions under which board members, employees, and their relatives can conduct business with the institution. Only after several bids have been collected and arm's-length business agreements have been signed should such transactions proceed.

To limit the potential for conflicts of interest problems, board members and administrators should annually submit the following information for board review:

- A list of their family members who are employed by the college, including names, titles, duties, supervisors, compensations, and relationships to board members or administrators

- A list of business interests that board members, administrators, or their family members have with the college, including annual sales, dates of agreement, relevant services or products, and company names

Board members and administrators should also consider the tax consequences of employing family members. The Internal Revenue Service could interpret business transactions with or employment of family members as violations of tax rules that prohibit colleges from distributing benefits and excess funds for personal gain. Board members who overlook such business dealings and employment practices could cost their college its nonprofit status.

Just because a college is a charity, the board should not exempt it from rigorous financial and management standards. Board members must review financial reports and major financial transactions with a critical eye, scrutinizing business dealings involving key administrators. Expense reimbursements and purchase authorizations for administrators, including the president, should not be made without due consideration. Clear lines of cosigner authority should be drawn to shield the college from charges of illicit spending and lack of financial oversight by the board.

Business Practices

Board oversight encompasses a college's business practices. Many small colleges fail to evaluate large campus investments scrupulously. When contemplating new construction, planners tend to overlook alternative locations, zoning requirements, architectural layouts, parking considerations, operational costs, and financing methods. Only when the county cites the college with a zoning violation, or parking shortages turn into traffic nightmares, or students trip over each other down short and narrow hallways do planners discover their design flaws. Given scarce resources, leaders must commit to customary business practices to assure the highest return on their decisions and investments. Among these practices are:

- Seek and evaluate alternatives.
  Early in the planning stages of a decision or project, the president and key leaders should brainstorm alternatives, compiling a cost and benefit analysis for each possibility. If opinions beyond those of chief officers are needed, the college should ask a consultant to assist with data comparisons.

- Look at the big picture.
  Leaders must consider the impact a proposed major investment will have on other systems and functions. A close look at the project's fit with the college's mission and location will help to ensure sensible and flexible building designs, adequate parking, and compliance with zoning regulations.

- Treat major financial decisions as investment decisions.
  After establishing goals for the proposed project, planners and financial leaders must figure and forecast the operational costs, determine the financial impact on other college functions and departments, and formulate budgets for each project alternative. Separate five-year forecasts of the costs, savings, revenues, and other tangible financial benefits associated with each alternative should be developed using the following guide:
  1. Calculate the net present value for each alternative.
  2. Figure out the probability that expected outcomes associated with each investment alternative will occur.
  3. Multiply the probability factors by the relevant net present values to determine the expected financial value of each alternative.
  4. Re-evaluate to confirm correct estimates.
  5. Rank order the alternatives according to their outcomes.
  6. Debate the top two alternatives.

- Justify the decision.
  Presidents should assume nothing but the burden of proof. Leaders must take it upon themselves to persuade their boards of the need for change through concise, coherent written statements and analyses. A board should not approve a decision or project unless it understands how it will serve the goals of its college.

Summary

Small colleges are crumbling beneath the weight of daily pressures and cowering at the prospect of yet another beating from the market. For leaders at these colleges, strategy has been reduced to a frenzied search for the next new dollar, without reasonable regard for management practices, market position, or long-term operational efficiency. More often than not, time, energy, and revenue are wasted on stop-gap financial measures. Even those colleges that have prospered under an intuitive leadership are not safe from closure, for success based on the hunches of particular leaders often ends with their tenure. Many an institution has faltered, if not fallen, during changes in management.

Strategy acts as insurance against vagaries in management. It complements a leader's intuition, and keeps chaos at bay. The president as keeper of the strategy will be a model of integrity, gaining his college safe passage to a world of financial stability. Most of the strategy and leadership tips in this chapter are simple, familiar to the greenest of leaders. But the work will certainly be slow and difficult at times. Ultimately, a course of action and peace of mind will emerge to the progressive manager who trades in an incrementalist mindset for long-term security.

Notes

1. George Keller, *Academic Strategy* (Baltimore, Md.: John Hopkins Press, 1983), p. 67.
2. Charles Lindbloom, *The Policy Making Process* (Cambridge, Mass.: Harvard University Press, 1968); Aaron Wildavsky, *Budgeting,* rev. ed. (New York: Transaction Books, 1986), p. 107.
3. Keller, *Academic Strategy,* p. 112.
4. Michael K. Townsley, "Brinkmanship, Planning, Smoke, and Mirrors," *Planning for Higher Education* 19 (1991): 27.
5. William S. Reed, *Financial Responsibilities of Governing Boards* (Washington, D.C.: Association of Governing Boards of Universities and Colleges and National Association of College and University Business Officers, 2001).
6. Robert Lenington, *Colleges Are a Business!* (Phoenix, Ariz.: Oryx Press, 1996), p. 34.
7. George C. Dehne, "Student Recruitment: A Marketing Primer for Presidents" (Old Saybrook, Conn.: GDA Integrated Services, 2001); Thomas Williams, "Proper Mix," *Business Officer,* March 2001, pp. 34–37.
8. Ruth B. Cowan, "Prescription for Small-College Turnaround," *Change,* January/February 1993, p. 37.
9. Lenington, *Colleges Are a Business!*
10. John Stevens, senior vice president and chief operating officer, Kaludis Consulting, Washington, D.C., interviews by author, September 11 and September 18, 2001.
11. Gary Wirt. vice president and director of admissions, Goldey Beacom College, Wilmington, Del., interview by author, October 11, 2001.

12. Keller, *Academic Strategy,* p. 61.

13. William Crouch, president, Georgetown College, Georgetown, Ky., interview by author, September 13, 2001.

14. Keller, *Academic Strategy,* pp. 123–25.

15. Ibid.

16. Peter F. Drucker, *The Practice of Management* (New York: Harper and Row, 1954; New York: Perennial Library, 1986): pp. 159–60.

17. James L. Fisher, interview by author, September 5, 2001.

18. Keller, *Academic Strategy,* p. 125.

19. Frederick E. Balderston, *Managing Today's University* (San Francisco: Jossey-Bass, 1975), p. 92.

20. Carnegie Commission on Higher Education, *Governance of Higher Education* (New York: McGraw-Hill, 1973), p. 37.

21. Ibid.

22. Fisher, interview by author, September 5, 2001.

23. John Nelson, senior vice president, Moody's Investors Services, New York City, interview by author, August 7, 2001.

24. Cowan, "Prescription for Small-College Turnaround."

25. Michael D. Cohen and James G. March, *Leadership and Ambiguity: The American College President* (New York: McGraw-Hill, 1974).

26. Victor J. Baldridge, David V. Curtis, George Ecker, and Gary L. Riley, *Policy Making and Effective Leadership* (San Francisco: Jossey-Bass, 1983).

27. Keller, *Academic Strategy,* p. 35.
    David R. Riesman (1998). *On Higher Education.* Transaction Publishers: New Brunswick.; page 297.

28. Lenington, *Colleges Are A Business!,* p. 7.

29. Herbert Simon, "The Job of a College President," *Educational Record* 58 (winter 1967): 69.

30. Cowan, "Prescription for Small-College Turnaround."

31. Scott Miller, president, Wesley College, Dover, Del., interview by author, August 10, 2001.

32. For a discussion of board financial oversight responsibilities, see Reed, *Financial Responsibilities of Governing Boards,* pp. 5–6.

Financial and Market Diagnostics

Any strategy worth its salt must rest on a reliable assessment of the institution's financial condition and market position. The data collection and analysis phase of strategic planning will involve gathering common-sense financial and market information, such as budget reports, financial statements, cash flow reports, trend analyses, cost reports, admission reports, and competitor performance (see chapter 9). The president reviews the data with a financial task force as the strategic planning process begins. To determine the best way of presenting collected information to both the president and the board, the chief financial officer should test several reporting formats. Most accounting software can be configured to convey basic financial information, downloadable to a spreadsheet. Custom reports can then be created to fit the institution's monitoring requirements. The monitoring system should track and report the performance of the institution relative to its financial strategy and to a set of external benchmarks.

Gathering financial data may prove especially difficult for small colleges, many of which have no reporting system for the analysis and monitoring of operations. The president may recruit auditors to help the chief financial officer not only with the data collection process, but also with the establishment of a formal monitoring system (and with any necessary software and spreadsheet operations). The work of data analysis and the development of a prudent strategy could be hamstrung by failure to establish a reliable way to track operations and financial progress.

Data collection occurs in two phases:

(1) A general diagnosis using strategic questions to establish a broad picture of the college's financial condition. This phase is crucial because such information will inform the leadership's actions during the construction of the financial strategy. Many questions will not require an exhaustive or expensive effort; most, in fact, will be answered simply "yes" or "no." The chief financial officer and the auditors should prepare

a joint report on the general financial condition of the college for the president's and the board's review. This general diagnostic process equips the president to perform the more detailed financial diagnostics to come.

(2) A detailed analysis involving four components of the financial system: revenue and expenses, cash, working capital, and permanent assets. The dollars, ratios, and financial trends provide a comprehensive picture of the current and historical condition of the college. This information will generate benchmarks for the monitoring system. Trend and ratio analysis may be the most significant part of the financial analysis because they can show whether finances are deviating from published norms or from internal expectations. The chief financial officer should track trends to spot major and undesirable changes. Conducting trend analysis after the disaster has happened only raises the question about who was keeping watch.

As with the first set of questions, the president may want the auditors' assistance. Appendix E, Financial and Marketing Diagnostic Checkoff, lists questions and issues that focus the analysis.

General Financial Condition

As a first step, the board and president need a snapshot of the college's operations, including views of the mission, audits, licensing, deficits, basic business practices, and basic financial position of the college. Answers to these questions—many of them obvious yet obscured in the daily fog of operations—form the baseline of the diagnostic endeavor. The goal is to learn what the college is doing and if it is operating effectively.

Mission and Strategic Goals

Do they accurately depict a college's present or future purpose? Will the strategic goals permit the college to achieve its given mission? If the mission and goals conflict, or are out of sync with the board's intentions, college operations will be anything but orderly. If synchronization drastically alters the college's mission, bylaws may have to be revised to comply with state licensing or corporate regulations. The college cannot operate without state licensure, which grants the authority necessary to offer educational programs and award degrees based on the college's mission, as stated in its corporate bylaws.

Accrediting Agencies

Accrediting agencies verify that college degree programs are legitimate and substantive, and together with licensing agencies, they control the institution's crown jewels. To win authority and secure accreditation, many colleges find themselves increasing investment in educational programs or in student or academic services. Whatever the requirement, the board and the president should acknowledge conflicts with these agencies and try to accommodate their demands. Resistance is futile.

Audits

Annual audits ensure the reliability of financial statements and the integrity of financial practices. If the college has not conducted annual audits, it must begin doing so. To clarify board oversight of the audit, and to reduce the likelihood of audit information being filtered by staff or administrative self-interest, the contract for the audit should be between the board of trustees and the auditor. The Enron debacle should make boards very cautious about audit reports that are tightly controlled by administrations.

Deficits and Growth Rates

After assessing the college's present condition, the president and the board must get a feel for the college's recent financial tendencies. Has the college run a deficit for two or more years? Have deficits recurred over five-year periods? If the college has been running regular deficits, it is probably ricocheting from one financial crisis to another. Is the growth rate for revenue less than the growth rate for expenses, and is the gap increasing? If the college does not run deficits but revenue and expense growth rates are out of balance and the gap is increasing, deficits will eventually appear. Sound financial strategy rests on the proposition that deficits rarely occur and that revenue and expense growth rates are either in balance or favoring revenue growth.

Instructional and Auxiliary Programs

Eliminating deficits goes hand in hand with adapting instructional and auxiliary programs to the realities of a sound financial strategy. Instructional programs are the financial drivers of the institution. If they produce a significant loss, they threaten the survival of the college. The same holds true for auxiliaries. If they lose money, they drain core services. Are these programs losing money? If no one knows, someone should find out.

Liquidity

Like a balanced operational budget, cash is essential to a college's solvency. The president and the board need answers to several simple questions: Does the college have sufficient cash to pay its bills and cover its payroll for the next several months? Will it have enough cash without having to borrow for the rest of the year? Frequent borrowing to make payrolls and bill payments may indicate a serious liquidity problem. The possible causes include failure to bill students regularly and/or to collect unpaid student balances; failure to draw down government financial aid allotments; and operations that do not produce excess cash.

Cash problems may be evident in payroll and payable offices. Are payroll taxes and benefit deductions deposited on time, and are bills paid on time? Or are they held due to insufficient cash? A Dunn & Bradstreet report will show if the college is slow in paying its bills. Late payments on taxes and benefit deductions must be corrected immediately. Failure to do so could have dire consequences.

Debt

Excess debt places the destiny of colleges in the hands of a third party: bankers, who can quickly become the dictators of college policies and operating conditions. College leaders must ascertain the amount of outstanding debt and establish a policy that delineates the circumstances in which debt may be reasonably incurred. Note that off-balance-sheet financing can obscure the true extent of debt obligations, but it must nevertheless be included in the total amount of outstanding debt.

State and Federal Financial Aid Funds

Government financial aid funds are critical in the revenue mix of every college. The leadership should scan the latest financial aid audits for any irregularities or management problems. Major problems with federal financial aid could lead to the loss of those funds or to onerous conditions imposed by the U.S. Department of Education. Before the transfer of funds, the ED could require that the college have a letter of credit equal to 50 percent or more of the financial aid amount—a devastating stipulation for a financially weak college. Any loss of financial aid could spell a small college's demise.

Incentives

Like all organizations, small colleges use incentives to encourage members to subordinate their personal interest to the goals of the organization. Decentralized authority, ambiguous goals, and collegial decision making can subvert incentive systems in larger colleges. By virtue of their size, small colleges are less likely to have autonomous departments that act outside institutional goals. Those small colleges with incentives that are inconsistently applied or distorted by self-interest may find their incentives losing power—a costly problem for colleges whose incentives are usually based on financial awards. The president, chief financial officer, chief academic officer, and other key institutional leaders should examine the consequences, intended or unintended, of the existing incentive system. Where incentives are working at cross-purposes with the goals of the college, they should be redesigned or abandoned.

Accounting and Budget Systems

To the surprise of their presidents and boards, some colleges fail to post monthly accounting records. (Problems with accounting records are usually evident in audit management letters.) Many budget systems are rudimentary at best, or nonexistent at worst. Accounting systems and the crucial functions they perform must be in place before a college can expect to implement financial strategy. They record financial transactions, track cash flow, delineate policies and procedures, and report on the financial condition of the college. Budget systems transform strategy into action by matching forecasts to plans, establishing performance benchmarks, and identifying responsibility areas relevant to the implementation of budget plans. Accounting and budget systems must work symbiotically. Financial strategy will be worthless without them.

For this reason, the president should ask auditors and the chief financial officer to report on both accounting and budget systems before planning begins in earnest. The report should cover all aspects of the finance office: payables, payroll, billing, accounting records, and software. It should identify report formats, procedures, policies, responsibilities, and deficiencies. Where deficiencies are reported, relevant solutions should be proposed. The president should meet independently with the auditors to evaluate the capabilities of the chief financial officer and his staff. Those who cannot perform effectively must be replaced, because financial duties are too important to leave in the hands of ill-prepared employees.

Specifics of Financial Condition

To understand a college's historical financial direction, the president and the board must consider trends in revenue, expenses, cash, working capital, permanent assets, and broad measures of financial performance. A look at trends will also indicate which changes in financial structure were intended and which were not. Leaders must understand what has been driving their institution's financial performance in order to make coherent, well-founded adjustments to it.

Audits represent a third party's report on a college's financial structure and should provide most of the necessary historical financial data. Because audits usually reflect financial data found in Integrated Postsecondary Education Data System (IPEDS) reports, cross-referencing of information from both sources enables comparisons of one college's financial performance to that of its competitors and benchmarking one college's financial performance against that of a "best-practices" college. Small colleges located in remote areas may find benchmarking difficult because they have no peers in their immediate vicinity. These colleges can consult sources such as John Minter & Associates for help with identifying peer benchmarks. In addition to the financial reports, three years of registration, billing, and human resources data will round out the trend analysis.

The chief financial officer should prepare the reports for review by the president and other institutional leaders. Given the labor and time involved collecting data— and the urgency of the cause—a CFO of a small struggling college may indeed need the help of auditors. Any changes made during the collection and analysis of *revenue and expenses, working capital and cash,* and *permanent capital data* should be incorporated in the final financial strategy.

Revenue and Expenses (see Appendix E)

Core Services: To analyze revenue and expenses generated from operations, the college's core services—instruction, research, or community service—must be determined. If allocation decisions have not benefited core services, the leadership must assess the effectiveness of its decisions. Without the discipline of a strategic plan, the budget process may haphazardly redirect allocations from core services to noncore services whose leaders do the best job of bargaining for increases. Core services allocation data should ultimately tease out two pieces of information: (1) current allocations of revenue and expenses, which will be compared to allocations several years earlier, and (2) historical allocation shifts, including rates of change by revenue or expense category and where new dollars went.

Student Flow: Small college leaders must consider the flow of students into and out of the college. Student flow is usually critical to financial condition and market position. Trend data should be analyzed with an eye to how numbers of incoming students, quitting students, and graduating students have changed over time by level (undergraduate or graduate), by instructional major, and by instructional program. Student flow ultimately drives operations, and relevant data will highlight those programs with strong and weak enrollment levels, high rates of attrition, and high or low graduation rates. The net income each program generates should indicate which level, programs, or majors have been most or least productive.

Well-defined data will not only indicate changes in student flow but will suggest their causes and their historical impact on revenue and expenses. Resource allocation will reveal whether enrollment flows have been supported and exactly how new dollars have been spent. Numbers of faculty and staff members, student-faculty ratios, student-employee ratios, class size, number of classrooms, square footage of classrooms, and capital assets will show how the college allocates resources by level, major, or program. (The college must eventually take this information one step further and lay out the revenue, expenses, price discounts, and net income produced by level, major, and program.)

Noncore Services: Small colleges must understand resource allocations to noncore services, including academic support and business or auxiliary services. Data will highlight expense allocations, number of employees, student-employee ratio, square footage of office space, and capital assets for noncore services. Data should show changes in allocation amounts to noncore services as well as how new dollars were spent. Trends in resource allocations (expenses, employees, square footage, and capital assets) between core and noncore activities should be compared. If the college is directing its largest increases to noncore activities, leaders must begin asking some hard questions.

Trends in Tuition Dependency Rate, Net Price, and Unfunded Aid: Tuition dependency will remain stable unless an institution has intentionally done something to change it. The college should be concerned if the rate has increased substantially on its own. The reason for the change—whether in the market or in the institution—must be discovered. Any increase in tuition dependency thrusts the college into a risky position vis-à-vis the market.

Net Price and Unfunded Aid: These are critical variables because they represent market decisions and reduction to cash generated by revenue. The institution should view trends of these variables in light of net cash generated to cover operations. Rising net price and unfunded aid rates that do not result in the significant improvement of a college's market position—reflected in unresponsive or declining enrollment levels or quality of students enrolled—may adversely affect the financial condition or reputation of the institution. The latter consequence translates into difficulty during recruitment of new students.

Auxiliaries: Auxiliary services generate important additional income to support core operations. Although auxiliary services need not generate huge amounts of income, their operating expenses should at least break even with their depreciated capital investment. Otherwise, they drain resources from core operations. If auxiliaries perform poorly, the college must conduct a separate study of their management and financial operations to determine how they can be improved. Small colleges cannot tolerate auxiliary services that deplete resources.

Net Income: Net income generated by operations must be evaluated on two levels: (1) Is net income positive? (2) Is revenue growth balanced with expense growth? If net income is not positive, or if it spikes up or down, the college must be unable to control either the flow of revenue to support expenditures or the rate of change in expenditures. Net income should be positive over time, and growth in revenue and expenses should be balanced. For small colleges with meager resources, bobbing from deficits to positive net income indicates that the institution is unable to build its reserves. As a result, the institution is more vulnerable to economic shocks. A college in this precarious financial position must develop goals for enrollment flows, resource allocations, and net pricing for tuition—all with the intent to achieve positive net income and a balance between revenue and expenses.

Working Capital and Cash (see Appendix E)

Net income and working capital are the main cash drivers for an institution. Net income generates cash from operations. Working capital moves cash from receivables and disburses cash for current liabilities such as accounts payable, accruals, and short-term debt. Net income and working capital must produce sufficient cash flows to support operations and outlays for capital expenses (debt service or direct investment). Working capital includes cash, receivables, inventory, accounts payable, accruals, unearned revenue, and short-term notes. Data on working capital can be found in the "current assets and liability" section of the statement of financial position (balance sheet) of the audit.

The trend table for cash should include cash and short-term investments. In addition, the college should track net cash flow from operations found in the audit's statement of cash flows if it complies with FASB Statement No. 117.[1] Net cash flow from operations is important because revenue does not always equal receipts and expenses do not equal disbursements. The leadership of a small college needs to understand that net income and net cash are not the same.

Cash analysis should set forth (1) the rates of change for cash, short-term investments, and net cash flow and (2) the *cash and short-term investments to total expenses ratio.* The trends and the rates of change will indicate the magnitude and direction of the changes in cash. The ratio will gauge whether cash is rising or falling relative to expenses. If it falls substantially below 16 percent, which is roughly equivalent to two months of cash disbursements, the college may have to resort to short-term borrowing for cash flow. KPMG and others even suggest that cash and short-term investments should represent at least three months of expenses to assure adequate reserves.

Beyond the simple trend analysis, the source of changes in cash should be identified. Were they due to increases in net income, changes in accounts payables or accruals, changes in receivables, or changes in short- or long-term debt? An association between cash and short-term investments *and* increasing payables or accruals suggests that bills are going unpaid. The college should carefully analyze the flow of funds into cash as well as the trend in cash following short- or long-term borrowing. What would the cash position be if debt had not increased?

The college should also go beyond the net cash flow from operations in the audit to examine the changes in total net cash flow in the audit. The audit statement on cash will help to answer several questions. Were increases or decreases to net cash flow due to changes in cash flowing from operations, from financing activities (contributions or changes in debt), or from investing activities (investments or purchases of assets)? What is the trend for these changes?

One other central question about cash needs analysis: Is there sufficient cash to cover the normal operations of the college without having to continually turn to banks for short-term funding? Inadequate cash is the one element in a college's financial structure that can quickly drive it over the brink. Cash, net cash flow, payables, and receivables must become key financial benchmarks, monitored regularly by the college. If the cash position is weak, the causes must be identified and remedial strategies implemented.

Receivables are problematic for small colleges that allow students to abuse payment plans. When students fail to make payments, the balance rolls to the next billing period. Over time, the college sees eroding cash levels, and the student sees that the college is not serious about bill collections. Many small colleges face a dilemma: payment plans entice students to enroll, but enforcing them may cause students to leave. Or, perhaps worse, late-paying students may gossip to potential students that the college aggressively collects overdue bills. Small colleges should understand that once they implement a reliable collection system, only a small core of delinquent payers would remain.

A classic measure for tracking adequacy of working capital is the *quick ratio* ([current assets minus inventory] divided by current liabilities); data for this ratio can be found in the audit. Current assets typically include cash and receivables, and current liabilities refer to payables and receivables. The ratio depicts the amount of cash that could be generated from cash and receivables to cover payables and accruals. If it is declining or less than one, the college needs to figure out the problem. Has cash declined, or have receivables, uncollectible receivables, or payables increased beyond the rate of change in expenses or tuition revenue? The ratio factors should be continuously monitored for problems.

Permanent Capital

Small colleges must be aware of the financial condition of permanent capital, for it supports future operations. A trend table should track property, plant, equipment, investments, debt, other major assets or liabilities, and net assets by category (unrestricted, temporarily restricted, etc.). The table should also include the *debt leverage ratio, return on net assets ratio, capitalization ratio, composition of net assets ratio*, and the *rates of change for each category of permanent capital*. Information on payout rates for the endowment, rates of return on investments, and a long-term debt list should complement the trend table.

Small colleges should list the details of all outstanding debt, including the lender, maturity, principal, debt service, interest rates, any conditions to the debt, and purpose of the debt. The list should include *all* forms of debt, including off-balance-sheet financing, which seems to act as an expense but in reality establishes future payment obligations much like debt. Such a list, if kept current and reported regularly to the board, will help a college keep track of its obligations. If debt increases to cover cash flow problems, the list will point out that change and facilitate the leadership's informed review and action. The college can also use the list to determine if debt should be refinanced when market interest rates are favorable.

Trend tables should be used to answer a series of questions:
1. What is the magnitude and direction of change in dollars and the rate of change for each category of permanent capital?
2. Which is increasing in scale and growing faster: debt, endowment, or plant?
3. Is the *debt leverage ratio* (net assets divided by long-term debt) declining, or is it below 2:1? If it is declining or is less than 2:1, the college may have become overly dependent on debt. It should seriously consider evaluating its debt structure and its strategy for funding assets.

4. Is the *return on net assets ratio* (change in net assets divided by total net assets beginning of the year) approximately twice the rate of inflation for the trend period? Return on net assets must be large enough to assure reasonable growth in the institution's resources.[2]

5. Is the *capitalization ratio* (modified net assets divided by modified total assets) between 50 percent and 80 percent, or is it changing direction? According to KPMG and Prager, this range provides sufficient flexibility for future investments.[3]

6. Is the *composition of equity ratio* (financial assets divided by physical assets) greater than one, or is it changing direction? KPMG and Prager contend that stronger institutions carry ratios greater than one.[4] A ratio of less than one may mean that the institution lacks the financial resources to take advantage of growth in the stock market and to respond to changes in the higher education market.

7. Are net assets increasing or decreasing in real dollar terms (valued after inflation)? If net assets are decreasing, then the college will be drawing down its financial reserves.

Besides establishing these basic benchmarks, a small college must ask the following questions about its investments and endowment:

- What is the rate of return on investments?

- How does the rate of return compare to a market benchmark—the S&P 500, for example? Investment benchmarks should be constructed to reflect the mix of investments held in the portfolio. For instance, if the portfolio is 40 percent equity stock and 60 percent bonds, the benchmark should reflect that mix.

- What is the payout rate on the endowment fund?

- Does the rate reflect a prudent course, such as 5 percent on a moving three-year average?

- What proportion of total revenue is produced by the endowment payout?

- Is the rate of return sufficient to maintain the proportion, or increase it? Given market uncertainties over the past several years, small colleges should re-evaluate their endowment investments, payout rates, and assumptions about long-term changes in the value of the endowment fund.

If answers to these questions indicate weakness in permanent capital, the college should address relevant problems and devise appropriate corrections in its financial strategy. More detail may become necessary as the college struggles to ascertain specific causes of the weaknesses. Auditors can be of assistance in this area.

Broad Measures of Financial Performance

Three approaches are suggested to measure financial performance: Moody's Investor Services measures, KPMG and Prager's financial ratios, and the CFI scoring system. Moody's measures are based on experience in rating private colleges. The KPMG and Prager ratios and CFI scoring system were discussed in chapter 6.

Moody's Investor Service Measures

As a college develops a comprehensive financial strategy, it can use important measures that credit-ranking agencies use to predict financial health. (Even if the college does not intend to enter the public debt market, it may need to borrow funds or maintain the good graces of federal student aid agencies.) The measures suggested here are based on the experience of Moody's Investor Services and on studies of financial indicators closely related to the financial condition of small colleges. Moody's defines a small college as enrolling fewer than 3,000 students.[5] The following ratios and measures, according to Moody's, are indicative of a small college's financial capacity to meet debt obligations.[6]

Financial Capacity to Meet Debt Obligations
1. *Free Expendable Financial Resources to Operations*: {total unrestricted net assets less net investment in plant} divided by total operating expenses.
2. *Total Financial Resources per Student*: {total net assets less net investment in plant} divided by full-time-equivalent students.
3. *Annual Operating Margin*: {adjusted total unrestricted revenue (limit investment income to 4.5 percent of previous year's cash and investments, and subtract net assets released for construction and acquisition of fixed assets) less total unrestricted operating expenses} divided by adjusted total unrestricted revenue.
4. *Average Operating Margin*: three-year average of the annual operating margin.
5. *Operating Margin Excluding Gifts*: (adjusted total revenue less gifts less total unrestricted operating expenses) divided by {adjusted total unrestricted revenue less gifts}.
6. *Actual Debt Service Coverage*: (annual operating surplus (deficit) plus interest and depreciation expenses) divided by actual principal and interest payments.

7. *Average Actual Debt Service Coverage*: three-year average of actual debt service coverage.

8. *Average Peak Debt Service Coverage*: three-year average of annual surplus (deficit) interest and depreciation expenses, divided by peak principal and interest payments.

9. *Return on Net Assets*: increase (decrease) in total net assets, divided by total net assets.

10. *Return on Financial Resources*: (increase [decrease] in total financial resources (total net assets less net investment in plant) divided by average total financial resources (the sum of beginning and ending total financial resources) divided by two.

11. *Free Expendable Resources to Debt*: (total unrestricted and temporarily restricted assets less net investment in plant) divided by direct debt.

John Nelson, senior vice president of Moody's, has found that the strongest indicators of a small college's financial ability to handle debt are its operating margin and expendable resources to debt ratios.[7] If a college has more than two years of operating margin deficits greater than 5 percent or a free expendable resources to debt ratio less than 10 percent, it should be alarmed. Nelson suggests that the values for the preceding ratios indicate the potential for financial trouble.[8] The values in Table 10.1—based on the fiscal year 2000 audited financial statements for 248 private four-year colleges and universities rated by Moody's as Baa (lowest rating before a listing of speculative grade)—also suggest boundaries for financial trouble.[9]

Other Diagnostic Measures

Three ratios—*debt leverage, capitalization, and composition of assets*—provide additional critical measures of the college's financial flexibility during periods of financial stress. For instance, when the *debt leverage ratio* (net assets divided by long-term debt)—which depicts the extent to which net assets are committed to debt—is below 2:1, the college may not be covering its debt in times of financial stress.[11] The denominator of this ratio—long-term debt—should include all forms of financial liability and off-balance sheet financing.

The *capitalization ratio* (net assets divided by total assets) measures the accumulated resources of the institution. A high ratio suggests that the institution has substantial financial flexibility—the "desirable" boundaries for this ratio range from 50 percent to 85 percent.[12] If the ratio is within these bounds, the college will

Table 10.1
Moody's Ratio Values for Small Colleges 2001–02[10]

Ratio	Values
Free Expendable Resources to Operations	.80
Total Financial Resources per Student	$20,427
Annual Operating Margin	1.69%
Average Annual Operating Margin	1.73%
Operating Margin Excluding Gifts	-3.73%
Actual Debt Service Coverage	$2.08
Average Actual Debt Service Coverage	$2.03
Return on Net Assets	8.46%
Return on Financial Resources	8.81%
Expendable Resources to Debt	1.34

(See appendix G for method to compute ratios.)

be able to respond to new opportunities. If the ratio is higher than 85 percent, the institution should consider using its excess net assets to take advantage of new wealth production opportunities.[13] A ratio less than 50 percent suggests that the college may not have the resources to respond to new market opportunities or to economic stress.

The *composition of assets ratio* (financial assets divided by physical assets) indicates the college's capacity to increase its financial reserves through its investments.[14] A ratio greater than 1 shows that the college is able to retain financial resources without devoting them to capital investment.[15] On the other hand, a ratio less than 1 suggests that the college deploys most of its permanent capital in fixed assets, which do not contribute to the bolstering of financial resources. The college should compare these ratios to determine how efficiently it is deploying resources.

CFI Scoring

A college should compute its CFI score not only because it is an important measure of financial condition. The components of the CFI ratios are important devices in building a financial strategy. CFI is computed from the primary ratio, net income ratio, net return on assets ratio, and viability ratio (see chapter 6). Each CFI ratio has a suggested value or range based on KPMG and Prager's experience. These ranges can become financial targets for improving CFI scores.

CFI Performance Boundaries

1. Is the *primary ratio* (expendable net assets divided by total expenses) greater than .40? Evidence suggests that with a score greater than .40 an institution has the flexibility to change with market conditions.[16] A ratio less than .15 suggests that the institution needs to cover expenses through short-term loans.[17]

2. Is the *net income ratio* ([operating revenue minus operating expenses] divided by total unrestricted operating income) greater than 2 percent? In this case, the college lives within its means and builds financial reserves.[18] The conditions related to net return on assets are covered in the previous section.

Is the *viability ratio* (expendable net assets divided by long-term debt) less than 1? If so, the college may not be able to respond to adverse conditions because it will have devoted its reserves to debt service.[19] KPMG believes that this ratio should fall within the range 1.25 to 2.0 for the institution to have adequate flexibility under adverse conditions.[20]

The CFI score itself is also bounded (see the scoring table in chapter 6). Scores above 3, especially scores substantially higher than 3, suggest that the college can consider how to deploy its resources effectively to strengthen its financial resources and its market position. If the score is less than 3, the president and the board need to take immediate action to improve the college's financial condition. A score less than 3 suggests that the college is vulnerable to unexpected changes in the economy and the market place. The college will need to construct a financial strategy that targets the weakest components within its CFI ratios. The result could be a major restructuring of the college to improve its productive efficiency and its position in the market.

A lower score, especially a score below 1, indicates that the college's very survival may be at stake. Drastic and immediate action might save the college. If the score has been less than 1 for several years, the college may face circumstances that force the board and the president to consider what actions will best serve the interest of their students rather than the preservation of the institution.

Market Analysis

Since the financial strategy and market strategy must be compatible, the college needs to understand its place in the market. Why do some applicants prefer to enroll in another college? Why do students drop out after a semester, a year, or shortly before earning their degrees? The chief academic officer, the financial aid director, and the chief enrollment officer are the key members of the market diagnostic team. They should conduct an exhaustive study of demographics, enrollment, attrition, and competitors.

Demographics

The market diagnostic team should profile the current enrollment pool by program and level (graduate or undergraduate), compiling demographics for each. Is the current student mix desirable—with its present combination of student characteristics, home vs. campus residency, full-time vs. part-time status, prior schooling, and test scores? If not, the market scheme should be adjusted or reconstructed to target the desired student pool.

Enrollments

What attracts students? Is it tuition discounts? the campus? amenities? a streamlined application process? a notorious faculty? renowned graduate and undergraduate programs? Each program at every level should generate a clear profile of participants. The market diagnostic team should question students and staff to determine what factors encourage registration. Though the happy student is the least likely to offer opinions, both current and former satisfied students should be interviewed where possible. Former students will share their experiences with friends and family— potential enrollees—so it is advisable to consult alumni. Even employers of alumni can offer valuable insights into the strengths of the college, given their take on the pertinent academic qualifications of their new or veteran hires.

Attrition

What makes students drop out? If the student attrition rate from the first to the second year is greater than 20 percent, that's high. The market team must find out why. Drop-outs should be interviewed and a marketing plan implemented—up to and including tuition discounts—to bring them back. Is the graduation rate less than 15 percent? Why? Maybe academic policy does not allow for courses to be offered frequently enough. Problems must be identified and remedied before new enrollments are dissuaded.

The admissions department should make a practice of following up by phone (no one reads letters) with all inquiries, admitted students, and enrolled students for a year. It should also keep a close watch on potential dropouts, arranging personal meetings where practical to encourage continued enrollment. Remember: Graduates are a college's best references.

Competition

The president and finance team should meet with relevant offices (admissions and development) and faculty to identify and classify the competition. Have new not-for-profit or national for-profit institutions entered the market? Not-for-profits might be thrown by an aggressive campaign—including direct mail, phone counseling, improved services, new advertisements, and/or new channels for advertisements—but for-profits won't be foiled so easily. They build market share very quickly. Strategic planning is essential to combat for-profits. A joint venture may be the only way to keep them from stealing the college's student pool.

Every competitor should be classified according to its marketing strategies, themes, and campaigns and then compared with the college on the same counts. How do competitors rank in terms of their programs, services, and amenities? Obviously, students who forsook the college for a competitor would have much insight to offer regarding the competitor's strengths. But interviews with the college's *current* dissatisfied students may be just as useful. From the application process, to course selection, to matriculation, to graduation, unhappy students won't withhold their opinions where conveniences are concerned. What about the competition's tuition, net price, revenue, gifts, endowment return, fund raising, and debt trends?[21] Such information can provide yield rates for each level of student matriculation, which will be useful later in the establishment of benchmarks in the college's competitive financial strategy.

As the college filters market goals from its research, it must remain amenable to various approaches to strengthening market position. Colleges often stick with the first potentially fruitful market approach they find, thereby closing the door on a host of alternatives. To help identify and evaluate alternatives, Robert Lenington suggests that colleges employ consultants, who can perform careful market and cost-benefit analyses of each new approach.[22]

If the college can determine why some students enrolled and graduated and why some students left, it has a chance of maintaining or rebuilding its market share. Building on strengths is a given. Enticing those who left or dropouts back with tuition discounts may be wise. But certainly, the financially troubled college would do well to tend its flock—however small—especially in the presence of new and existing predators.

Other Operational and Governance Issues

Procedures that guide and regulate the behavior of the board, the president, and other key institutional leaders underpin the financial integrity of the institution. As chapter 9 suggests, policies and procedures must assure that omission or commission does not jeopardize the integrity of the college. Not-for-profit colleges have a special duty to regulate activity so that surplus funds are not diverted for personal benefit. Therefore, boards should make sure that policies exist that require their members, the president, and key officials of the institution to sign statements regarding conflicts of interest. Guidelines should also be in place about business transactions among the institution, board members, key administrators, and family members. Board oversight of key administrators' purchases rounds out the common-sense practices that will assure the college's compliance with tax regulations.

Federal student aid and federal grant regulations require most colleges to conduct audits, which provide disinterested third-party reviews of financial records, policies, and procedures to confirm their compliance with generally accepted accounting procedures and regulations. William Reed strongly recommends that the audit or finance committee meet privately with auditors "to talk candidly about institutional financial management."[23] As these two organizations note, "Only through open, regular, frank, and confidential dialogue will the audit or [finance committee] be in a position to utilize the knowledge of outside auditors in assessing internal controls, management, . . . and the impact of each on the quality and reliability of financial statements."[24]

Furthermore, the board should assure itself that risks from financial operations are at a minimum by checking to see that regulations exist for payroll, student billing, payables, accounting, purchasing, cash transactions, and investments. These regulations should specify responsibilities and controls that follow "generally accepted accounting principles."

Summary

The measures and commentaries described in this chapter give presidents, boards, and chief officers some guidelines for assessing the financial and market conditions of their institutions. No two colleges face identical financial scenarios. Though financial measures and market tactics will not apply across the spectrum of financially distressed colleges, the overall message applies to all: Financial strategy depends on a leadership's knowledge of both its financial tendencies and its market position. There is no easy way to handle the diagnostic information. The college's leadership simply must tackle the work, cognizant of the likelihood that careful data collection and assessment will pay huge dividends in the future.

Notes

1. Financial Accounting Standards Board, "Statement of Financial Accounting Standards No. 116, Accounting for Contributions Received and Contributions Made," no. 127-A, June 1993.
2. Ronald E. Salluzzo, Philip Tahey, Frederic J. Prager, and Christopher J. Cowen, *Ratio Analysis in Higher Education*, 4th ed. (New York: KPMG LLP and Prager, McCarthy & Sealy, LLC, 1999), p. 17.
3. Ibid., p. 59.
4. Ibid., p. 61.
5. John Nelson, *Private Colleges and Universities Outlook 2001/02 and Medians* (New York: Moody's Investors Service, 2001), p. 9.
6. Ibid., pp. 13–14.
7. John Nelson senior vice president, Moody's Investors Services, New York, N.Y., E-mail to author, November 8, 2001.
8. Ibid.
9. Nelson, *Private Colleges and Universities Outlook 2001/02 and Medians*, p. 9.
10. Ibid., pp. 10–11.
11. Salluzzo et al., *Ratio Analysis in Higher Education*, p. 71.
12. Ibid., p. 59.
13. Ibid., p. 60.
14. Ibid., p. 61.
15. Ibid.
16. Ibid., p. 16.
17. Ibid., p. 16.
18. Ibid., p. 15.
19. Ibid., p. 22.
20. Ibid.
21. Online sources of financial and enrollment data include: John Minter and Associates, www.jma-inc.net; GuideStar, www.guidestar.com; and NSF's WebCASPAR database. Data are also available from state postsecondary agencies.
22. Robert Lenington, *Colleges Are A Business!* (Phoenix, Ariz.: Oryx Press, 1996), p. 36.
23. Reed, William S. *Financial Responsibilities of Governing Boards* (Washington, D.C.: Association of Governing Boards of Universities and Colleges and National Association of College and University Business Officers, 2001), p. 96.
24. Ibid.

Financial Strategy

The small college that expects to meet the challenges of the next decade must incorporate financial strategy into its plans. Chapter 10 laid out a pivotal piece of strategic planning: the collection of financial and market data. Data collection is a considerable undertaking, and it is the only alternative to the hip-pocket strategizing that once characterized financial planning and management. Out of necessity, many institutions will take potentially unbearable financial risks in the 21st century. In attempts to keep pace with changing market demands, for example, small colleges will assume increasing debt. Those with adequate immediate resources to support debt service will fare well, but those that depend on revenue growth will approach the brink of catastrophe if estimates fall short.

Effective leadership combined with revenue increases and expense cuts can transform financially distressed colleges.[1] Financial stability depends on positive flow from net income, achieved through a balance of revenue growth and expenses.[2] Financial strategy succeeds only if a charismatic leader melds financial data, marketing, operational management, and finance into a comprehensive plan.[3]

Financial strategy is much more than dollars, cents, and spreadsheets. It is a careful weave of a college's eccentricities, a realistic interpretation of its financial history, and the determination of many to transform financial potential into financial performance. Financial strategy at small colleges must fit into a strategic plan that rests on four legs: "a creative admissions office (or marketing); flexible, market-sensitive academic programs; a financial buffer (in the form of a strong financial structure); and a disciplined budget system."[4] A successful financial strategy will expand financial resources, optimize net pricing, cut expenses, control debt, build contingency funds, and manage a disciplined budget system—all through effective management.

Financial Resources

Financial resources—working and permanent assets—are the lifeblood of the small independent college. They must be strong, and they must grow. They are paramount in a college's quest to fulfill its mission and achieve its strategic goals. Recall the financial measures in chapter 10; they must be computed and deconstructed if leaders hope to gain full understanding of their college's financial resources and drivers. Gauging the magnitude and direction of the relevant ratios and ratio components will yield valuable insights into a college's ability to adapt to crises and new opportunities. Ignoring flexibility measures could seriously impair financial responsiveness.

Once leadership assesses the college's financial resilience (or lack thereof), it must apply a cohesive strategy to strengthen financial resources. Operations at small colleges, especially tuition-dependent colleges, must contribute substantially to resources. Receivables must not be bogged down by a high rate of uncollected student accounts or excess bookstore inventory; they must support a strong cash position. Auxiliary services, such as dormitories, food, bookstore, and health services, should produce a positive income large enough to cover depreciation and administrative charges. Financial assets should exceed or equal physical assets so as to promote financial flexibility. Net assets should grow relative to operational expenses to ensure that the college continually improves its financial condition. These components of resource strategy should blend together in a symphony. To manage them independently would be to compose a cacophony.

To grow financial resources, the college must adopt revenue production strategies. Classic growth options have a proven record; however, nearly every college has employed one or more of them (if not all of them) at one time or another. The last college to use classic growth options is much like the last investor to figure out the turn in the stock market; by the time this investor parts with his money, there is no longer any value to be gained from the investment. So that even the last college to try a classic growth option has a chance at success, we will put a different spin on the classic options here.

And after discussing classic growth options, we will consider several emerging options. From joint ventures, to for-profit operations, to investments, to market strategy, colleges can choose from an array of novel opportunities. Prudent experimentation—given the risk of new approaches combined with the recent fluctuations of the stock market—will ensure that the college breaking from a string of failed attempts at growth achieves maximum flexibility.

Financial Strategy through Ratios and Benchmarking

Ratios and performance benchmarks could be used to build a financial strategy (see chapter 10). Since these ratios have a performance benchmark (Moody's Investor Service Medians or KPMG/Prager), they can become strategic goals. For example, the benchmark for the annual operating margin for small colleges is 1.69 percent. If the ratio value for the college falls below the benchmark, the college's goal could be to raise the operating margin to the benchmark level. Another example is a CFI score that is less than 3. The strategic goal would raise the score above 3 because this score is an indicator of financial distress.

The objectives would deconstruct ratios or the CFI score to identify factors that must be changed in order to raise values. For instance, the net income ratio has many points of entry to improve performance. A college could increase revenue, reduce expenses, build the endowment fund, and improve management of financial assets. The CFI score can be improved either by working to increase the numerators or to decrease the denominators for the four ratios that form the score: primary reserve, net income, return on net assets, and viability. The primary reserve ratio can be increased by increasing unrestricted net assets or by reducing total expenses. The same type of analysis could follow for the other CFI ratios.

The same deconstruction and goal building can occur with marketing and personnel ratios. Low admission yields mean that the college is receiving many inquiries but few applicants. The college can refocus this ratio by changing its inquiry and admission strategy. High staffing ratios relative to competitors may mean higher expenses. If the college wanted to change the staff-to-student ratio, it would change either the number of staff or the number of students. There is a caveat to changing this ratio, however. The college may have a high staff-to-student ratio as part of a marketing plan that attracts students. In that case, the ratio should be changed only after considering the consequences.

Ratio and benchmarking as a path to financial strategy requires good data, careful analysis, and an understanding of the consequences. These conditions especially apply to benchmarking. The origin of benchmarks and their relationship to the college must be known. Otherwise, the college may discover that ratio and benchmarking strategies lead to decline rather than to improvement.

Classic Growth Options

From new instructional programs (master's level), to new degrees (technology-based), to new student markets (adult and working students), to new schedules (accelerated and modular classes), independent colleges have exhausted the tried and true growth options. The MBA, for example, has been the cash cow of many independent colleges for two decades. But some of the options are beginning to show their wear. Growth has slowed and even declined at many colleges that offer MBA programs, accelerated courses, and degrees for working students.

Colleges must do more than carve niches and duplicate successful programs. Markets call for originality. When a group of competitors offers redundant degrees, advantages, and services, the gains associated with the "enhancements" diminish for each college. Leaders must develop new programs and find new ways to deliver services.

Degrees at for-profit colleges resemble those of not-for-profits, but with a fundamental difference. For-profit leaders constantly scan corporate, student, and government markets for profiles of the ideal graduate, responding swiftly by revamping old programs and devising new ones, modifying services, and refining policies and procedures—and they complete their innovative work within months, not years.[5] Speed, responsiveness, and excellence must become the watchwords for all small colleges seeking to revive student interest and bolster revenue.

Speaking of student interest, a college's image can make or break enrollment projections. The student who enjoyed the last four years of academic life at Awesome College may help a younger friend or relative enroll next year. If hundreds of happy students encourage hundreds of friends to enroll, the college has just saved significant resources that would have otherwise gone into recruiting them.

The college that carefully researches and develops a program, writes a curriculum, and hires instructors in plenty of time for the program's implementation will portray an image of order and preparedness to interested students. Those that scramble at the last minute, sending in graduate students to teach until new instructors arrive, come across as thoughtless, disorganized, money-grubbing institutions. Changes to programs and procedures entail enough stress in and of themselves; colleges would do well not to complicate the picture with a poor image.

Focus on Strength

A planning officer at an Ivy League university told me that financial strategy must focus on building core sources of revenue. Revenue is generated by a variety of income streams, including tuition, fees, grants, contracts, gifts, and auxiliary sales. Only a few of these streams produce the largest share of revenue. The balance represents minor contributions, and while they should not be ignored, they also should not consume the majority of the administrative team's time and effort. The main goal of any good financial plan is to concentrate on the primary flow of income into the college.

When the main flow is from tuition, the college needs to make sure that it sustains and increases its market share. It can do this through new programs or by tying down enrollment feeder patterns. Regarding the latter, the college could arrange for high schools or youth clubs to participate in courses or projects on the campus.

The administrative team should spend most of its resources on its most important income flows and see that they grow and remain strong. There is nothing more disheartening for a small college than to watch its main source of income fade away because it was ignored or because the administrative team turned to other minor projects.

Focus but Diversify

It is an old investment adage that all good financial plans are diversified, so that the collapse of one sector of the market does not markedly degrade the value of an investment portfolio. The same holds true for small colleges. While a small college needs to focus its attention on its core income streams, it must also make sure that its core income does not depend on a single segment of the market or a single source, such as gifts. Colleges that receive a large portion of their gifts from a single benefactor are vulnerable if something happens to the benefactor. The bad news is that benefactors do die, and the heirs may not care about the college.

Nursing and engineering programs are classic examples of instructional programs that are susceptible to quick and unpleasant changes in student demand. Colleges with these programs can have many good years of steady income and then discover in a short span that student enrollment drops 20 percent or more overnight. Excessive reliance on a program like nursing or engineering can prove devastating to a small college.

Diversifying income streams can involve several strategies. The college can add programs that draw students from different segments of the market. For instance, colleges might want a mix of programs that attract traditional or adult students. They may also consider a mix of undergraduate and graduate programs that enroll students from different age groups and capacity to self-fund their education. The point is that diversification does not mean moving into untried areas. Diversification can mean that the college finds alternative sources for its main income stream. By expanding its options, the college will reduce the risks resulting from changes in the economy or other unexpected events.

Investments

The bear market of 2001 taught institutions some hard and lasting lessons about investments. The endowment and investment funds of most small colleges constitute a limited portion of total assets, so these colleges must follow the rule of the prudent investor. Small colleges with endowments valued at less than $3 million that got caught up in the technology frenzy made the mistake of entering the market at the top. They saw their thin safety margins shrink by 50 percent or more. They compounded their errors by holding the investments, thinking they would rebound to their original values. Because the market typically generates a 10 percent return, simple compounding suggests that it will be years—perhaps decades—before the losses are recouped. Small colleges must strive to build wealth in order to survive the vagaries of the marketplace.

Though most colleges and investors today are well aware of these basic investment rules, the small college that adopts investment as a growth option ought to ensure that these rules are in place to guide every investment decision:

1. Never risk more than the college can afford to lose.
2. Venture capital, while producing huge returns, carries equally huge risks and may take years to produce any return.
3. Avoid unfamiliar investments.
4. Diversify by investing in index funds or in a mix of equity and bond funds that balance risk against the market.
5. If using outside investment firms, the board should monitor investments.
6. Understand that investments carry transaction costs that diminish return values.
7. No-load funds or new equity indexes can provide low expense ratios and match a diversified portfolio.
8. It typically takes between $12 and $20 of investment to generate $1 of payout, depending on the endowment draw rule. Manipulating investments is not a sound tactic for increasing current income.
9. Investment reports should compare the college's portfolio against a benchmark. Examples for fully diversified portfolios include the S&P 500 or a benchmark that represents the total market, such as the Russell 3,000 or the Wilshire 5,000.

New Programs

When contemplating a program shift, the president and key leaders should identify the problems with existing programs. Perhaps they are current, but not properly run. Perhaps a large public university nearby offers new programs that could be more efficiently and personably run by the small independent college. Several new or improved programming options should be prepared for the review of the president and key leaders.

The president should appoint a task force to develop the concept for each option to be investigated. Each task force will

- describe the relevant student market and the new program's appeal;

- design marketing and curriculum strategies;

- propose changes to policy and procedures (and to existing programs, where appropriate) that will streamline and encourage student participation;

- prepare a three-year enrollment forecast and a revenue/expense budget;

- compile written job descriptions and lists of pertinent new equipment, space, or custodial needs;

- identify anticipated problems (and solutions where possible); and

- draft an implementation schedule.

The finance office will then evaluate the budget, estimate the payback of implementing the new programs, and compute the net present value for the review of the president and key leaders. Approved programs can then be ranked according to their respective net present values, dates of introduction, and potential problems associated with their implementation. Selected programs will then be formally slated for start-up. Program goals should be established and budgets, policies, and procedures should be finalized before being marketed and advertised according to budgets. Once a program head, faculty, and program monitoring system are in place, the program can be cleared for implementation.

Site Strategy

For-profit colleges and the most aggressive independent colleges add sites to improve revenue and net income. A regional site network involves the most significant extension of a college's presence, perhaps throughout a large state or even across state borders. The potential for revenue growth from site strategy is substantial, especially for small colleges that want to cater to the commuter student market.

Commuters want sites closer to home and work, and successful planners must meet that demand with an ideal site, top-quality management, and, of course, appropriate accreditation and licensing. (Colleges opening their first ancillary site should consider hiring a consultant to develop plans and handle accrediting and licensing issues.)

A college must first identify the ancillary location and decide what programs it will offer there. Then, for each site contemplated, the president will charge a task force to:

- characterize the relevant student market;

- research the competition and its pricing structure(s);

- estimate space requirements and cost estimates (including rent and new construction comparisons) for classrooms, service rooms, storage rooms, and offices;

- estimate equipment, supplies, and maintenance requirements and costs;

- identify accreditation and licensing issues;

- forecast and characterize such elements as budgets, enrollments, class sizes, bookstore services, policies, and types of instructors;

- consider who should lead development of the site itself and who should manage it once operations begin; and

- project site completion and opening dates.

With these parameters and deadlines in hand, the site plan should be finalized; the budget, enrollment, schedules, policies, and lists revised as necessary; accreditation, licensing, and tax requirements met; the location confirmed; and site construction or adjustments to rented sites begun. A monitoring system should be in place to track the site's performance in light of its competitors. By the time of the first site's opening, college leaders probably will have begun plans for the next site.

Many institutions make the mistake of opening multiple sites and reveling in the proceeds without giving careful consideration to site management. If the main campus leadership merely grafts ancillary management into departments without careful consideration of authority and accountability issues, ancillary management will assume a passive, disconnected form. It is not enough for problems at a new site to temporarily rouse the interest of a distant leadership. Inter- and intrasite management must be continuous, coordinated, and energetic. Crisis control does not count. Successful site management requires a site manager, a main campus manager, an operational plan, performance benchmarks, and delegated authority.

Consider the example of a small independent college in the mid-Atlantic region that established three sites central to the three largest counties in the state. It enrolled fewer than 1,000 students when it began expanding, and enrollments have increased 7.5 times in the last 20 years. One of its most successful sites operates out of a community college that also houses sites run by two public universities. For every student enrolled there by the public universities, the independent college enrolls eight.

The college credits its success to responsive programs and almost familial relationships among faculty, staff, and students. When adversity strikes, students can fall back on a predictable support system. The college even revised its withdrawal policy, making students with family emergencies or job changes eligible to receive refunds for incomplete courses.

Aggressive Competition

Competition creates a rich marketplace for colleges that work to provide superior programs and services at reasonable prices. With an aggressive direct mail campaign, the small independent college with a competitive product can draw sticker-shocked students away from pricier, arrogant institutions. Inquiring students should be contacted personally, as should dropouts, recent graduates, and employed alumni. Single-course or semester discounts can be offered, or funds can be established specifically for the purpose of enticing these students. The college should contact businesses, government agencies, labor unions, and professional organizations offering discounts to employees or members who sign up for coursework (block pricing as a tuition strategy is discussed later in this chapter). Warrants can easily be designed to track authorized discounts.

Expanded Fund Raising

Fund-raising serves a crucial purpose by helping to insulate institutions against economic and enrollment fluctuations. If colleges lack fund-raising skills or resources, they should outsource their fund-raising and alumni relations operations. Successful fund-raising campaigns that aggressively target board members, reliable donors, alumni, and senior administrators can be established to offset unfunded tuition discounts, pay down debt, or fatten a college's endowment fund.

Emerging Growth Options

Joint Ventures

Enterprising colleges form joint ventures that capture the advantages of scale economies and risk reduction as they enter new or untried markets. Higher education abounds with joint ventures. Stanford and Harvard offer Internet courses; MIT and Cambridge form joint institutes; Pearson Publications has joint ventures with Cambridge, the University of Michigan, Regents College, and 24 Jesuit colleges and universities to offer online programs; and PBS collaborates with various colleges on telecourses.[6] Even with the shake-out in technology ventures, institutions are scrambling to work together to tap new markets before businesses do.

The variations on the who's, how's, and why's of joint venture formations are endless. Two guiding principles apply across the board: (1) Joint ventures are legal contracts, and colleges should enter negotiations with the close involvement of legal counsel. (2) A joint venture should be negotiated at arm's length so that each party serves its own interests, not relying on the good intentions of the other party.

Before initiating a joint venture, consider these questions:

- *Have other colleges set up a similar joint venture?* If so, visit them. Ask about their experiences and any problems they've encountered. Obtain a copy of the venture agreement.

- *Is this joint venture untried?* If so, get information about the other party. Has it worked with other colleges? Were the relationships amicable? Were there problems?

- *How will operations be structured?* An operational statement should clearly explain the management structure, directors, policies, reports, personnel policies (especially key employees), and goals.

- *How will cost splitting and revenue sharing be defined?* Several formulas exist for cost splitting: the institution providing the service carries costs, costs are split equally, or costs are proportional to effort. Revenue sharing may include: revenue following cost, revenue being shared equally, or revenue being proportional to effort.

Every joint venture should follow these basic guidelines:

- Define the initial investment by members.

- Determine how new members are added.

- Establish a governance procedure, especially regarding voting rights.

- Decide whether participation in new ventures will be mandatory or voluntary.

- Audit operations.

- Establish rules for changing, withdrawing, or dissolving the venture.

- Define and revise performance benchmarks.

- The college that has no experience with a joint venture should hire a consultant to help review performance.

New Legal Entities

Tax law does not restrict colleges to not-for-profit corporation status when they create new operations. Joint ventures, expense consortia, service centers, and remote instructional sites could all be organized as for-profit corporations. The not-for-profit portion of the college could contain board membership, own all or part of the new corporation, or simply be an investor in the for-profit corporation.

For-profits and not-for-profits differ in the following ways. For-profit corporations can raise capital through the sale of equity because they can distribute earnings. Not-for-profit organizations, which are restricted from distributing earnings, raise capital in debt or gift form. For-profits can incur debt and solicit gifts, too, but benefactors receive no value for their gifts. Not-for-profits cannot be owned by a for-profit corporation. If a for-profit wants to buy a not-for-profit college, the not-for-profit's corporate status must be dissolved, and the for-profit will have tax liabilities associated with the not-for-profit's net assets having accumulated tax-free.

Not-for-profit colleges have tremendous flexibility when establishing new operations. The college will have more control over work rules, management, and operations in a new structure than it has had within the boundaries of its original status. Regardless of which type of structure the college selects for its extensions, it should examine the impact of newly formed tax entities. If the new entity provides instructional services, it will need to meet licensing and accreditation requirements; it may make more sense to contract with the college for such services. The venturing or expanding college should consult tax accountants and specialists in licensing and accreditation to determine the relative costs and benefits of using the existing corporate structure or forming a new one.

Market Strategy

Market strategy may seem out of context with financial strategy, but their relationship is important. Markets are a major driving force in the financial performance of a small independent college, shaping not only student enrollment but also gifts, grants, and research. Financial strategy in turn informs market strategy, with financial aid funds determining the composition of the student body and the proportion of full-pay and full-time students, for example.

Much like the financial resource components described above, market and financial strategies are often designed and implemented independently. As a result, a college's marketing strategy, uninformed by a financial perspective, will fail to generate the benefits of a well-designed net price strategy. But a financial strategy cannot succeed in the absence of an effective market strategy.[7] The small college must be conversant in its market and keenly aware of its place in it. Market indifference could easily lead to financial catastrophe.

Pricing and Tuition Strategy

Pricing strategies follow directly from market strategy and should play an integral part in the financial strategies of most colleges. Among small colleges, pricing strategies tend to revolve around net price. Tuition discounts build enrollment by targeting a student population and defining it in terms of price and quality. An effective net price strategy depends on the success of a college's marketing strategy, its ability to determine student price sensitivity, and the prudent distribution of financial aid.

Planners must coordinate market and pricing information to avoid wasting time and money on net price strategies that do not fit the student population or the institution. Indiscriminate tuition discounts—better known as "trolling for students"—will not boost quality enrollment. They will eat away at budgets with little or no payoff. As budgets implode and revenue declines, academic quality will suffer and enrollments will stagnate.

Net pricing strategies are financed by a college's charitable wealth and its ability to generate support in the form of gifts, endowments, or other institutional assets. As the relative scale of financial resources declines, net subsidies also decline, leaving small colleges with a bag of aggressive discounting policies. Tuition discounts must then be offset by unfunded institutional aid (cash discounts not recovered by the institution). This practice consumes revenue, and without sufficient resources many colleges turn to debt to support operations. These are the colleges that bob in and out of deficit—depending on the stringency of their expense controls and the flow of gifts.

Some colleges that do not have an explicit net price strategy extend one implicitly by charging fixed nondiscount tuition rates that carry huge discounts to the market. Provided that these colleges serve large transfer markets, and that other colleges do not follow suit, nondiscount strategies can work. There is just one problem: Nondiscount price strategies apply across the board; they cannot target for academic quality or for characteristics such as student interest in particular programs or services. Tuition discount planning must judiciously anticipate not only student characteristics, but graduation rates, funds for instruction, academic support, plant and maintenance, and net marginal revenue.[8]

Experience suggests that forming a tuition discount team is advisable. This team includes the chief financial officer, the financial aid officer, the chief admissions officer, and the chief academic officer.[9] The tuition discount team should collect trend data on:

- the current mix of students (academic characteristics, program enrollment, and level of degree);

- the current cost of discounting policies (including marketing and recruiting costs);

- the proportion of full-pay students; and

- competitors' student mixes and tuition discounts.

The team should also establish goals for its own college's student mix, net marginal revenue, and proportion of full-pay students. Given the potential cost of the linchpin discounting policy, the president should review all goals associated with it.

Colleges can employ three different tuition discount strategies: preferential, differential, and leveraged.[10] Preferential discount packages go to students who meet certain academic criteria. The awarding of differential discount packages depends on a combination of academic merit and need. Leveraged discount packages—the most difficult to design—include a matrix of awards based on enrollment history, the effect of past financial aid offers on yield of students or subgroups from various economic and academic levels, and a forecast of short- and long-term effects of financial aid policy on cost and net revenue. According to

Tom Williams of Noel-Levitz, colleges can advantageously devise leveraged discounts that conform to current market and financial conditions.[11]

The tuition discount team must ask several questions as it designs a strategy. Is the average tuition discount of the graduating class substantially less than that of the incoming class? The college must recognize cost differences in tuition discounts from year to year. How many students would comprise total enrollment? An effective policy will result in a student body that better fits the college. Attrition should decline under the new policy, which could result in cost savings in recruiting new students to fill vacancies. What are the one- and five-year impacts of financial aid policies on enrollment and net revenue? The college should not blindly implement an untested policy.

Many small colleges have discovered with chagrin that tuition discounts may positively affect revenue while negatively affecting cash. Those colleges are enrolling more students but collecting smaller tuition amounts. If they respond reflexively by reducing their discounts, another problem will arise: the lowered discounts will throw off pricing relationships among competitors. Small colleges can reduce the stress of tuition discounting by funding the discount. However it chooses to manage its discounting policy, the small college must work to achieve a desirable student mix and generate sufficient cash to support operations.

Since a financial aid policy carries daunting data demands, prudent financial leaders will seek assistance during its construction. Beyond the basic structure of the plan, the college will need a system to track awards, students enrolled, retention, income generated, and graduation rates. The tuition discount team should continuously monitor and modify the pricing strategy, updating discounting forecasts based on the impact any modifications will have on enrollments and net revenue.

Net Price: Fund the Discount

The biggest problem with tuition discounts at small colleges is that they are unfunded. Revenue may increase, but cash constitutes a smaller percentage of it, and revenue may ultimately fall below expenses. Colleges can avoid the net price predicament by shrinking the discount, but backing off tuition discounts can affect the competitive condition of the college. Aligning sticker price with net price could upset the delicate balance between price and perceived quality (see the discussion of tuition strategy in the next section). Or, colleges could raise funds to offset the discount, increasing the annual campaign target and using the difference to cover the unfunded portion of the tuition discount. The endowment fund could also be increased so that the payout can cover the discount over the long term.

Tuition Strategies

If the college has excess capacity, many competitors, open enrollment (or very low selectivity standards), and easily transferable students, it most likely operates in an elastic market; many tuition-driven colleges do.[12] Price reductions in such a market should result in higher enrollment and greater revenue, provided that (1) the price reduction takes net price into account and (2) students know of the price reduction. In 1996, the *Chronicle of Higher Education* reported that "enrollments surged after large tuition cuts at private colleges."[13] However, a college must be very careful that price reductions do not confuse its student market, because price and quality are closely linked.

Tuition cuts typically balance sticker price reductions with corresponding reductions in institutional aid, a low-risk tactic that often results in virtually unchanged net prices. A more aggressive approach that might work for as long as it takes other colleges to follow suit is to drive sticker price below current net price, eliminate institutional aid, and advertise the change. Another tactic for nonselective colleges would be to increase sticker price and net price by the rate of inflation, a more conservative approach that takes longer to produce a relative price change. Selective colleges that employ this option may want to set a price position target relative to that of their competitors. Finally, colleges can discount tuition to fill dormitory rooms, thereby increasing auxiliary revenue while cutting tuition revenue. Once dormitories are filled, the strategy can be discontinued. This trade-off strategy is useful only when increased auxiliary revenue is greater than the discounted tuition revenue.

Independent colleges that use the inflation strategy will see tuition at competing colleges rise over time, leading eventually to a shrinking tuition gap. Even tuition at public universities will rise to the level where the independent college is holding tuition increases equal to the rate of inflation. The independent college can then aggressively market its price, targeting public university student pools. Many students will transfer to an independent college if price is comparable, service is better, or degree work takes less time to complete.

One small college used the inflation tactic, marketing its program to potential students of a public university's master's program in education. The independent college offered better service, convenient academic schedules, and an insignificant price difference. Many students transferred to the independent college, and over five years, the public university program's enrollment level dwindled to a handful. The independent college's revenue, increased tenfold and came to hold the largest market share of local market students.[14]

Another price strategy—block pricing for employees of businesses and governmental agencies—grants tuition reductions to working students. This market is immense. Businesses in 2000 spent more than $4 billion reimbursing their employees for tuition.[15]

Businesses or government agencies initiate most block price discounts, usually on a small scale and dependent on a relationship between the college and the outside entity. In most cases, working students are treated like any 18-year-old who seeks admission. Each student is approached individually, and market strategies are directed toward individuals. There is no coherent strategy for going after the working student market. Colleges simply ignore the advantage of enrolling large blocks of students at a discount. But large blocks could lead to substantial savings. Advertising and recruitment costs could be reduced. Working students are more motivated, so attrition would decline. They do not require the amenities that traditional students seek. The college can increase market share, which enhances market reputation, which stimulates future students to enroll.

Block pricing suggests that there are many creative solutions to price cutting or discounting. Tuition cuts and pricing strategies may become more prevalent if competition for students continues to increase. If for-profit colleges emerge as a force in higher education, price could become a major tool they use to build market share. In that case, small colleges that share the marketplace with for-profits will have to become more adept at pricing.

Pricing must include cost controls, because expanding enrollment holds no value if the cost of providing services outstrips the revenue increase. Price cutting can be a boon to small colleges, but it is risky, especially for those colleges with no reserves. Price cutting by way of net price or other pricing strategies can undermine cash flow. One problem with price cuts versus tuition discounts is that lower sticker prices may attract less academically prepared applicants. One year of price cuts may temporarily boost enrollment of the desired caliber of students, but continued discounts may actually shrink the applicant pool of these students. Prospective students often see sticker price as an indicator of academic quality—both theirs and the college's. The lower the sticker price, the less academically prepared the applicants may be.

Cutting Expenses

Most colleges—with their bureaucratic offices, overlapping points of control, and miasmic protocols—are ripe for cost cuts. Howard Bowen's law that revenue rises to meet expenses and Robert Zemsky's and William Massy's administrative lattice and faculty ratchet indicate that powerful incentives grow expenses faster than inflation at many colleges. [16] The prevalent bureaucratic model—with its redundant levels of authority, multiple layers of administration, numerous points of control, self-interested administrators, and ever-expanding staff and offices—contribute to cost intensity.

Cutting expenses usually offers the best chance of improving a college's services. The benefits may not be obvious, but many colleges are burdened by inefficiencies in administration, instruction, and student services. The most difficult part of trimming costs is not figuring out what to cut. The biggest challenge is doing it. There are a million obstacles to changing the status quo.

But cutting costs can yield significant returns, provided that two rules apply. First, someone must be responsible for developing and carrying out the plan. A task force may be created to draw in important segments of the institution, but one person must head it. Second, the individuals responsible for plan development and implementation must be held accountable for their work. If the task force as a whole dilutes individual responsibility, the president will have no one to reprimand or congratulate but the entire group.

Re-engineering

William Massy has said that "U.S. higher education may be the envy of the world, but, as with many industries before it, the time has come for restructuring." [17] One of the primary tools for revamping operational processes within an organization is business process re-engineering—"the fundamental rethinking and radical redesign of processes. . .[with a goal to] achieve dramatic improvement in critical measures of performance." [18] Parallel with the goals of a small college, re-engineering cuts costs while streamlining and improving services.

Small colleges, even those operating under massive deficits, tend to cling to outmoded processes that qualify for re-engineering. Consider, for example, the traditional admissions-registration chain, which typically involves filing papers and shuffling students from one office to the next. Each office processes papers, checks papers, and monitors policy to assure compliance, and the cost of such a paper trail—from the staff doing the monitoring and processing to the files that hold the paper to the offices that hold the staff and the files—can be staggering. Each office needs extra staff to handle surges of students (who don't trickle in consistent numbers through *any* process). Each office experiences workload surges as well, so that one office may sit quietly while another works frantically. Many an annoyed student standing in line at one office has watched staff in another office reading, playing cards, or conversing over coffee.

The admissions-registration process begs for change, but forces of habit prevail. Admissions offices must meet with students. Advisers—not admissions officers— must advise students. And no one but the registrar may enter courses in the official course file. In some small colleges, the registrar's office does little more during registration than enter courses into computers. But many ancillary campuses permit a student counselor to conduct the entire admissions-registration process. The counselor takes the admissions form, sets up course schedules, and accepts payment. Why not implement such a simplified process at the main campus? Small colleges could streamline many of their processes in much the same manner at tremendous savings.

Technology has done little to untangle the bureaucracy because computers continue to support rather than replace manual operations. Colleges must allow technology to handle more of the processing.[19] As technology takes over the role of administrative policy enforcer, staff as service agents can begin to reacquaint themselves with students. The payment office can become strictly a billing office. Overstaffing will be substantially reduced—even if the registrar continues as preserver and monitor of the integrity of records—with fewer staff working more effectively. Leadership will be crucial as they break in new, more efficient traditions.

Students refuse to suffer the inefficiencies of circuitous administrative processes. In fact, with credit transfers being accepted more readily than they used to be, students now vote with their feet for colleges that will treat them not as impediments to already convoluted policies and procedures but as valuable customers. For-profit colleges are ahead in this game.[20] Students willing to suffer the pain of degree work but not the pain of bureaucracy will escape to for-profits, where helping the student is not secondary to upholding administrative rules and regulations.

Organizational Paradigm Shifts, published by NACUBO in 1996, contains an excellent synopsis of the rationale for and steps to re-engineering.[21] Leaders must identify the institution's major process chains, that is, the sequences of activities among several offices geared toward a specific end. A task force for each chain then considers a series of questions: Who does the process serve? What in the process can be eliminated or consolidated so that single customer agents can replace three and four? How can information technology manage policies and procedures more directly? Can the college model the efficient processes of other institutions? Based on this analysis, the task force should recommend cost reductions, service improvements, performance standards, implementation deadlines, monitoring procedures, and a map of the overhaul process.

Restructuring

This strategy eliminates management layers, consolidates responsibilities, and reconfigures work. Restructuring can improve efficiency by re-engineering work or taking common-sense action to make the college function better. When it is frequent, unannounced, and used to control management, restructuring is not a positive strategy but can strike a Machiavellian chord, sowing chaos, fear, and conflict. Productivity will dissipate if the leadership's sole purpose is to disrupt cabal formation and isolate instigators of dissension. In the worst sense, restructuring concentrates power in a preferential few rather than decentralizing power to eliminate redundancy and complexity.

Legitimate restructuring should begin with a review of existing roles, relationships, spans of control, management accountability, and number of management layers.[22] Leaders must identify those redundant or contradictory roles and relationships that can be eliminated without disrupting core services. Next, leaders apply re-engineering to design new service-delivery processes, concentrating service delivery in centers staffed with highly trained people who are accountable to a central director. Excess staff will be let go through attrition, retained staff will be retrained, and new staff will be recruited according to quality and trainability. Finally, restructuring will require monitoring and refinement to contain power-seeking tendencies, where duplicitous behavior becomes the norm.

Outsourcing

This powerful tool can help colleges turn costly services into sources of income through expense cuts and/or the creation of scale economies. Small colleges can outsource auxiliary services like food services, dormitories, health services, and bookstores; financial and administrative services like security, custodial services, accounting, billing, collections, purchasing (consortia), advertising, site operations, personnel operations, and computer services; and instructional services like computer instruction, which could go to a nearby college with a large investment and a strong, relevant reputation.

Success depends on the outsourcing contract and the college's diligent oversight of outsourced operations. These conditions are so important that the outsourcing college should hire a consultant to develop the contracts and a manager to oversee all outsourced operations. Leaders should also initiate and maintain relationships with other colleges that have outsourced similar services, reviewing their contracts if possible and asking what they would change in their contracts if they could.

Performance benchmarks, penalties for failure to achieve them, and a schedule for performance reviews should be established with and for the contracted service organizations. College leaders must be sure to have a high-level manager at the outside agencies with whom to discuss problems. Contracts should be renewed subject to performance reviews, not automatically. Mandatory security checks and monitoring of security guards and custodians at the outside agencies, as well as a requirement that they carry liability and theft insurance, will help protect the college's interests.

Scale Economies

An institution should strive to reach an operational scale in which the average cost of operations is at or approaching a minimum. Generally, costs will continue to decline until enrollment reaches between 1,500 and 2,000 students. [23] For some four-year colleges, scale economies grow up to an enrollment of 1,100 students. "There is a cost disadvantage of about 12 percent for operating at half this size."[24] The small college that enrolls fewer than 1,000 students needs to develop strategies to improve its scale economies or else it may find it difficult to keep pace with expenses and price its product attractively.

In addition to expanding enrollment and outsourcing, a college can form consortia with other small colleges to build up its scale economy. In a consortium, the sharing of administrative and student services reduces each partner's average costs. General accounting services, student payments, and administrative computing systems are a few of the services that could be transferred to a consortium. A consortium can also share services that are outsourced.

Debt Strategy

Debt is not inherently bad. It can provide small struggling colleges the leverage they need to transform themselves. Not-for-profit institutions of higher education have no access to equity markets for capital formation; they use gifts and debt to form capital. Though gifts carry the advantage of requiring no repayment, their flow depends on a college's access to a wealthy and generous donor pool. Colleges without wealthy donors must use internal funds, forgo the capital investment, or turn to debt. Debt can facilitate the spreading of an equipment or facilities investment across several generations of students.

Colleges without access to debt markets that make capital-intensive investments must deplete either financial reserves or current operational resources to do so. The reallocation of operational resources to finance a capital investment puts a heavy burden on current students to generate assets that will be used by future students. The worst-case scenario is the college that forgoes capital investment due to inadequate internal resources or lack of access to debt markets. This college will suffer competitively.

During the next decade, small colleges will face tremendous pressure to make capital investments. Considerable evidence suggests that all levels of higher education need to upgrade buildings and equipment to accommodate both modern technology and student demands for comfort, personal services, and a homey atmosphere. Colleges built 40 years ago were designed when technology was mere science fiction and students were grateful for residence in a monastic cell.[25] To keep up with changes in technology and student expectations, colleges must design facilities that can be easily reconfigured more often than every half-century. In the first decade of the 21st century, enrollments are projected to grow at a fast pace of 20 percent due to an increase in the number of high school graduates.[26] More colleges will be renovating and expanding than ever, and the impoverished among them will be forced to either employ debt or drop by the wayside.

Debt gives small colleges the opportunity to keep programs and services current, but it must be used judiciously. Debt becomes hazardous when used repeatedly to bail a college out of a bad financial situation, or when based on bad predictions. Bradford College is a classic example of the college that borrows and loses big on a whim; Bradford closed two years after building new dorms that were supposed to boost enrollment (see chapter 8).

A small college considering new debt must prudently analyze its current debt load, being careful to include off–balance sheet financing. Debt outside the classic instruments of notes, mortgages, and bonds can be indistinguishable from normal operating expenses, yet these new forms are still long-term obligations that must be met. Complementing the debt list (see chapter 10) should be a spreadsheet showing the cumulative long-term payout schedules for all net debt payments, adjusted for revenue or pledges obligated to the payments. Once the spreadsheet is complete, evaluation of the debt's potential impact begins.

Before considering an increase in debt, the college must decide how to fund it. If the current debt leverage ratio (net asset divided by total debt) is substantially below 2:1, and/or the viability ratio (expendable net assets divided by long-term debt) is substantially less than .40, the college should reduce its current debt load before undertaking new debt. If debt load is greater than 2:1 and the viability ratio is greater than .40, the college should take the following steps to plan for debt:

1. Prepare another spreadsheet containing current and new debt payments (include off-balance sheet financing).

2. Evaluate the impact of the new debt on debt leverage and viability ratios, the budget, and the college's cash position.

3. Consider a fund-raising campaign to offset principal or future debt payments (all things being equal, the best debt strategy for small colleges is to minimize debt through major gifts or fund raising).

4. Evaluate revenue-generating projects carefully, using present net value to estimate valuation, and bound projects with upper and lower projections. Basing debt-related decisions on a single best-case scenario does not allow for unexpected events that could change a project's revenue flow.

5. Carefully analyze the conditions of the debt instrument.

6. Submit a plan to the president and finance committee for review that includes paybacks, costs, conditions, and the fit with current debt obligations.

Long-term debt, especially when it is increasing, can create a drag on the economics of cash-starved small colleges. Debt service appropriates funds that could otherwise be used for operations. In many instances, small colleges trade maintenance of existing buildings or expansion of core services for new construction. This debt strategy is unproductive to say the least, with beautiful new buildings springing up next to eyesores that house failing instructional services.

Cash-starved small colleges are also prone to delinquency, the surest route to closure. These institutions must find ways to reduce their risk. The best strategy is to minimize debt by complementing debt investments with fund raising.[27] They also could design and place debt-funded facilities in locations that appeal to the real estate market so that if financial forecasts don't pan out, the investments can be sold. With foresight, debt can be managed even in uncertain times.

The NACUBO publication *College and University Business Administration* explains debt financing in higher education, describing types of debt instruments, regulatory conditions, and procedures.[28] Before financing capital with debt, the president and chief financial officer of a small college should review this publication carefully.

Contingency Funds

Paul Brinkman has found that many financially distressed colleges can survive with the help of contingency funds, which provide reserves for colleges to dip into during periods of economic stress.[29] The purpose of a contingency fund is to limit a college's chances that enrollment or other unexpected events will force it into a period of uncontrollable deficits or even lead to its demise.[30]

The contingency fund can be considered a quasi-endowment under board control. Colleges build such reserves by investing a portion of net income prudently, so that funds are accessible within 12 months if necessary. (This time frame assumes that economic downturns will be apparent to key leaders.) In the absence of contingency funds, colleges often make sweeping cuts to academic, plant operations, and administrative services—cuts that can adversely affect the college's ability to manage its resources, serve its students, and provide safe and appealing facilities.

Mergers

Mergers offer a strategic opportunity for some small colleges to strengthen their financial condition and their position in the market. James Martin and James E. Samels contend that imminent bankruptcy does not have to be the only reason for merging colleges. They cite 10 principles for merging: enhancing complementary missions; encouraging mutual growth; strengthening academic offerings; revitalizing the financial base; stabilizing enrollment and market share; improving administrative efficiency; generating economies of scale; making public relation opportunities; expanding the alumni base; and creating new synergies.[31] When a merger is not compelled by financial exigency, it may prove difficult for both parties to agree. Colleges, unlike businesses, are not owned by someone. Administrators, staff, faculty, students, and alumni have a vested interest in maintaining the unique identity of the institution, and they can create roadblocks to a decision to merge.

Martin and Samels suggest that each party to a merger should be guided by four rules:

- Each college should hire legal counsel, particularly one qualified in merging colleges.

- Each college should perform a careful "due diligence" review of all aspects of the merger.

- The merger agreement should precisely define all conditions to the merger.

- The merger agreement should clearly describe how disputes are resolved during the transition phase of the merger.[32]

- If the work is done well, and each institution gains from the merger, then the new college should be stronger, more resilient, and more attractive to students than the individual colleges.

Management Commitment

Claiming a strategic plan for the sake of an accreditation report doesn't ensure its validity. Senior managers must treat strategic planning not as a mere process, but as an evolving concept that demands undivided attention and devotion.[33] "Processes" involve "steps" that anyone can list. Anyone can gather, edit, publish, and file reports to be forgotten. A valid strategic plan requires review and monitoring by the president and senior managers. They must continuously match progress against strategic goals, identify areas of weakness or obsolescence, and adjust goals accordingly. Plan activities should be formally monitored quarterly—in addition to emergency meetings—and officials should meet annually to assess plan progress.

The following principles deserve repeating: The college must be able to react expeditiously to market and financial vicissitudes. Budgetary and financial controls must be in place that involve limits on spending, rules on new expenditures, and sanctions for exceeding budgetary limits without authority. Such controls are the central focus of financial management in small colleges. A college must constantly test its financial, market, and academic assumptions.[34] Administrators and managers must not bypass the intellectual work of testing hypotheses. Finally, the college must have a system of incentives in place that encourages faculty, staff, and administrators to accomplish institutional goals.

Budgets

Budgets are the instrument for transforming the abstract resources of the financial structure into current action with future consequences.[35] Budgets themselves are more than an abstraction. Although they appear on the surface to be little more than estimates and allocations, budgets are the human dimension of making an organization carry out the will of the leadership. They are crucibles for conflict and compromise as participants attempt to influence the direction of the organization. Budgets are definitely an instrument of power, because a budget defines the narrow range within which faculty and staff can act.[36] Budgets express the future as understood by the leadership and translate forecasts into action statements of enrollment, research, donations, endowment yields, expense allocations, cash flows, and the conversion of permanent capital into current production. In many small colleges, the budget is much more prosaic, being little more than a guess about the future combined with the hope that revenue will cover next year's expenses. For these colleges, the budget explicitly addresses only revenue, expenses, and some sort of enrollment forecast. Everything else—cash flow, receivables, and payables—is implicitly taken for granted. The assumption is that revenue and expenses will work as they always have. Capital spending is an ad hoc decision made independently of the budget. Capital projects' ramifications on the budget are assumed to take care of themselves. In some ways, small-college budgets are a throwback to the era when colleges were religious institutions. The leadership assumes that somehow faith in the goodness of the college will overcome all obstacles.

If budgets are to be an effective tool for preserving and strengthening the integrity of the financial structure, they must look beyond the challenge of finding the next dollar of revenue to cover incremental operating costs. When budgets ignore the working and permanent capital structure, they ignore its effect on the institution's well-being. Focusing only on revenue and expenses assumes either that operations produce sufficient resources to sustain the college or that the financial reserves embodied in the capital structure are adequate to maintain its productive capacity.

Complex budget planning models have been developed for large independent universities, such as David S.P. Hopkins and William F. Massy's monumental planning model for Stanford University.[37] Although these models are beyond the capabilities of small colleges, which may not have the people, the computing power, or the funds to manage an elaborate budget planning system, small colleges must still go beyond revenue and expenses when they construct their budgets. Budgets can become a comprehensive statement about the financial structure of a college by comparing the condition of the financial structure to the competition or to a benchmark group of colleges. Such a comparison can point to weaknesses in the structure.

Financial and Business Monitoring

Monitoring the financial structure is an imperative for a small college that wants to ensure that it has the financial resources to fulfill its mission. Monitoring can not be an occasional activity. With their thin financial reserves, small colleges cannot afford to ignore their financial structures. The same holds true for small colleges with larger reserves. Economic conditions change too rapidly and too subtly to assume that the internal dynamics of a particular financial structure remain valid under all circumstances.

John Minter has found that signs of trouble are usually apparent well before the college finds itself in dire circumstances. [38] But someone must be awake at the switch or the opportunity to intervene might be lost. A regimen that tracks trends and ratios of the four critical components of the financial structure can provide an early warning system. The monitoring plan outlined in table 11.1 can be expanded to fit the needs of a particular college.

Trends for these measures (ratios, actual dollar amounts for the numerators and denominators, and rates of change) should be tracked over a minimum of three years. Deviations between one-year and three-year rates of change should be a cause for alarm if the one-year rate drops below the three-year rate. The chief financial officer should also graph these ratios and the actual dollar amounts. Minter notes that graphs are a good way to illustrate financial condition and to quickly spot impending problems.[39] When trend lines indicate current problems or point to future problems, the chief financial officer needs to bring this to the attention of the president.

Since small colleges' financial reserves are so meager, small discrepancies between forecasts and fiscal performance can be disastrous. The longer it takes to discover the problem, the more difficult it is to solve the problem. Options disappear during the fiscal year as discretionary funds are spent. Conversely, the pleasant possibility of extra funds can be dashed if the anticipated surplus is only a guess. Checking actual performance against the budget at the end of each registration and each month will impose control.[40]

In addition to their financial monitoring role, the president and the chief financial officer also must make sure that the college scrupulously follows regulations or depository requirements related to taxes, employee benefits, hiring practices, and federal aid. Business offices must deposit tax and benefit withholdings on time. Pay and benefits for key administrators must be tested for excessive or inequitable compensation. Hiring practices—applications, hiring standards, testing, and termination procedures—must conform to federal and state regulations. In addition, the college must dispense financial aid carefully and keep accurate records of all transactions. In fact, record keeping is an imperative in today's regulatory climate. Otherwise, the college is at the mercy of federal audits and penalties that could jeopardize its tax status and financial condition.

Table 11.1
Critical Financial Monitoring System

Measure	Benchmark
Revenue and expense growth rate equilibrium	One-year and three-year rates balanced (with expenses including depreciation and a nominal net income of 2%)
Net price trend	One-year and three-year rates equal to rate of growth in instruction, academic, and institutional support services.
Annual operating margin	Greater than 2%
Cash to expense ratio	Greater than 8.03%
Viability ratio	Greater than 1.25
Return on net asset ratio	Greater than 8.46%
Net assets, assets, and liabilities (actual dollars)	Assets must be greater than liabilities, and net assets should trend upwards. If trend lines suggest that liabilities will cross assets in the future or that net assets are turning down, a major problem is emerging.

The best advice for small colleges that may not have the expertise to deal with these matters is to have auditors regularly review financial aid practices, prepare federal reports (income and benefits), and conduct compensation and benefit tests.

In addition, the college should provide for a regular review of personnel practices. Keeping current with governmental regulations can have a significant impact on administrative costs; ignoring regulations can be disastrous.

Keys to Financial Strategy

A financial strategy provides the resources necessary to accomplish a college's mission and ensure its financial viability for future generations. Inadequate financial resources will prevent a college from delivering educational, research, or other services to students, parents, and the community. The keys to a successful financial strategy are not esoteric. They follow from economic theories like that of Charles T. Clotfelter, financial models like that of David S.P. Hopkins and William F. Massy, financial performance systems like that of KPMG/Prager, and credit rating programs like that of Moody's Investor Services.

To implement a successful financial strategy, a small college must take into account the following keys to financial strategy:

1. Eliminate deficits from operations, subject to producing a positive net income.

2. Balance revenue (including excess funds for positive net operating income) with expense growth rates.

3. Build a coherent net pricing strategy or raise funds to reduce unfunded financial aid.

4. Focus strategy on main income flows into the college.

5. Diversify the main income flows to reduce risk.

6. Trade gifts for debt to raise the debt ratio above 2:1.

7. Build budgets that:

   - include forecasts, goals, and plans for working capital (cash, receivables, payables, accruals, inventory) and permanent capital (endowment, debt, and net asset position);

   - add employees discriminately;

   - contain expense growth;

   - estimate revenue conservatively and prior to the budgeting of expenses;

   - increase revenue scrupulously (not arbitrarily) to support expenses; and

   - revamp incentives when they fail to improve effectiveness.

8. Build a capital reinvestment fund for renovations and equipment replacement.

9. Build a contingency fund.

10. Establish a monitoring system for financial performance using ratios, trends, and benchmarks based on industry standards suggested by Moody's, KPMG/ Prager, or other reliable sources.

11. Install budget controls by:
    - establishing protocol for handling over-expended budgets;
    - tracking variances between actual and forecast revenue and expenses;
    - having a plan for variances (positive or negative); and
    - limiting addition of new employees during the fiscal year.

12. Conduct regular budget, financial condition, and financial strategy meetings to review goals and policies using appropriate financial ratios, the CFI scoring system, and trend analysis.

13. Bill students monthly and enforce collection procedures.

14. Set a bad-debt goal not to exceed, for instance, 2.5 percent of receivables.

15. Commit to cash and short-term investment goals to equal at least 8 percent of expenses.

16. Require auxiliaries to achieve a net income minimum goal that covers direct expenses, depreciation, and fixed expenses from the college.

17. Reorganize or outsource auxiliaries, administrative services, or other operations that fail to meet financial goals.

18. Expect alumni relations to produce income equal to their costs, plus some portion of total revenue.

19. Set net income goals for athletics.

20. Incorporate options in the financial strategy that promote flexibility during times of economic stress.

As suggested earlier in this chapter, the president and senior officers must make a serious commitment to the financial strategy. They must disseminate it throughout the institution, conveying it personally—not by mail or e-mail—to all who will bear responsibility for its implementation. If the leadership takes the strategic plan seriously, so will the larger college community. The president must display faith in the strategy by following established protocols during times of economic uncertainty.

He or she must hold staff members accountable for errors and reward them for contributions. The president must scrutinize proposed alterations to the college's financial course. After all, planners should have anticipated economic shifts and designed the strategy to withstand them.

End Games

For some colleges, the odds are too overwhelming. Deficits, cash shortages, shrinking enrollment, and the use of debt to fund ongoing operations push the college to fail. If a college lacks the financial resources to carry out its mission, it must look at its options with a critical eye. It is unfair to students to offer an inadequate education or to push them out when the college suddenly closes its doors. Boards that are contemplating exit strategies should look at mergers and the impact of closing the college.

If the college has residual value—property, a student market, licensing and accreditation of programs—then it may be attractive to another college. However, it can not wait until it is desperate before it considers a merger. Partners may believe that they can get a better deal by waiting for liquidation. Robert Lenington says that mergers can be a viable option assuming an institution has an appropriate mission, a good program, and a service that is in demand. And all of the constituencies associated with an institution in financial difficulty are best served by merger if the alternative is the eventual financial collapse and demise of the institution. Allowing an institution to fail financially and then have society pay for the start-up and development of similar operations elsewhere is wasteful."[41]

If the college has little or no residual value, then it may have no choice but to close its doors. This decision calls for more than merely locking the doors and handing the keys to the banker. As a board confronts the demise of the college, they have a duty to look after the welfare of the students and the employees by observing the following principles:

- Do not close the doors part way through a semester.

- Find another college that will accept students' records.

- Help students' transfers to another college.

- Notify students so that they can make their own plans.

- If funds are available, arrange for outplacement for faculty and staff.

- Transfer financial records and archives to storage for safekeeping.

- Provide auditors with copies of all tax records.

- Determine the disposition of personnel records.

- Hire counsel to handle relationships with creditors.

- Sell remaining assets, and funds for outstanding liabilities.

Preventing foreclosure is only possible if a college takes steps before distress becomes crisis. If foreclosure is threatened, it is too late to take remedial action. A college must act as soon as it detects serious problems with its financial or market conditions. Strategic planning, leadership, management, and good business practices must have time to take effect.

Notes

1. Alan Hamlin and Curtiss Hungerford, "How Private Colleges Survive Financial Crises," *AGB Reports* 31, no. 3 (May/June 1989): 17–22.
2. David S. P. Hopkins and William F. Massy, *Planning Models for Colleges and Universities* (Stanford, Calif.: Stanford University Press, 1981)
3. Robert Lenington, *Colleges Are A Business!* (Phoenix, Ariz.: Oryx Press, 1996).
4. Michael K. Townsley, "A Strategic Model for Enrollment-Driven Private Colleges," *Journal for Higher Education Management* 8, no. 2 (Winter/Summer1993): 58.
5. Richard S. Ruch, *Higher Ed, Inc.* (Baltimore, Md.: John Hopkins Press, 2001), p. 82.6.
6. Susan Carr, "PBS Sticks to Its Strategy for Telecourses, Unafraid of Competition From the Internet," *Chronicle of Higher Education,* July 13, 2001, pp. 1–4; Beth McMurtrie, "Jesuit Colleges Try to Bring Their Values to Online Education," *Chronicle of Higher Education,* May 12, 2000, pp. 1–6; Alina Tugend, "MIT and U. of Cambridge Announce $135-Million Joint Venture," *Chronicle of Higher Education,* November 19, 1999, pp. 1–2; Goldie Blumenstyk, "How a Publishing Empire Is Changing Higher Education," *Chronicle of Higher Education,* September 8, 2000, pp. 1–9; "Harvard and Stanford to Offer Online Business Courses," *Chronicle of Higher Education,* January 5, 2000, pp. 1–2.
7. Lenington, *Colleges Are A Business!*
8. Thomas Williams, "The Proper Mix," *Business Officer* 32, no. 9 (March 1999), pp. 34–37.
9. Ibid., pp. 34–35.

10. Ibid., p. 35.

11. Ibid.

12. Michael K. Townsley, "The Effect of Competitive Structure on Price Elasticity in Local Markets of Higher Education in the Commonwealth of Pennsylvania" (Ph.D. diss., University of Pennsylvania 1994).

13. Anne Marie Borrego, "Study Finds Strong Growth in For-Profit Higher Education," *Chronicle of Higher Education*, July 19, 2001.

14. Robert Zemsky and Penney Oedel, *The Structure of College Choice* (New York: College Entrance Examination Board, 1983).

15. *Lifelong Learning Trends* (Washington D.C.: University Continuing Education Association, 2000), p. 56.

16. Howard R. Bowen, *The Costs of Higher Education* (San Francisco: Jossey-Bass, 1981); Robert Zemsky, "The Lattice and the Ratchet," *Policy Perspective* (Pew Higher Education Research Program) 2, no. 4 (June 1990): 1–8; William F. Massy, "A New Look at the Academic Department," in *The Higher Education Research Program* (Philadelphia: University of Pennsylvania).

17. William F. Massy, "Remarks on Restructuring Higher Education," in *Straight Talk About College Costs and Prices: Report of the National Commission on the Cost of Higher Education* (Phoenix, Ariz.: Oryx Press, 1998), p. 84.

18. *Organizational Paradigm Shifts* (Washington, D.C.: National Association of College and University Business Officers, 1996) p. 11.

19. Massy, "Remarks on Restructuring Higher Education," p. 89.

20. Ruch, *Higher Ed, Inc.*

21. *Organizational Paradigm Shifts*, pp. 14–17.

23. Paul T. Brinkman and Larry L. Leslie, "Economies of Scale in Higher Education: Sixty Years of Research," *Review of Higher Education* 10 (fall 1986): 1–28.

24. Malcolm Getz and John J. Siegfried, "Costs and Productivity in American Colleges and Universities," in *Economic Challenges in Higher Education*, ed. Charles T. Clotfelter, Ronald G. Ehrenberg, Malcolm Getz, and John J. Siegfried (Chicago: University of Chicago Press, 1991), quotation on p. 355.

25. Eva Klein and John H. Augustine, "Debt Financing and Management," ch. 10 in *College and University Business Administration*, ed. Caroline M. Grills (Washington, D.C.: National Association of College and University Business Officers, 2000).

26. "Higher Education Enrollment," ch. 2 in *Projection of Higher Education Statistics to 2010* (Washington, D.C.: U.S. Department of Education, National Center for Education Statistics, 2001), nces.ed.gov/pubs2001/proj01/chapter2.asp.

27. Townsley, "A Strategic Model for Enrollment-Driven Private Colleges," p. 59.

28. Klein and Augustine, "Debt Financing and Management."

29. Paul T. Brinkman, "College and University Adjustments to a Changing Financial Environment," in *The Economics of American Universities*, ed. Stephen A. Hoenack and Eileen L. Collins (Albany, N.Y.: State University of New York Press, 1990), p. 228.

30. Townsley, "A Strategic Model for Enrollment-Driven Private Colleges," p. 59.

31. James Martin, James E. Samels, and associates, *Merging Colleges for Mutual Growth* (Baltimore, Md.: Johns Hopkins University Press, 1994), p. 13.32. Ibid., pp. 22–41.

33. Susan Fitzgerald, "Moody's Rating Approach For Private Colleges and Universities" (New York: Moody's Investors Service, September 1999), p. 1.

34. James L. Fisher, interview by author, Baltimore, Md., September 5, 2001.

35. Aaron Wildavsky, *Budgeting*, 2nd ed. (New Brunswick, N.J.: Transaction Books, 1986), pp. 8, 86.

36. Michael K. Townsley, "Deficit Prevention: Budget Control Model for Enrollment- Dependent Colleges," *Business Officer* Vol 28, no. 4 (October 1994): 40-44.

37. Hopkins and Massy, *Planning Models for Colleges and Universities.*

38. John Minter, president, John Minter and Associates, e-mail to author, January 15, 2001.

39. Ibid.

40. Townsley, "Deficit Prevention," p. 40

41. Lenington, *Colleges Are a Business!,* p. 41.

Small College Turnarounds: How They Did It

George Keller has warned that "a specter is haunting higher education: the specter of decline and bankruptcy."[1] Although some small colleges are unable to survive financial distress (see chapter 7), others have stared down the "specter," made a commitment to change, and lived to tell about it. This chapter offers four reassuring stories of turnaround and survival. These small independent colleges—Georgetown College, Chatham College, Marylhurst College, and Wesley College—prove that with hard work, decline and financial distress don't have to mean bankruptcy or closure.

Themes of vigilance, leadership, and wise financial planning are fundamental to each story. Colleges exist in a precarious education market. Without caution, agility, and steady guidance, many would fall to competitors or to a volatile economic climate. Think of financial distress as a vast pool of quicksand, the path around it poorly marked. The unwary traveler missteps and disappears. The foolish traveler tries to take a short cut and disappears. Even the experienced traveler, having avoided the quicksand before, traipses along not carefully enough and disappears. Credible sources thought that Bradford College had made a successful turnaround, but within seven years, thanks in large part to foolhardy guidance, the college sunk (see chapter 7).[2]

Georgetown College

Bill Crouch, president of Georgetown College, may be one of the most innovative college presidents in the country.[3] He combines an awareness of what a small college must do to strengthen its reputation with the fiscal discipline to keep it going. Georgetown College is located on 104 acres in the bluegrass horse country of Lexington, Kentucky, within the "Golden Triangle" of Cincinnati, Louisville, and Lexington. The largest automotive plant in the United States is nearby, manufacturing and shipping its product from the great river cities.

Like many colleges on American frontiers, Georgetown has religious roots. The Kentucky Baptist Education Society opened the college in the winter of 1830 and chartered it in 1859. Like most colleges of this period, Georgetown offered a liberal arts education based on the classics, but it distinguished itself by offering academic and cultural blends of northeastern and southern influences. During the Civil War, the college closed as Kentucky became one of the early battleground states. Until the mid-20th century, Georgetown remained a liberal arts college. After it began offering professional degrees in the 1950s, enrollment grew, and so did the campus.

But enrollment began to decline in the 1990s, and it declined quickly. From 1990 to 1993, enrollment dropped 15 percent, from 1,595 to 1,370.[4] As enrollment plunged, deficits grew—a combination that inspired Georgetown's board to seek new leadership. When Crouch arrived in 1994, he set four goals for the institution and began immediately to convince the board, the faculty, the students, and alumni that Georgetown could be the best college in its competitive niche.

His first goal was to modernize the plant and equipment. Second, he would fatten the endowment fund so that the college would be able to entice the best students. Third, he would instill the fiscal discipline needed to maintain financial stability. Fourth, he would improve faculty salaries in recognition of its contribution to the college and in anticipation of hiring other high-caliber instructors. Bill Crouch, rising to one of George Keller's leadership standards, would be a "quality monger."[5]

Crouch secured an "A" bond rating from Moody's when a large bond issue was sold, forcing Georgetown to keep itself in financial order. He had Georgetown sell the naming rights to its stadium—used for summer training by the Cincinnati Bengals—to the Rawlings Corporation. He turned over alumni association operations to an outside agency, securing for Georgetown the agency's expertise in both fund raising and national advertising. He conducted major fund-raising campaigns himself to shore up a lame endowment fund, taking advantage of the Golden Triangle's horse country and manufacturing wealth.

At the heart of Crouch's strategy to stabilize Georgetown's financial structure has been an annually updated 10-year forecast used to set targets for tuition increases and income and expense growth. When new expenses or investments are planned, they are tested against the forecast. Crouch is recognized as a leader among small colleges for his innovative work at Georgetown. He has demanded that his college operate under tough, self-imposed financial guidelines, and Georgetown is all the better for it.

Chatham College

Chatham College is one of the oldest women's colleges in the country.[6] The campus in a pleasant section of Pittsburgh incorporates the former estate of financier and industrialist Andrew Mellon.

Chatham, like many women's colleges, has been hard pressed to continue as a single-sex institution. It has been challenged for 40 years by its size and, more recently, by the declining appeal of colleges that are exclusively for women. By 1993, enrollment had fallen from nearly 700 students to 623 students—barely enough to justify keeping the college doors open.[7] The women's movement was originally a boon to enrollments at women's colleges, but with the power of choice came interest in coeducational academic life.

As enrollment shrank, so did Chatham's operating deficit. But its annual deficit grew through most of the 1980s, and in the early 1990s it ballooned to more than $3 million.[8] The board now faced the question of Chatham's viability. Boasting residence on Andrew Mellon's estate may have garnered the college a patina of wealth and strength at one time, but Mellon's historic contribution to the country's wealth probably meant little to prospective students. Recognizing its financial plight, Chatham sought to strengthen itself with a programming shift to coeducation. But amid protests by students who refused to forego the historic imperative of the college, the plan was rejected.

During the coed controversy, the board had fortuitously chosen Esther Barazzone as the next president. A scholar in European intellectual history with a doctorate from Columbia University, Barazzone invigorated the college with her problem-solving approaches. Her multifaceted strategy was to stimulate growth in the undergraduate program, expand the college's continuing education and master's degree programs, add sites, cut expenses, and eliminate the deficit.

Barazzone initiated campus-wide centers for innovation—including the Center for Women in Politics in Pennsylvania, the Pittsburgh Teachers Institute, and the Global Focus program. These centers spurred welcome publicity and made Chatham and its mission better known in the larger community. She guided the college through the addition of more than 40 new traditional undergraduate programs, and she boldly opened the continuing education and master's degree programs to men. Now men could reap the benefits of a Chatham education without diminishing Chatham's primary daytime role as a traditional women's college. While introducing these changes at the main campus, Barazzone led the effort to establish a new site in fast-growing Wexford, Pennsylvania. To Chatham's advantage, she had met one of the great challenges to small colleges: offering personal service at an ancillary campus.

By the early 1990s, new programs and new sites had doubled enrollment. But as Alan Hamlin and Curtiss Hungerford found in their study of college turnarounds, only a strategy based on growth *and* targeted expense reductions will speed recovery.[9] Expense cuts can make or break a college and its president because they typically are made in an atmosphere of conflict and despair. But Barazzone achieved a savings of nearly $2 million by cutting administrative and faculty expenses by 20 percent while keeping Chatham afloat and maintaining its focus on innovative excellence.

In keeping with debt reduction and enrollment growth, Barazzone initiated successful fund-raising campaigns to help revitalize the campus. With the construction of new buildings and the restoration of older ones, Chatham began to shed any image it may have projected of a run-down institution struggling to survive. The Chatham story illustrates that when campus renovation is well managed, it not only puts a fresh face on the buildings and grounds for all donors to see, but it infuses a college and its community with a new spirit. Barazzone communicated and carried out her plans with candor and confidence, and the Chatham community both fueled and rewarded her with theirs.

Perhaps even more crucial to Barazzone's mission than the support of faculty and students was the board's trust in her leadership. The board was recognized for three significant steps it took during Chatham's revitalization.[10] Board members had met directly with the college community in a series of "visioning" exercises aimed at outlining the challenges and the opportunities for change. They had restructured the bylaws to affirm the president's authority relative to the board and the faculty. And most important, the board had demonstrated its resolve to make changes by hiring a worthy president and vesting her with the authority to take progressive steps. As the board chair reported, the president had at first been "concerned she would have problems...with a 'stodgy board'" as she worked to get her initiatives passed.[11] But to everyone's advantage, board members had given her a free hand, and she repaid them with her diligence, her drive, and her uncommon diplomacy.

With board approval, and in keeping with her standards of excellence, Barazzone has contributed vibrancy and breadth of purpose to a small, caring women's college.

She has contributed essays about her work at Chatham to major publications, and she has been named a member of many professional and community boards. For all the work of its leadership, Chatham is gaining recognition. The college has earned, among other awards, the Special Commendation for Distinguished Achievement in Undergraduate Education from the Association of American Colleges and Universities. But the students offer perhaps the most valuable recognition of Chatham's turnaround. In a clear expression of Barazzone's success at combining college growth with personal service, Jennifer Rys of Cleveland says, "My classes are small. My teachers all know me. Even teachers you don't have classes with know you."[12]

Marylhurst College

In 1859, the Sisters of the Holy Names of Jesus and Mary followed Richard Henry Dana's route to the West through the treacherous currents of Cape Horn. Their mission: to offer God's services to the pioneering women who had made the long wagon trip to Oregon. As entrepreneurs of the Catholic Church in Oregon, the Sisters established orphanages, a school for girls, and St. Mary's Academy in Portland. In 1893, St. Mary's began to offer bachelor's degrees—a leap forward for women's education in Oregon. The nuns, having succeeded in providing affordable education to women, eventually moved their academy in 1930 to Marylhurst, a suburb overlooking the city of Portland.[13]

The Sisters offered their services to schools and colleges like Marylhurst at no cost. They required only shelter, food, and the opportunity to serve and educate young people—in this case young Marylhurst women—according to the teachings of the church. Orders like the Sisters of the Holy Names of Jesus and Mary were the bedrock of Catholic education until the 1960s. Vatican II, a growing feminist movement, and the general social upheaval of the times drained religious orders. Young sisters embarked on journeys of self-discovery, leaving convents to the care of older nuns.

As nuns retired from educational service and retreated to their convents, student pools in the feeder schools dwindled as female students moved to larger coeducational colleges and universities to complete their educations. Marylhurst, having lost most of its students and its inexpensive yet most experienced labor source, the nuns, eventually closed as a women's school. Later, under the direction of a lay board, the college reopened as a coeducational college with no tenured faculty.

Marylhurst's coed reincarnation did not significantly increase its fortunes, however. Enrollment continued to stagnate, with most students attending part-time. As deficits mounted, the threat of default on federal loans forced the college to look outside the order for a new leader. They turned to Nancy Wilgenbusch, dean of continuing education and vice president of marketing at St. Mary's College in Omaha, Nebraska.

Wilgenbusch found Marylhurst in disarray, its buildings and grounds seedy from years of neglect, its curriculum a veritable hodgepodge. Students had customized degrees on whims, stretching personal service to its limit, and they, along with Marylhurst's reputation, were suffering for the abuse. It would take a miracle to reverse the damage to finances, the campus, and the educational system, and Marylhurst turned to Wilgenbusch for just that.

Fortunately for the college, it had found a president with the same spirit, loyalty, and straightforwardness that Marylhurst's founding nuns had projected. She set about changing Marylhurst's image—a task that initially involved convincing many Portland residents, who thought the college had been closed since the 1970s, that it was indeed open. Wilgenbusch spoke to any civic or service group that would have her, eventually generating enough gifts to begin sprucing up the campus. Beyond inspiring donations, Wilgenbusch's public engagements led to business alliances that would later bring new revenue streams to the college.

Wilgenbusch's overall strategy has extended well beyond a facelift for the facilities. She has hired the very best faculty members and administrators (the vice president of finances and facilities comes from Stanford). She has streamlined Marylhurst's curriculum and developed new brochures and viewbooks that emphasize the link between courses, degrees, and the student market. Using six principles as her guide, Wilgenbusch has significantly restructured Marylhurst's financial operations:

1. Mission determines finances.
2. Knowledge is power.
3. Inflation caps tuition.
4. No tuition discounting.
5. Gifts are dangerous.
6. Budgets are promises.[14]

The most interesting rule is that "gifts are dangerous." Wilgenbusch believes that excess reliance on gifts can place the college at risk because those gifts may dry up.[15] Small colleges that depend on substantial gifts from a single benefactor can be at considerable risk. Many small gifts from middle-income families can evaporate during periods of economic disruption.

Under Wilgenbusch's leadership, every part of the college is financially accountable. Departments that propose new instructional programs must file a business plan that shows expected return on investment. The finance office tracks the fiscal performance of each department in terms of its contribution to the college's margin. When an instructional department reports a decline in enrollment or margin, it must file a report explaining the problem and proposing a solution. The department is then held accountable for the implementation of its turnaround plan.

Every asset is expected to perform to its maximum. Rooms or buildings that are empty part of the week are leased to outside organizations, maintaining a revenue stream in the absence of direct educational service. Wilgenbusch has further bolstered revenue by identifying holes in the marketplace and developing relevant new programs to fill them. Despite fears of enrollment or margin declines due to competition between new and existing programs, and despite the risk of profit sharing (inherent whenever a college contributes significant resources to a new program), enrollment has tripled under Wilgenbusch's guidance.

Nancy Wilgenbusch has delivered on her miraculous intentions to bring Marylhurst out of the red and into the black, but she has faced criticism for her efficiency. Some faculty members think she runs the college too much like a business—a complaint commonly directed at presidents after they overhaul a troubled academic institution. Faculties want to retain the benefits of the current structured approach yet return to the good old days of lax financial procedures and self-serving administrative standards. They forget the penury wrought by years of this management style.

Decision making in a vacuum of faculty and student interests exemplifies Michael D. Cohen and James G. March's "garbage can model," which likens collegial decision making to a manipulative game that rarely serves academic interests.[16] Large, rich independent universities may be able to afford the waste of resources associated with a full-blown collegial decision system—in which precious time and energy are invested alternatively listening and arguing, obstructing and conceding—but small colleges cannot. Their resources are too dear, their financial condition too fragile to wait for faculty egos to reach consensus.

Wilgenbusch, while ascribing to the philosophy that leaders ought to be accessible to their front-liners, has steadfastly demanded that all parts of Marylhurst be held accountable for their actions. Concerns about new projects should lead to adaptation, not to prolonged consideration by many, and certainly not to a sapping monopolization of a president's time and energy. Wilgenbusch has balanced leadership of a small college with concern for its faculty and community. She has, for example, built up pay and support for full-time and part-time Marylhurst employees. Her overall success is gaining far-reaching recognition. Marylhurst has won a "Best Practices" award from the Council for Adult and Experiential Learning as well as a "Best Value" ranking from *U. S. News and World Report*.

Wesley College

Wesley College is the oldest independent college in Delaware. Located in the state capital of Dover, Wesley is within walking distance of many pre-Revolutionary War sites, including Woodburn, the governor's mansion. Caesar Rodney, a signer of the Declaration of Independence, came from Dover. John Dickinson, a delegate to the Constitutional Convention, lived on one of the many plantations nearby. Delaware's southern cities, including Dover, retain a southern flair that is reflected in the slow pace and the sound of people's accents.

The president of Wesley College, Scott Miller, does not fit this relaxed stereotype, however. A fast-paced leader, he assumed control of the moribund college in 1997. He is so animated in his enthusiasm for his growing campus that a visitor might expect him to leap over his desk on his way to construct a new building. His rare energy has been a powerful asset to a college that once was sinking into financial oblivion.

By 1997, Wesley had barely survived an enrollment shrinkage of more than 20 percent.[17] In response to questionable terminations, former faculty members had filed lawsuits against the college and its then-president, who met meeting dissension with fire and brimstone. A new college nearby sought to usurp the continuing education market that had been keeping Wesley afloat. The college had always survived rough patches through the beneficence of United Methodist Church (John Wesley himself had founded Barratt's Chapel just down the road). But once-willing friends had become wary of backing Wesley. The blows from low enrollments, bad leadership, lawsuits, and competitors were apparent on campus, where even the buildings were beginning to look downtrodden. As rumors spread, bets were accumulating as to how long the college could survive before it had to merge.

Enter Scott Miller. He found the money to settle lawsuits and begin building renovations. He gained the favor of the powerful Gannett newspaper, the *News*

Journal, which championed his efforts to change Wesley's image. The positive media attention was instrumental in establishing Wesley as a leader in Dover and attracting the interest of wealthy benefactors. In fact, one generous supporter happens to be chair of Wesley's most formidable competitor. But completing the small college's transformation from penury to prestige took more than facelifts and testimonials.

Miller moved ahead with his long-term strategy. He doubled enrollment in the traditional programs, building a powerful revenue base and ensuring that Wesley no longer has to troll for applicants. He narrowed Wesley's market by gearing advertising toward students with strong academic backgrounds and adequate financial resources. The numbers bear out that those students tend to complete their coursework: Wesley's retention rate has risen to 88 percent.

Another factor in boosting Wesley's revenue has been Miller's initiation of a feeder system. In partnership with the Boys & Girls Clubs of Delaware, Wesley invites 400 high school students to use the campus for their activities. The college receives revenue that offsets the cost of the building, and it also benefits from having potential students actively engaged on its campus.

A third facet of Miller's strategy has been to create an ancillary campus for students in upper Delaware. Within a mile of the college that sought to lure Wesley's continuing education students away from Dover, the site has forced its competitor to keep tabs on its own market. The jury is still out on whether this tactic will relieve some of the local pressure on Wesley and whether it will help to grow enrollment.[18]

To round out his strategy, Miller has found creative ways to fund the college's debt. He has employed off-balance-sheet financing to cover the cost of new construction. The cost of financing does not disappear, but it is replaced by finance charges; the goal is to generate enough revenue from the construction to compensate for them. But even if enrollments decline, Miller has a backup plan for the new buildings. They will be designed for alternative use as offices or housing, and the rents would offset the construction costs.

Wesley College's turnaround can be attributed largely to Miller's energy and informed creativity. His aggressive problem-solving approaches have transformed Wesley from a directionless campus mired in controversy into a well-respected institution, and his sound judgment regarding markets and financing have rebuilt a distressed financial structure. Despite the risks—Wesley's liabilities as a proportion of assets jumped from 33 percent to nearly 43 percent over three years—Miller has used debt judiciously to build revenue, not to finance pipe dreams.

Make Way for a Turnaround

Financial distress begins with a series of accelerating deficits and enrollment declines. It ends with a merge, a closure, or a turnaround. These four stories involve presidents who convinced board members, faculty, and students that change was necessary. From new leadership, to restructured protocols, to cutbacks, the college community must sometimes swallow bitter pills to stave off financial death.

The new president must be dynamic, determined, and capable, for he or she will need to convince others that the college's financial resurrection is possible. The president will act upon arriving to the college, having already assessed its true financial condition through homework and meetings with auditors, accrediting agencies, and licensing agencies. Obviously, the board should be included in the diagnostic interviews, with the president keeping in mind that board members may be poorly informed—or even uninformed—of the college's true financial condition.

From interviews with the board president, to the treasurer or chair of the finance committee, to the janitor of the boardroom, the president must determine what problems remain hidden from view. Are there accrediting, licensing, or governmental problems? Do executive committee members have drastically different interpretations of the college's financial predicament? Do their individual goals for the college differ from their collective goals? What can they contribute to the turnaround? Nothing will debilitate a new president more than beginning a turnaround based on one set of conditions and goals, only to discover the real set later on.

The president should interview people in charge of finance, academics, plant operations, and other critical operations, assessing the competence of each department head in light of the coming changes. While interviewing, the president should be noting his surroundings. Are the buildings in shambles? Are they cramped for space? Are any or all of them candidates for renovation or restoration? Will new construction be necessary?

After gathering information, the new president should "make a splash," in the words of Wesley College's Scott Miller. Saving the full-blown strategy for later, the president should win the support of the college community, rallying students, faculty, and the public for a comeback. Next comes the least favorite job of college presidents: replacing bad leadership with good, standing in personally when appropriate (for example, as academic head), delegating temporary leadership to others in the administration, or soliciting the help of outsiders (for example, financial assistance from auditors) until new department heads can be found.

In the spirit of Nancy Wilgenbusch's "knowledge is power" principle, the president must share financial information with constituents. Everyone needs to understand the true financial condition of the college as well as how to contribute to a turnaround. A step-by-step synopsis of the president's plan, conveyed with reassurance and verve, will help clear the way for the president to begin the turnaround process.

After diagnosing the college's condition and proposing a restorative plan to interested parties, the president must be free to "treat the patient." James L. Fisher advises the board to remove any obstacles to the president's legitimate authority, including policy decisions or bylaws.[19] It would also be prudent for the board to analyze its own relationship to the college's governance structure. The board must be comfortable with the turnaround plan and must manifest its confidence by affording the president enough authority to see the plan through. The success of Chatham College demonstrates the value of mutual trust and respect in the board-president relationship.

Given the authority to begin the turnaround, the president must be sure that both faculty and administration will work cooperatively toward change. Small colleges, says Fisher, cannot afford the ambiguity and chaos of a rivalrous faculty-against-administration governance structure.[20] John Stevens observes that the governance structure of many small colleges is a mishmash of autocratic and participatory influences.[21] Without an obvious and consistent leadership style, a college turnaround will grind to a halt. He believes that participation and accountability can work under the appropriate leadership. Task forces can create and implement plans, and task force leaders will be ultimately accountable for outcomes. (Accountability, by the way, should include a process for rewarding successful outcomes.)

Turnaround Strategy

The specifics of a turnaround plan should be well defined and tested against established financial principles. From Georgetown to Chatham to Marylhurst to Wesley, the presidents of these four successful turnaround colleges spoke to the rigor of a successful financial strategy. Both Bill Crouch of Georgetown and Nancy Wilgenbusch of Marylhurst exemplify the prosperous financial mentor who brings clear plans to embolden slackened financial structures.

First, a president must ensure working assets and donor goodwill as he or she transitions a college from penury to prestige. A financial strategy that lacks the capital to get the ball rolling will amount to no more than good intentions—and perhaps a merge or a closure. Second, a president must identify a viable market. An isolated campus with no enrollment pool won't make much of a turnaround. Third, and not least important, the college needs a positive community or market perception. Some colleges die an image death, with community members mistaking the campus for a quaint collection of partially erect old buildings, soon to be knocked down and replaced with a Target and a great big parking lot.

Following Wilgenbusch's example, the turnaround president must engage every willing ear in the community. From service to professional organizations, from churches to college-sponsored luncheons to candle parties, the message must be broadcast that this college is undergoing a transformation and that employees, applicants, and the public can look forward to a viable provider of educational service. Wesley College's experience with the *News Journal* shows what can happen when a local newspaper adopts the local college and spreads word of its transformation. At the very least, appearances will receive a boost, and unexpected revenue resources may be generated.

These four colleges illustrate five additional points about financial strategy during a turnaround:

1. *Reinforce strengths.* For Georgetown, access to a wealthy and growing economic market was a strength. Chatham focused on its reputation as a college for women and Wesley on its favorable reputation with its church sponsor and its endorsement by a regional newspaper.

2. *Rebuild the strongest financial source.* All four colleges emphasized enrollment by seeking new programs or new feeder patterns.

3. *Diversify income.* Licensing a training field to a professional football team (Georgetown), developing centers and institutes for women (Chatham), offering new programs not offered by other colleges (Marylhurst), and providing a venue for youth programs (Wesley) enabled these colleges to diversify their income. Each college also increased gift giving while remaining tuition driven.

4. *Manage debt.* These colleges either found income streams to cover debt (Georgetown's affiliation with the Cincinnati Bengals) or off-balance sheet financing offset by new revenue sources (Wesley's new dorms, which generated new income based on existing enrollment growth). They also designed projects with alternative functions (Wesley's dorms will be attractive as corporate offices).

5. *Run a disciplined budget and financial management system.* These colleges constantly monitored performance and sought the best managers to produce accurate and timely records.

Many colleges in the past decade have gone through financial resurrections. A college reaches a point of decline, finds a new leader, and grows enrollments, eventually outgrowing financial distress but then reaching an enrollment plateau. For many small colleges, enrollment plateaus translate into higher costs and subsequent tuition increases, leading ultimately to an ironic constraint of enrollments due to market inability to bear the tuition increase. Plateaus may tilt downward because graduations and attrition may shrink the base. From 1988 to 1997, only 15 independent colleges were not constrained by enrollment plateaus; their annually compounded growth rates were above 10 percent.[22] It is difficult to say what accounted for their sustained growth, but evidence suggests that in some cases, the president and the faculty were responsible and accountable partners who did not allow the college to slip backward into collegial governance. The small college tied to a system of serving multiple interests will deplete its own time, energy, and resources, thereby reducing its ability to respond to market shifts in a timely manner.

Whether due to chaos or inertia, stalemates and lead feet are anathema to college turnarounds. Department heads must work in conjunction with the president and board in the name of progress. For the college in financial distress, change is all that will separate an open door from a closed one. It must be heralded on all fronts with enthusiasm, participation, determination, and accountability. Progress, change, and transformation are mere euphemisms for the uncomfortable yet continuous process by which a leader tests a small college's most cherished beliefs and clichés.[23]

Notes

1. George Keller, *Academic Strategy* (Baltimore, Md.: Johns Hopkins Press, 1983), p. 3.
2. Ruth B. Cowan, "Prescription for Small-College Turnaround," *Change* 25, no. 1 (January/February 1993): 38.
3. The information about Georgetown College is based on the author's interview with Bill Crouch,
4. "Sheet 15565881.wk1: Opening Fall Enrollment: 1967–1997," National Science Foundation WebCASPAR Database System, http://caspar/nsf.gov/.
5. Keller, *Academic Strategy*, p. 133 .
6. The information about Chatham College is based on the author's interview with Esther Barazzone, October 4, 2001; the Chatham College Web site; "Chatham College Turnaround Lauded," *Pittsburgh Tribune-Review*, February 12, 2001; and Esther L. Barazzone, "Back from the Brink," in *Presidential Essays: Success Stories that Make a Difference at Thirteen Independent Colleges and Universities* (Indianapolis: USA Group Foundation New Agenda Series, 2000).
7. "Sheet 15565881.wk1: Opening Fall Enrollment: 1967–1997."
8. "Sheet 08180820.wk1: Unrestricted and Restricted Fund Types: 1987–1996," National Science Foundation WebCASPAR Database System, http://caspar/nsf.gov/.

9. Alan Hamlin and Curtiss Hungerford, "How Private Colleges Survive Financial Crises," *AGB Reports* 31, no. 3 (May/June 1989): 17–22.

10. Allan Splete and Robert C. Dickeson, "Five Boards that Lit a Spark," *Trusteeship*, January/February 2001, pp. 30–31.

11. "Chatham College Turnaround Lauded," City Tribune-Review, February 12, 2001.

12. Ibid.

13. The information about Marylhurst College is based on the author's interview with Nancy Wilgenbusch, August 28, 2001; college publications; and an extensive article about the president and Ron Feemster, "Faith in Financials," *University Business* 3, no. 3 (April 2000): 34-39.

14. Feemster, "Faith in Financials," p. 39.

15. Ibid.

16. Michael D. Cohen and James G. March, *Leadership and Ambiguity: The American College President* (New York: McGraw-Hill, 1974).

17. "Sheet 15565881.wk1: Opening Fall Enrollment: 1967–1997."

18. The competing college has begun construction of a large campus on the main thoroughfare in Dover. Sometimes tit for tat can get out of hand.

20. James L. Fisher, interview by author, Baltimore, Maryland, September 5, 2001.

21. John Stevens, senior vice president and chief operating officer, Kaludis Consulting, Washington, D.C., interviews with author, September 11, 2001, and September 18, 2001.

22. See "Sheet 15565881 wk1: Opening Fall Enrollment: 1967 to 1997."

23. James L. Fisher, interview by author; James L. Fisher, *Power of the Presidency* (New York: American Council on Education and Macmillan Publishing Co., 1984).

Chapter 13

What Are the Prospects for Small Colleges?

Small independent colleges offer what most parents want for their children: an enjoyable college experience in which enlightened faculty members teach classes and anticipate student needs and a protective campus community that guides students as they mature. There is a catch, however. The Utopian college experience does not come cheap. And not only are parents and students unwilling to pay a high price for it; many independent colleges simply can't afford to offer it.

The Utopian college caters to its students' desire for homey quarters and contemporary degree programs. In addition to McDonald's, The Gap, multiplex theaters, electronic boutiques, shopping malls, and hot entertainment spots, students want degrees that will be valued seriously in the labor market. They want freedom from outdated rules and regulations; recruitment, admission, registration, matriculation, and graduation ought to follow an efficient, convenient course. But as colleges expand tuition discounts in order to build enrollment and lure the best scholars, they struggle financially to offer anything more than hard-scrabble educations with the barest amenities, let alone superior educations that meet every student's whim.

The actual small independent college, to its chagrin, offers a college experience that few self-respecting teenagers seek: encumbered with outdated technology, one-size-fits-all degrees, uncertain transition to work, group showers, broken furniture, shared rooms, inadequate electrical and Internet services, leaky pipes and roofs, dirty classrooms, and (worst of all) nothing to do and no place to hang out. Location, resources, and image have conspired against the marketing teams at many small colleges for the last decade, and enrollments and revenue have fallen in stride. Through most of the 1990s, 30 percent of colleges with fewer than 2,000 students reported deficits.

Philip Tahey, who co-authored KPMG and Prager's book on financial ratios, is amazed at the resilience of small colleges that report deficits year after year and should have merged or closed but that scrimp and cajole enough money to stay open.[1] Unlike small community hospitals, small colleges have not been forced to merge by auditors, or changes in federal reimbursements, or competition, and they have garnered enough support to keep going. Yet because so many have barely the resources to operate, a single precipitating event during a second decade of fiscal distress could force a major restructuring within the small college market niche. A variety of scenarios exist:

- Competition drives down net price, and small colleges cannot meet cash needs or debt obligations.

- Competition strips continuing education revenue used to subsidize traditional day programs.

- Interest rates rise unexpectedly, and small colleges are unable to make full payment on debt service.

- Changes in federal rules reduce the amount of financial aid colleges can receive from the Department of Education.

- Student demographics change, and small colleges do not have the means to serve the changing market.

- Student expectations drive up the costs of providing services, and small colleges cannot afford to remain competitive.

- Auditors and financial agencies tell boards of directors that small colleges are no longer economically viable, and they need to find support from stronger institutions.

What Do the Data Suggest?

A good economy floats all boats, as the financial expression goes. Most independent colleges, regardless of size, did quite well during the last four years of the 20th century. On average, net income grew, and revenue outpaced expenses. Even the smallest colleges seem to manage operational income better than do their larger cousins; the proportion of institutions with negative slopes for net income was inversely related to college size. Small colleges still operate on very thin reserves, however, with net assets and investments providing little insurance against unforeseen changes in marketplaces or the larger economy.

The stock market began to spiral downward in mid-2000, taking the economy with it, and the plunge intensified with the terrorist attacks on September 11, 2001. If stock markets fall again in 2002, we will see the first consecutive three-year stock market decline since the start of the Depression. The last fiscal year of financial data used here ended June 30, 2000, just before the economic downturn. Anecdotal evidence suggests that many institutions of higher education have not, as of the end of fiscal year 2001, accounted for the market's impact on their investment portfolios. Come June 30, 2002, when portfolios are finally marked to market, the news for some institutions could be quite bad.

There may be a silver lining, however. Miserable economic times and a concomitant rise in unemployment usually translate into growing enrollments, provided tuition revenue grows fast enough to offset losses in grants, gifts, or investment revenue. Given that the economy is definitely not the same as it was in 2000, it would be improvident to prognosticate on the future for small colleges. It is fair only to say that small colleges will either putter along as they have in the past, or succumb to the downward pressure and slide over the brink.

Advantages and Disadvantages of Small Colleges

Uncertainty about the future of small colleges is not something new. In the late 1960s, Christopher Jencks and David Riesman saw large public universities usurping chunks of the student markets usually served by smaller independent colleges and nationally recognized independent institutions enticing the best students and growing financially powerful through strong endowments.[2] What is new—and what Jencks and Riesman did not speculate—is the possibility that small colleges would disappear altogether.

Small independent colleges have persisted against the odds because students tend to fear the alien environment of large universities located far from home, and they opt instead to prepare for the job market in the less anonymous, more comfortable setting of a local independent college.[3] Jencks and Riesman believe that the survival of most small colleges, especially those lacking a national academic reputation, depends on the size of the gap between independent and public tuition rates. Were the gap to grow, parents would simply have to send their children to public universities, proximity and comforts be damned.[4]

The world that Jencks and Riesman saw for small colleges five decades ago, in which small independent colleges offer a viable alternative given a reasonable price, persists today. But new threats and newcomers to the marketplace have complicated the scenario. For-profits, cutting edge technology, and rising student demand for personal services are only the beginning.

Disadvantages

Micro colleges, which enroll fewer than 500 students and have inadequate financial reserves, are sharply limited by their size. They must engage in net price battles in order to maintain a trickle of enrollments. They have few alumni and fewer donors on which to base a stable financial structure. John Nelson cites under-financing (due to tuition dependence and/or meager financial reserves) and minuscule enrollments as indicators of financial instability, with an attendant likelihood of long-term financial strain. [5] These colleges are just too small. They don't have the slack to survive financial crises or respond to market fluctuations.

Compounding the size problems for these colleges is location, location, location. Many small independent colleges are buried in rural towns where student markets have shrunk so much that they can no longer sustain the operations, let alone the financial integrity, of the colleges. Others are located optimally in or around major cities, but they face vicious competition from public universities, for-profit enterprises, and wealthy independent institutions. Well-financed institutions sap the traditional markets and ravage the continuing education markets of small colleges. In eroding the continuing education market, the competition drains the revenue stream small colleges use to subsidize traditional programs.

Just as financially vulnerable as the typical market-sapped small colleges are the micro colleges tied to particular sectarian groups. These colleges are usually very small, very poor, and sorely neglected by their mother churches. Over the last half-century, sectarian loyalties have waned among Catholics and members of old-line Protestant sects, so that neither parents nor students view small religious colleges as viable alternatives. If they appeal to an enclave of true believers, colleges tied to an orthodox religion have a chance of surviving; consider, for example, colleges that reliably serve members of the Church of Latter Day Saints. But many a fundamentalist college has watched its academic mission crumble in time with the fame and fortune of its founder.

Whether fundamentalist or traditional, a run-of-the-mill tuition-dependent college will struggle with invisibility in the marketplace. Many small colleges cannot spur significant market interest because their reputations are circumscribed to such small groups of students. Colleges lacking distinctive academic programs and sufficient economies of scale will charge relatively high tuition rates. Add to the ordinariness a discounting policy that keeps net price constant over time, and you have colleges that fit the Jencks and Riesman paradox: survival demands higher prices, but higher prices and a faded image translate into diminished interest of potential students (and their parents).

The crushing blow to many small colleges is their inability to finance the personal services and attention that their small size implies and that their students desire. Under-financed colleges will find that low reserves and debt capacity preclude the new construction and service overhauls necessary to compete for students. By default, they will enter the market offering a high-priced degree and services that fall short of those at wealthier institutions. As consumers—of room, board, recreational facilities, game rooms, shops, and entertainment—rather than investors in education, potential enrollees will walk if consumables don't match expectations.

Colleges' ability to satisfy students will intensify as demographics change over the next decade. Promising enrollment growth estimates shroud a growing number of unprepared applicants. The traditional assumptions about what basic academic skills first-year students should possess have declined over the last quarter-century, and they will be called further into question as more students who fail to meet secondary school standards enter the higher education market. Small colleges barely capable of delivering an education to students with modest academic ability will be hard-pressed to accommodate academically lagging populations.

Advantages

Despite the liabilities associated with small colleges, we must flip the coin and remember that small colleges have prospered through the decades *because* of their size. Small classes and personal treatment entice students and parents who count guidance, encouragement, and protection as crucial elements of a successful undergraduate career.[6] Alien values, uncertainty, unharnessed immaturity, and anonymity can be checked at the door. Instead, students at small institutions will experience a pervasive faculty attentiveness that will nurture them as they grow into well-rounded, productive adults.[7]

The public generally regards small colleges as safe harbor from an aggressive culture rumored to exist in larger or more demanding universities. As such, students from smaller colleges progress to graduate work and careers in the national labor market following a gentler, yet still appropriately demanding, introduction to higher education.

Larger universities can't hold a candle to the small local college as far as commuters and continuing education students go. In choosing the local college, commuters save having to pay room and board, as well as the costly travel expenses associated with visiting home for the holidays. Local continuing education students can drive 10 minutes from their jobs to their classes, instead of 40 minutes down an interstate during rush hour.

From location, location, location we turn to bureaucracy, bureaucracy, bureaucracy. Far from the politics and paperwork of the large university are the direct levers of power of the small college, whose president can easily access decision makers and make immediate adjustments (from the minuscule to the monumental) to instructional programs, administrative policies, and student services. Depending on the will of the leadership, and presuming no governance deadlocks or power struggles, small colleges have the agility to resolve discord swiftly and to leap at new opportunities. More than one small college has nimbly picked itself up and moved to accommodate market demand.

What Could Happen to Small Colleges?

Only time will tell whether the disadvantages outweigh the advantages for small independent colleges. The rich will thrive, the poor and mismanaged will fail, and those in between face a long and hard struggle with net price, competition, rising costs, technology, economic stagnation, falling yields from gifts and endowment funds, and higher debt loads.

The challenges to higher education over the next decade could touch, if not destabilize, the financial structures of every small college. As student demographics shift, so too must the demands on faculty, the content of instructional programs, and the intensity of degree requirements. For example, small colleges will struggle to accommodate larger numbers of primarily Hispanic and African-American students, as well as migrants, who may be less prepared to pay for and complete their coursework. But with accountability and testing standards in grades 3 through 12 finding wider acceptance, that struggle may ease after a time.

All in all, potential student population sizes that approach those of the baby boom generation, along with a consistent demand for adult higher education, will favor the small college. Combine with population growth an astute leadership that carefully blends and monitors financial, market, service, and academic strategies, and you will have the level of market responsiveness necessary to invigorate even the faintest of colleges. Without clever leaders, market savvy, and adequate resources, however, small colleges will enter the next grueling decade with much vulnerability.

From the brand name to the sectarian, let us next explore the potential impact of 21st- century challenges on different types of small colleges, surmised from the data, experience, and observations of noted leaders and analysts in higher education.[8]

Brand-Name Colleges

Brand-name colleges recruit nationally, charge premium tuition rates, have esteemed academic reputations, and prepare their students for top-notch graduate and professional schools. [9] Gifts and income from endowments provide a major proportion of their operating revenue, which in turn permits the colleges to grant large tuition discounts and subsidize academic services, administrative services, and plant operations. Substantial tuition discounts usually lead to excess market demand, from which colleges can pick the best students.

Brand-name colleges should do well in the next decade, provided they continue to offer a reputable product and consumers remain willing to pay a premium for it. If prices rise dramatically, however, say to compensate for shortfalls in gift or endowment income, and public universities offer comparably reputed academic programs, small brand-name colleges may find themselves digging more desperately into their (or other market sectors') applicant pools for students.

Presidents of brand-name colleges must ensure that endowments generate sufficient funds to subsidize operations; that gift income grows despite a flat economy; and that educational services, student services, and plant operations meet student expectations and remain competitive. Failure to anticipate the changing economic environment will undermine this sector's heretofore strong market position.

Convenience Colleges

Located in densely populated areas near accessible expressways, convenience colleges (otherwise known as nonselective colleges) offer no-frills education and open admissions.[10] Tuition at convenience colleges represents 70 percent to 90 percent of total revenue. Endowments are small. And because students who opt for convenience colleges aren't looking for deep and lasting connections with faculty or classmates through extracurricular study, sports, or clubs, loyalty as expressed through gift income is minimal. The cost of fund raising may in fact outrun the amounts collected in the effort.

Convenience colleges must grow (and they do so primarily through the referrals of satisfied students) in order to cover expenditure increases and keep tuition rates down. The trick is to grow fast enough that tuition increases don't outpace the inflation rate. Tuition pricing is simple: price is a function of enrollment growth and expense increases. Over the long term the price gap between convenience colleges and traditional colleges should expand, and the gap between convenience colleges and public universities should shrink, making tuition discounts less necessary at convenience colleges. If convenience colleges were to raise prices, however—to accommodate changing student needs, for example—the price gap trends would reverse, and their competitive edge would be lost.

Recent high school graduates who favor accessibility and low stress have contributed to the student population, but the bulk of enrollees have been first-generation college students and middle managers in the mid-20s to late-30s age range who work and attend classes part-time. Goal-driven and satisfied with classroom instruction, the majority of students at convenience colleges have demanded relatively little of their colleges. The typical student wants small classes, flexible schedules, convenient locations, friendly staff, easy registration procedures, simple payment plans, degrees with few electives, and high-speed courses.

As the decade progresses, however, the segment of the convenience college population recently graduated from high school will grow, as will the number of minority and migrant applicants. Younger students will approach the college experience with fewer goals than the traditional student, yet will require more attention and home comforts. Minority and migrant populations will need extra help meeting writing and math standards. The convenience college is ill equipped philosophically and financially to provide the level of student services and academic support needed to direct wayward or educationally deficient students. If forced to ramp up prices to pay for new services, nonselective colleges just might price themselves out of their ideal market position.

Changing demographics might cost convenience colleges more than their competitive edge; federal financial aid may be at risk. Less mature and minimally educated students will have higher dropout rates. The Department of Education frowns upon awarding aid to colleges that enroll droves of students and then graduate only a few. [11] For a convenience college to lose access to financial aid, which for many students bridges the tuition gap between convenience colleges and public universities, would be devastating.

No longer can leaders rely on seat-of-the-pants growth estimates and retrospective strategizing. No longer can financial administrators treat their budgets as checkbooks, adding new cash to the balance with every registration. Presidents and administrative teams of every convenience college will have to build financial reserves while keeping pace with market demands and vigilantly monitoring financial, market, *and* academic performances. Leaders of "mom and pop" enterprises will have to be especially careful to interject discipline and accountability into budgetary and strategic planning processes.

Population growth in the next decade will be anything but continuous and straightforward. But given the adaptability and friendliness of convenience colleges toward various populations—recall their successful shaping of degrees, programs, and services to adult and commuter students—convenience colleges are certainly up to the task.

Regional Selective Colleges

Regional selective colleges, if they are successful, have developed a distinctive niche and reputation within a geographic market that feeds colleges from a large student population base. Enrollments reach between 1,100 and 1,800 students, an optimum economy of scale range for small independent colleges. Many students, satisfied with their education at selective colleges, move on to nationally ranked graduate schools, while others enter second-tier graduate schools or professional schools.

Current levels of gifts and endowments, while flowing steadily, don't thrust these selective colleges into the rarefied air of national markets, but current alumni and donor bases generate enough gift wealth to support capital projects and permit the accumulation of financial reserves. But a sustained economic downturn coupled with changes in tax laws could change all that. To protect against the threat of falling gift and endowment levels during the next decade, the already volatile rates of change in tuition levels at selective colleges will spike, destabilizing their market position. Students may opt for cheaper independent colleges or public universities. Shrinking enrollments on top of large declines in gift and endowment income could definitely drive small regional colleges to the brink of financial distress.

Selective colleges tend to depend more heavily on tuition than do brand-name colleges, with more than 50 percent of their revenue coming from tuition. Heavily tuition-dependent regional colleges do not have sufficient reserves to sustain price wars or to finance the drastic cost increases necessary to meet changing student demands for posh, protective living conditions. Less selective colleges with especially paltry reserves will have to find creative solutions to survive, heeding one of George Dehne's dictum that colleges use symbols to effectively portray their missions.[12] Cost cuts alone won't do the trick; colleges don't want to eat their seed corn, and students of the next decade will scoff at an impoverished college life.

And then there's the other half of the demographics double whammy. Students lacking academic skills will not fit into the educational philosophies or missions of selective colleges, which view themselves as mini-brand-name colleges. Those students who do make the cut at top-notch selective colleges will be sought, if not successfully lured, by brand-name colleges that will compete outside their niche for academically and/or financially prepared students.

Less selective regional colleges that depend on continuing education students to subsidize their traditional day programs will find themselves in desperate competition with convenience colleges, which boast 30 percent lower sticker prices. Because convenience colleges do not regularly offer tuition discounts, less selective colleges could compete by using tuition discounts to match their net prices with convenience colleges' sticker prices.

Unfortunately, continuing education students may fail to see the real price similarity between a selective college's net price and a convenience college's sticker price and will think only in terms of sticker price when comparing the two. (Continuing education students tend to enroll late, missing the opportunity to go through the normal financial aid process and reap the benefit of net pricing.) Furthermore, if less selective regional colleges offer too large a price cut to continuing education students, they may find their traditional full-pay day student populations inquiring about the in-house continuing education programs.

Less selective regional colleges and continuing education programs can adjust to the new demographics if college presidents and continuing education directors endeavor to model convenience colleges and for-profit institutions. They will have to provide friendly, comfortable environments where students can socialize while earning reasonably priced, marketable degrees.

If overall student market growth is not evident in a selective college's geographic sector, or if the selective college fails for whatever reason to respond quickly to market demand, it may need to consider strategic reorganization to improve services and reduce costs (especially the college with a weak financial base). Partnerships may offer new academic products useful for serving students who need more academic support. Consortia could help spread operational costs. Mergers just might improve operational efficiency.

Regional selective colleges ought to employ presidents with the spirit and finesse both to direct operations and to woo donors. Because revenue is dearer to these colleges than to their more exalted cousins, presidents will expend considerable energy motivating staff and faculty to perform to their highest standards. Working within the guidelines of a strategic plan, selective colleges will be able to build on current successes, respond quickly to changing student needs, and retain a distinctive market niche.

Catholic Women's Colleges

An anachronism back in the 1960s, when changes in the Catholic Church and in the aspirations of women foretold a dreary future, independent Catholic women's colleges have not made much progress in the last 40 years. Most exist on the fringe of old eastern and midwestern cities; some are tucked away in sylvan dreamscapes. All have offered protected, contemplative, and rigidly disciplined environments for the daughters of second- or third-generation Europeans who, before the 1960s, were just beginning to join the broad middle class. College applicants had attended diocesan high schools, taught by the same religious order of nuns who ran the colleges. Enrollment levels held steady, the cost of education low because nuns lived a life of subsistence, and wealthy donors helped out on occasion.

The women's movement of the late 1960s and early 1970s hurt Catholic women's colleges in two ways. First, young women began rejecting the confines of what was, for all intents and purposes, a convent. Second, the colleges' inexpensive labor supply began to evaporate as nuns left the orders and were not replaced by younger religious women. These trends have only intensified over the decades. Today, when young Catholic women do enroll, it is often at the behest of parents looking for safe places to enroll their daughters. The typical enrollee puts up with the college for a year or two, then transfers at the first opportunity. High attrition rates make full enrollment a very difficult and costly goal for the college.

Many Catholic women's colleges have sustained their traditional day programs with continuing education degrees that enroll both men and women, and continuing education enrollments have often outnumbered day program enrollments. The continuing education tactic has worked for years but is now threatened by public universities and better-known independent colleges that offer comparable programs. As a result, revenue from continuing education has eroded, landing many of these colleges in severe financial distress. Try as they might to remain on the offensive with new programming, their resources are so diminished that most will ultimately fail as independent institutions.

A college of this type near a metropolis would seem to occupy an ideal position, with ready access to a large Catholic market. But, again, interest among modern young women is low. And then there's the location problem: Catholic colleges in large cities often locate themselves on top of each other. Philadelphia, for example, boasts five Catholic women's colleges, each within a half-hour of the others. All five are residential, and most remain under the control of a religious order. They simply ravage each other's market share.

For small Catholic women's colleges isolated in rural settings, the feminist movement has been disastrous. Most such colleges have not had a continuing education market with which to supplement their day programs. Those lucky enough to have such a market have been overwhelmed by larger, wealthier colleges. Many have closed. Only a few still hang on.

Small Catholic women's colleges, especially the tuition-dependent ones that have weak or absent financial reserves, will continue to atrophy. Their only hope is to find partners or consolidate with nearby institutions. An "Oxford variant" could grow out of the dreary mix, with individual colleges loosely organized around a central administration. The colleges could provide academic services, while the "university" manages everything else. Regardless of the arrangement, no college is promised its same form, cost structure, or even location.

Sectarian Micro Colleges

Sectarian micro colleges enroll fewer than 500 students and often are located in sparsely populated rural areas. Originally, close ties to a protestant church yielded subventions that helped support educational programs, and sectarian loyalties in general were strong, but both have waned over the years. This set of micro colleges hangs on by a thread.

Occasionally, new presidents attract money or launch programs that briefly reverse years of dismal financial performance. But reality makes a quick comeback in the form of donors who are not wealthy enough to infuse the college over the long haul, or new programs that simply feed on enrollments from existing programs. The college returns to its struggles, with faculty, administrative, and staff compensation packages at a familiar 50 percent below the average. (Employee turnover is low, however, given employees' ties to the area and their lack of employment options.)

Presidents, boards, and key administrators of these colleges embody the abject poor in Eric Hoffer's lexicon.[13] Inured to their circumstances, they show little interest in changing their ways. Instead, the leadership focuses on the "concrete and immediate" essentials—making payroll, paying bills, finding the next student. Sectarian micro-colleges have hitherto sidestepped one crisis for another, but they may finally succumb to the competition and the changing demographics to come.

Coeducational Catholic Colleges

Coeducational Catholic colleges maintain closer ties with their churches than do sectarian colleges, even though some churches don't directly contribute financial support. Most funding comes instead from student tuition, with some indirect support from the order. Many coed Catholic colleges are old-line commuter colleges and bear a resemblance to convenience colleges. Unlike convenience colleges, however, coed Catholic colleges have not successfully handled their weaknesses: insufficient financial reserves, inability to discount or to charge lower prices, and intense competition among themselves, to name a few. Jencks and Riesman in the 1960s noted something that remains true today for Catholic colleges: They have a relatively high "natural" rate of mortality[14] (see chapter 7 for the Trinity College story and chapter 12 for the exertions required of Marylhurst College to survive).

Growing numbers of Hispanic students who are uncomfortable with Catholic northern European traditions will continue to befuddle coed Catholic colleges in the next decade, making them the first type of small college likely to fail. If they cannot diversify in response to their changing market pool, coed Catholic colleges could merge together into a large Catholic network—but interfaith rivalry regarding heritages and myths will likely keep them apart.

Rural Micro Colleges

Local rural colleges, located in small or mid-sized towns predominantly in the southern, eastern, and midwestern United States, enroll fewer than 500 very local students. High school students who live much more than a stone's throw away (50 miles, really) won't know anything about these colleges, for recruiters are not paid enough to travel that far.

Rural college curricula are standard, practical, and bare-boned. Keeping technology current and modernizing degrees to satisfy job markets are tall orders for these micro–colleges. They don't have the funds or debt capacity to purchase new equipment or hire new faculty. Young adults who forsake their small towns for big city employment, whether down the road or across the state, contribute to a steady trimming of the local student market.

As evidenced by their mere existence, rural colleges have occupied beloved places in their communities. The braid of college, community, and career is so tightly woven that college board members can depend on local business leaders (a.k.a. alumni) to pony up a few dollars during hard times. But without a viable market or a competitive market presence, these colleges will fade fast, especially when the local boosters disappear. An entrepreneurial president might morph a few of them into something useful, by perhaps attaching them to local high schools or community colleges, but for the majority, the future holds little promise.

What Can Small Colleges Do to Prosper?

Astute and rational leaders will attend to details and work very, very hard to ensure the mere *survival* of their small independent colleges in this next decade. For small colleges to *prosper*—for them to acquire the resources necessary to provide quality education while responding to intensifying competition, student demands, and various impending economic and tax challenges—their leaders must be well acquainted with the ingredients of financial strength and market savvy (regardless of how distasteful they may be at first).

Chief academic and financial officers must work as a team with a president who motivates everyone to "perform beyond the ordinary."[15] Even the most charismatic president will find the challenges of the next decade difficult to surmount, especially where markets and finances are depleted. Nevertheless, as they gear up in the 21st century, leaders can take knowledge and inspiration from the observations, experiences, and suggestions of learned consultants, financial analysts, and presidents, distilled in Table 13.1 at the conclusion of this chapter.

Conclusion

Beyond their ability to serve and protect their students, small colleges persist, according to David Riesman, because public institutions are not politically mandated to build smaller institutions that cater to homogeneous student populations.[16] Though most small independent colleges don't face an imminent danger of being swept away, their missions and financial integrity will face powerful challenges in the years to come.

Those Catholic, sectarian, and rural colleges—or even entire sectors of the college market—that are poorly financed, lack distinctive market placement, and cannot modernize key personal services will be most vulnerable. If economic events diminish the ability of these colleges to compete, the first decade of 2000 could see huge declines in levels of service provided to students across the nation.

After competitive and market pressures push colleges (or whole sectors) into decline, cash shortages could force them to close. Loan calls, loss of confidence among donors, enrollments that fail to generate sufficient cash, student neglect of bills, and government agency denial of college access to financial aid funds constitute just a few of the sudden causes of cash shortages. In most cases, however, evidence of decline has been readily apparent for some time, and following a college closure, many lament that "someone" should have done "something" to stop it.

Alternatives to closure—mergers, partnerships, or new leadership—are vulnerable to loyalties and location restrictions. Mergers and partnerships are especially hard to pull off because no concentrated ownership remains to make profit-maximizing decisions. Urban or suburban colleges may be the best candidates for mergers or partnerships, provided that they offer valuable services and that their leaders are poised to act quickly. Colleges isolated in rural regions with declining student markets and no way to fund emergencies through donors may find closing a relief, let alone their only option.

The small college waiting for a federal bailout shouldn't hold its breath. The federal government—which awards nearly $600 million in Pell grants alone, excluding college work-study funds, supplemental educational opportunity grants, and subsidized loans (Stafford and Perkins loans, and unsubsidized Plus loans)—is not likely to tolerate arguments that college closures will constrain student choice or limit access to education.

First, the government would argue that it already supports choice through award monies that students can use at any college. A particular college's (or an entire sector's) inability to entice students falls far outside the government's rescue scope. Second, though small independent colleges answer a need for accessible centers of higher education in geographically isolated areas, the lack of such access simply doesn't carry enough weight to spur the government's notice. Besides, states have answered the accessibility problem themselves by investing heavily in conveniently located community colleges and public universities. Why should the government interfere? All told, small colleges present as neither a large nor a united constituency capable of rousing the government's protection.

Whether a precipitating event will force massive changes in the small college market is not readily evident. Problems emerging in the for-profit sector from the Enron scandals—with auditors failing to act aggressively against shaky business enterprises and credit rating agencies ignoring financially dubious business models—may lead to harsher audit rules and tougher reports from auditors and credit rating agencies. If that is the case, financially distressed colleges will find themselves in the same unenviable position as did small hospitals that brutally learned of their financial debility from auditors in the 1980s and 1990s.

Small colleges can save themselves, but they need to step up to the task *now*. Leaders must diagnose current financial, market, and academic conditions;

construct a viable and integrative strategy; inspire the college, from its board members to the community at large; and finally, implement and monitor the strategic plan. Strategies come with risk. Colleges will enter into debt to finance revenue projects with fuzzy financial forecasts; recruit international students from politically volatile regions of the world; offer tuition discounts that negate cash flow increases; approve student payment plans without effective collection policies; or condone off-sheet financing that hides true credit position—all *at their peril*.

So how will small colleges fare during the next decade? Data suggest that many have drifted from deficit to deficit on meager resources. Yet somehow they have mustered the financial wherewithal to make it to the next crisis. Will the 21st century find small colleges slipping completely over the brink of financial distress? Or will they continue to muddle along in search of the next miracle or handout? Might they stumble into a new golden age?

We can only begin to answer these questions if we divide small independent colleges into three categories: those that are rich, those that are financially distressed and whose leaders recognize them as such, and those that suffer financial distress under a clueless leadership. The rich college will fare well regardless of minor crises. The financially distressed college, however, will need to forego luck for a sharp leader who can avoid brinkmanship. In the absence of shrewd leadership, old ways will persist and new pressures will arise, forcing small hard-pressed colleges into mergers or out of existence. Nevertheless, short of bankruptcy, there is nothing pressuring small troubled colleges to make dramatic changes. Absent the demands of creditors or patrons, these colleges will stumble along on their own path satisfied with taking the scraps leftover in the market.

Table 13.1
Building a Financially Strong Small College

Strategy
- Construct a strategic plan integrating finances, academic programs, student services, marketing, and administrative services.
- Incorporate a monitoring plan.
- Annually review the plan in response to economic conditions, the student market, and other salient factors.

Finance
- Either fund net price discounts or grow net price as fast as inflation.
- Generate operating margins, including depreciation.
- Balance revenue and expense growth rates, including net income in expenses.
- Use net income to build financial reserves.
- Build cash reserves.
- Grow receivables no faster than tuition revenue.
- Track uncollectible receivables closely.
- Minimize debt by funding all or a portion of capital expenses.
- Conduct fund-raising campaigns, hiring external agents to manage them if necessary.
- Generate a positive net income from all auxiliaries (after depreciation).
- Find alternative uses for fixed assets to generate additional revenue.
- Achieve and maintain a CFI score greater than 4.
- Use budgets to forecast, guide, and provide references for financial performance.
- Monitor the budget and financial ratios against performance benchmarks.
- Use trend analysis to spot changes in financial or operating conditions.
- Hold accountable administrators or others responsible for budgets.

Academic Programs
- Formulate market-responsive academic programs.
- Design straightforward policies and procedures.
- Modify programs regularly to compensate for changes in job and technology markets.
- Customize academic programs so that they provide greater benefits to students.
- Use trend analysis to monitor class size, faculty work, student performance, and the financial performance of departments, divisions, and/or other academic subdivisions.
- Remember the primary mission of the college: to provide a credible education program.

continued

Student Services

- Design a student service strategy that allows for personal attention and student development.
- Foster links between academic programs, graduate schools, and employers.
- Encourage a community of students through living, academic, and recreational activities.

Marketing

- Identify preferred enrollees—their location, their motivation to attend, their price sensitivity, their expectations about academics and the college, any barriers keeping them from attending, and any relevant academic or personal characteristics.
- Compile a database of prospective and current students' characteristics.
- Develop a marketing strategy built around student preferences, academic programs, and exactly how the college will tend to students and customize services.
- Communicate to prospective students through campaigns that spell out the college's value, personalized services, and fulfilling communities.
- Use symbols beyond the written word to convey and reinforce the college's mission.
- Establish a program to minimize attrition or bring former students back.
- Craft a financial aid program that targets preferred students.
- Design a marketing campaign that links public relations to traditional advertising, bringing prospective students and colleges together (for example, through services provided to high schools).
- Keep on top of new revenue-generating opportunities.
- Monitor admissions, enrollment, marketing, and financial aid campaigns.
- Create a distinctive niche for the college that will enhance its reputation.

Administrative Services and Governance

- Simplify everything, consolidate where reasonable, and cut expenses.
- Eliminate as many obstacles to student admission and registration as possible.
- Treat the student as customer, and provide one-stop shopping.
- Make administrators accountable for their work and their offices.
- Reward people for good work.
- Seek partners in strategy.
- Work under a strong governance structure that clearly defines respective roles for board members, faculty members, and administrators.

Notes

1. Philip Tahey, interview by author, Williamsburg, Virginia, January 15, 2002.

2. Christopher Jencks and David Riesman, *The Academic Revolution* (Garden City, N.Y.: Doubleday Anchor Books, 1969).

3. Ibid., p. 196

4. Ibid., p. 289.

5. John Nelson, Senior Vice President, Moody's Investors Services, interview by author, New York, N.Y., August 7, 2001.

6. Jencks and Riesman, *The Academic Revolution,* p. 196; George C. Dehne, "Another Look at the Future of the Private College," GDA Integrated Services, 2001, at: www.gdais.com/new_research/research_another_look.html

7. Ibid.

8. Esther Barazzone, president, Chatham College, Pittsburgh, Pa., interview by author, October 5, 2001; David Chopko, venture capitalist, interview by author, November 19, 2001; William Crouch, president, Georgetown College, Georgetown, Ky., interview by author, September 13, 2001; George Dehne, president, George Dehne & Associates, Old Saybrook, Conn., interview by author, August 27, 2001; James Doti, president and Donald Bren Distinguished Professor of Business and Economics, Chapman University, Orange, Calif., interview by author, October 10, 2001; Greg Kirk, partner, Deloitte & Touche, Philadelphia, Pa., interview by author, August 9, 2001; Susan Lee, foreign student and scholar advisor, University of Delaware, Newark, Del., interview by author, September 14, 2001; Michael McPherson, president, Macalester College. St. Paul, Minn., interview by author, August 31, 2001; Scott Miller, president, Wesley College, Dover, Del., interview by author, August 10, 2001; John Nelson, senior vice president, Moody's Investors Services, New York, N.Y., interview by author, August 7, 2001; Naomi Richman, senior vice president, Moody's Investors Services, New York, N.Y., interview by author, August 7, 2001; John Stevens, senior vice president and chief operating officer, Kaludis Consulting, Washington, D.C., interviews by author, September 11 and 18, 2001; Peter Stokes, executive vice president; Eduventures, Inc., Boston, Mass., interview by author, September 17, 2001; Nancy Wilgenbusch, president, Marylhurst College, Portland Oreg., interview by author, August 28, 2001; Thomas Williams, president, Noel-Levitz, Iowa City, Iowa, interview by author, September 24, 2001.

9. "In Search of Strategic Perspective: A Tool for Mapping the Market in Postsecondary Education," *Change* 29, no. 6 (November/December 1997): 23–39.

10. Ibid.

11. U.S. Department of Education, "Student Assistance General Provisions: Final Rule," *Federal Register,* Part IV, 34 CFR Part 668, 1997.

12. George C. Dehne, "Another Look at the Future of the Private College," GDA Integrated Services, 2001, at: www.gdais.com/new_research/ research_another_look.html.

13. Eric Hoffer, *The True Believer* (New York: Harper Perennial, 1951).

14. Jencks and Riesman, *The Academic Revolution,* p. 104.

15. George Keller, *Academic Strategy* (Baltimore, Md.: Johns Hopkins Press, 1983), p. 125.

16. Jencks and Riesman, *The Academic Revolution,* p. 288.

Appendices

APPENDIX A: TREND TABLES

Marketing Trends	years					change	
	1	2	3	4	5	1	5
Marketing—Undergraduate							
inquiries							
applicants							
admitted							
matriculated—new students							
yield—inquiries							
yield—applicants							
yield—admitted							
Marketing—Master's							
inquiries							
applicants							
admitted							
matriculated—new students							
yield—inquiries							
yield—applicants							
yield—admitted							
Marketing—Doctorate							
inquiries							
applicants							
admitted							
matriculated							
yield—inquiries							
yield—applicants							
yield—admitted							
Marketing—Total							
inquiries							
applicants							
admitted							
matriculated—new students							
yield—inquiries							
yield—applicants							
yield—admitted							
Selectivity Measures—Undergraduate							
yield—admitted							
average SAT score							
average high school GPA							
average high school rank							
Transfers							
percent transferred							
average SAT score							
average transfer credits							
Market Share—Relative to Competitors							
college enrollment							
total enrollment competitors							
total market enrollment							
college's share							

		years				change	
Marketing Expenses & Costs	1	2	3	4	5	1	5
advertising							
direct mail							
recruiting							
other marketing							
staff & administrative expense							
other marketing expense							
total marketing expense							
marketing cost per new student							
Competitor Analysis							
Competitors (separate section for each major competitor)							
enrollment							
tuition							
net price							
net income							
cost per student							
net assets							
student faculty ratio							
student—administration ratio							
student—staff ratio							
average faculty pay							
average administrator pay							
average staff pay							
Students, Classes, & Student/Faculty Ratio							
Enrollment, Sections, & Class Size							
undergraduate							
master's							
doctorate							
total							
Class Sections							
undergraduate							
master's							
doctorate							
total							
Average Class Size							
undergraduate							
master's							
doctorate							
total							
Faculty & Student Faculty Ratio							
Faculty							
undergraduate							
master's							
doctorate							
total							
Student Faculty Ratio							
undergraduate							
master's							
doctorate							
total							

APPENDIX A: TREND TABLES

Personnel Trends	years					change	
	1	2	3	4	5	1	5
Counts							
administration							
staff							
faculty							
undergraduate							
master's							
doctorate							
subtotal							
total personnel							
faculty—by rank							
instructor							
assistant							
associate							
full-professor							
total							
Expenditures							
administration							
staff							
faculty							
undergraduate							
master's							
doctorate							
subtotal							
total personnel							
faculty—by rank							
instructor							
assistant							
associate							
full-professor							
total							
Cost Per Position							
administration							
staff							
faculty							
undergraduate							
master's							
doctorate							
subtotal							
total personnel							
faculty—by rank							
instructor							
assistant							
associate							
full-professor							
total							

	years					change	
Basic Performance Data	_1_	_2_	_3_	_4_	_5_	_1_	_5_
Enrollment Flow							
new students							
enrollment							
average class size							
tuition & fees							
net price							
discount							
net cash provided by operations (audit)							
Financial Statement							
Revenue							
tuition & fees							
grants & contracts							
gifts							
other							
total revenue excluding auxiliary							
Expenses							
core services							
instruction							
research							
public service							
academic and student support							
scholarships							
institutional support							
total expenses excluding auxiliary							
Net before auxiliary							
Auxiliary net							
Net before transfers							
Transfers							
Net							
Working Capital							
Current Assets							
cash							
receivables							
uncollectible receivables							
pre-paid expenses							
inventory							
other							
total							
Current Liabilities							
payables							
accruals							
notes payable							
retirement and benefit liabilities							
other							
total							
Net Current Assets & Liabilities							

APPENDIX A: TREND TABLES

Permanent Capital	years					change	
	1	2	3	4	5	1	5
Assets							
net investment in plant, property, etc.							
investment restricted to plant							
quasi-endowments							
endowments							
other investments							
total							
Liabilities							
long-term debt							
other liabilities							
total							
Net Assets							
unrestricted							
temporarily restricted							
permanently restricted							
total							
Relative Weights							
Revenue Weights							
tuition & fees / total revenue minus auxiliary revenue							
grants & contracts / total revenue minus auxiliary revenue							
gifts / total revenue excluding auxiliary							
other & fees / total revenue excluding auxiliary revenue							
Expense Weights							
instruction/total expenses minus auxiliary							
research / total expenses minus auxiliary							
public service/total expenses minus auxiliary							
core services/total expenses minus auxiliary							
academic & student support/total expenses minus auxiliary							
scholarships / total expenses minus auxiliary							
institutional support/total expenses minus auxiliary							
plant / total expenses minus auxiliary							
Total Revenue Minus Auxiliary/Total Expenses Minus Auxiliary							

APPENDIX B: RATIOS

Market Information

1 Inquiry Yield
ratio: number of applicants divided by number of inquirers
purpose: useful for planning and to measure efficiency of marketing
computation

numerator = number of applicants	A
denominator = number of inquirers	B
ratio:	A/B

2 Selectivity—Admissions Yield
Source: Moody's—page 12
ratio: number of admissions divided by number of applications
purpose: useful for planning and to measure efficiency of marketing
computation

numerator = number of admissions	A
denominator = number of applications	B
ratio:	A/B

3 Matriculant Yields
ratio: number of enrolled new students divided by applicants
purpose: useful for planning and to measure efficiency of marketing
computation

numerator = number of matriculants	A
denominator = number of admitted students	B
ratio:	A/B

4 Graduation Rate
ratio: number graduating within six years divided by size of enrolling cohort
purpose: useful for planning and to measure if college is performing its main function
computation

numerator = number of graduates within six years	A
denominator = size of enrolling cohort for graduates	B
ratio:	A/B

5 Attrition Rate for First Year Students
ratio: 1- (first year students remaining second year divided by size of enrolling cohort)
purpose: for planning and to determine if large proportion of students are leaving college
computation

numerator = number of first year students enrolling second year	A
denominator = size of enrolling cohort	B
ratio:	A/B

APPENDIX B: RATIOS

6   **Tuition Dependence**
    Source: NCHEMS—page 15
    ratio: tuition & fees/total unrestricted revenue
    purpose: to determine dependency on tuition and implies amount of income diversification
    computation
    tuition and fees   A
    total unrestricted revenue   B
                                        ratio   A/B

Operations

7   **Revenue Flexibility Ratio**
    Source: NCHEMS—page 24.
    ratio: total unrestricted revenue divided by total revenue
    purpose: measure income that is under the control of the college
    computation
    add unrestricted revenue
    subtract gains & losses
    subtract: net assets released for construction & acquisition of fixed assets
    numerator = total: unrestricted revenue   A
    demnominator = total: expenditures   B
                                        ratio   A/B

8   **Expense Flexibility Ratio**
    Source: NCEMS—page 23.
    ratio: full-time faculty plus operations and miantenance of plant divided by total expenditures
    purpose: measures proportion of expenses that is fixed at most colleges
    computation
    add full-time faculty
    add: operations & maintenance of plant
    numerator = total: fixed commitments   A
    denominator = total: expenditures   B
                                        ratio   A/B

9   **Revenue Weights or Source of Funds (general form)**
    Source: Chatobar—page 197
    weight: revenue category divided by total revenue subtract gains & losses
    purpose: measures how revenue flows into the college
    computation
    numerator = revenue category: ex. tuition and fees   A
    total revenue
    subtract: gains & losses
    denominator = adjusted revenue   B
                                        ratio   A/B

10   **Expense Weights or Use of Funds (general form); see following four ratios for examples**
     Source: Chatobar—page 198
     weight: expense category divided by total expenses excluding auxiliary services
     purpose: measures how expenditures are allocated
     computation

     numerator = expense category: ex. instruction   A
     total expenses
     subtract: auxiliary services
     denominator = adjusted expenses   B
                                                 ratio   A/B

11   **Educational Core Services Ratio**
     Source: KPMG/Prager—page 49
     ratio: educational core services divided by educational and general income
     purpose: measures instruction, research, & public service as percent of expenses
     computation
     add instruction
     add research
     add public services
     numerator = total educational core services expense   A
     add total unrestricted revenues and gains
     add investment return in excess of spending rate
     subtract auxiliary revenue
     denominator = educational and general income   B
                                                 ratio   A/B

12   **Educational Support Ratio**
     Source: KPMG/Prager—page 51
     ratio: educational support ratio divided by educational and general income
     purpose: measures academic support & student services as percent of expenses
     computation
     add academic support
     add student services
     numerator = total educational support   A
     total unrestricted revenues and gains
     add investment return in excess of spending rate
     subtract auxiliary revenue
     denominator = educational and general income   B
                                                 ratio   A/B

13   **General Support Ratio**
     Source: KPMG/Prager—page 52
     ratio: institutional support divided by educational and general income
     purpose: measures burden of administrative costs on expenses
     computation
     numerator = institutional support   A
     total unrestricted revenues and gains
     add investment return in excess of spending rate
     subtract auxiliary revenue
     denominator = educational and general income   B
                                                 ratio   A/B

14 **Operations and Maintenance of Plant Ratio**
Source: KPMG/Prager—page 53
ratio: operations and maintenance of plant divided by educational and general income
purpose: measures burden of plant expenses on total expenses
computation

numerator = operations & maintenance of plant   A
total unrestricted revenues and gains
add investment return in excess of spending rate
subtract auxiliary revenue
denominaor = educational and general income   B
                                    ratio   A/B

15 **Plant Coverage Ratio**
ratio: operation & maintenance of plant divided by plant assets (depreciated)
purpose: older plants should demand more maintenance
computation

numerator = operation and maintenance of plant   A
denominator = plant assets net of depreciation   B
                                    ratio   A/B

16 **Age of Facility Ratio**
Source: KPMG/Prager—page 113
ratio: accumulated depreciation divided by depreciation expenses
purpose: estimate of the age of the plant
computation:

numerator = accumulated depreciation   A
denominator = depreciation expense   B
                                    ratio   A/B

Operating Margins (Net Income)

17 **Annual Operating Margin**
Source: Moody's—page 13
ratio: adjusted total unrestricted revenue minus total unrestricted expenses
        divided by adjusted total unrestricted revenue
purpose: measure operational performance through excess revenue from operations
computation
adjusted total unrestricted revenue
add total unrestricted revenue
subtract: net assets released for construction & acquisition of fixed assets
subtract: gains & losses
add: .045 x (cash + investments) from previous year
denominator = subtotal: adjusted total unrestricted revenue   B
subtract: total unrestricted operating expenses
numerator = total: adjusted total unrestricted net   A
                                    ratio   A/B

18 **Average Operating Margin**
   Source: Moody's—page 13
   purpose: keep a 3 year running average on the operating margin
   computing note: 3 year average of annual operating margin

	year 1	year 2	year 3	average
annual operating margins				

19 **Operating Margin Excluding Gifts**
   Source: Moodys—page 13
   ratio: (adjusted total unrestricted revenue minus gifts minus unrestricted operating expenses)
       divided by (adjusted total unrestricted revenues minus gifts)
   purpose: measure operating performance purely on revenue generated from services
   computation
   adjusted total unrestricted revenue (see Annual Operating Margin)
   subtract: gifts
   numerator = adjusted total unrestricted revenue minus gifts   A
   denominator = subtract total unrestricted operating expenses (C.1)   B
                                   ratio   A/B

Tuition & Fee Ratios

20 **Net Tuition & Fees Ratio—Form A (net of institutional aid)**
   Ratio: net price divided by tution and fees
   purpose: measure tuition & fees net of institutional aid
   computation
   denominator = total tuition and fees   B
   subtract unfunded institution aid
   subtract funded institutional aid
   numerator = net tuition & fees   A
                         ratio   A/B

21 **Net Tuition & Fees Ratio—Form B (net of unfunded institutional aid)**
   Ratio: tuition net of unfunded institutional aid divided by tuition and fees
   purpose: identify impact of unfunded institutional aid on net tuition & fees
   computation
   denominator = total tuition and fees   B
   subtract unfunded institution aid
   numerator = net tuition & fees price (net of unfunded institutional aid)   A
                                   ratio   A/B

Working Capital Ratios

22 **Cash Income Ratio**
   Source: KPMG/Prager—page 41
   ratio: net cash from operating activities divided by total revenue subtract gains & losses
   purpose: identify proportion of cash generated from operations
   computation note: net cash from operations is found in the cash flow statement of the audit
   computation
   numerator = net cash provided by operating activities   A
   total unrestricted revenue gains and losses
   add investment return in excess of spending rate
   add net released from restrictions
   subtract unrestricted realized gains (if known)
   subtract unrestricted unrealized appreciation (if known)
   denominator = total unrestricted income excluding gains   B
                         ratio   A/B

23 Cash Expense Ratio
ratio: cash & short-term investments divided by total expenses
purpose: identify cash sufficiency to support expenditures
computation

numerator = cash & short-term investments	A
denominator = total expenses	B
ratio	A/B

24 Current Ratio
Source: Chatobar—page 193
ratio: current assets divided by current liabilities
purpose: identify if there is sufficient current assets to support current liabilities
computation (refer to audit statement of financial position)

numerator = current assets	A
denominator = current liabilities	B
ratio	A/B

25 Available Funds Ratio
Source: Chatobar—page 194
ratio: cash & short-term investments divided by current liabilities
purpose: identify if there is enough quick liquidity to support current liabilities
computation (refer to audit statement of financial position)

cash	
add short-term investments	
numerator = available funds	A
denominator = current liabilities	B
ratio	A/B

26 Receivables Ratio
ratio: receivables divided by tuition & fees
purpose: determine what proportion of tuition & fees are receivables—useful for cash flow planning
computation

numerator = receivables	A
denominator = tuition & fees	B
ratio	A/B

27 Uncollectible Receivables
ratio: uncollectible receivables divided by receivables - useful for cash flow planning
purpose: what proportion of receivables is bad debt
computation

numerator = uncollectible receivables	A
denominator = receivables	B
ratio	A/B

28 Payables & Accruals Ratio
ratio: payables and accruals divided by total expenses
purpose: identify how much of expenses becomes payables & accruals—useful for cash flow planning
computation

numerator = payables & accruals	A
denominator = total expenses	B
ratio	A/B

29 Inventory Ratio
ratio: inventory per audit to auxiliary sales
purpose: measure inventory control
computation

numerator = inventory per audit   A

denominator = auxiliary sales per financial recores   B

ratio   A/B

Debt Measures

30 Viability Ratio
Source: KPMG/Prager—page 23
ratio: expendable net assets (unrestricted net assets plus temporarily restricted net assets subtract
(net property, plant, and equipment) plus long-term debt divided by long-term debt.
purpose: estimate the capacity of the college to support long-term debt, if operational income changes
computation

unrestricted net assets
add: temporarily restricted net assets
subtract: net property, plant, & equipment
add: long-term debt

numerator = total: expendable net assets   A

denominator = long-term debt   B

ratio   A/B

31 Risk Ratio
Source: NCHEMS—page 21 & KPMG/Prager—page 69
ratio: interest expense divided by total expenditures
purpose: determine the impact of interest payments of total expenditures
computation

numerator = interest expense   A

denominator = total expenses   B

ratio   A/B

32 Actual Debt Service Coverage
Source: Moody's—page 13
ratio: annual operating surplus (deficit) plus interest and depreciation expenses divided by
actual principal and interest payments
purpose: determine capacity of college to support debt service payments, if operational income falls
computation

total operating revenue
subtract: total operating expenses
subtotal: annual operating surplus (deficit)
add: interest & depreciation expenses

numerator = total: annual operating surplus (deficit)   A

denominator = actual principal and interest payments   B

ratio   A/B

33 Average Actual Debt Service Coverage
Source: Moody's—page 13
purpose: track debt service through 3 year moving average
computing note: 3 year average of actual debt service coverage

                                                        year 1   year 2 year 3   average

average actual debt service coverage

34 **Average Peak Debt Service Coverage**
    Source: Moody's—page 14
    purpose: track impact of peak debt service over 3 year moving average
    computing note: 3 year average of annual operating surplus (deficit) plus interest and depreciation
              expenses, divided by peak principal and interest payments (during 3 years)

computation	year 1	year 2	year 3	sum
annual operating surplus (deficit)				
add: interest and depreciation expense				
numerator = total: adjusted annual operating surplus (deficit)				
denominator = peak principal & interest payments (during 3 years)				
ratio				

Long-Term Assets

35 **Composition Ratio**
    Source: KPMG/Prager—page 61
    ratio: financial assets divided by physical assets
    purpose: useful for tracking changes in relationship between financial and physical assets
    computation

numerator = financial assets	A
denominator = physical assets (property, plant & equipment)	B
ratio	A/B

36 **Capitalization Ratio**
    Source: KPMG/Prager—page 60
    ratio: modified net assets divided by modified total assets
    purpose: useful for tracking changes in net assets to total assets
    computation

numerator = modified net assets (remove goodwill & intercompany receivables)	A
denominator = modified total assets (remove goodwill & intercompany receivables)	B
ratio	A/B

37 **Endowment Yield**
    ratio: endowment gains & losses divided by endowment value beginning of year
    purpose: track investment performance
    computation

numerator = gains, losses & yield
denominator = endowment value beginning of year
ratio

Net Asset Relationships

38 Free Expendable Resources to Operations
Source: Moody's—page 13
ratio: total unrestricted and temporarily restricted net assets subtract net investment in plant
divided by total operating expenses
purpose: helps understand how net assets are expanding in relation to expenses
computation

total unrestricted net assets
add: total temporarily restricted net assets
subtract: net investment in plant

numerator = total: free expendable resources   **A**

denominator = total operating expenses   **B**

ratio   **A/B**

39 Total Financial Resources-per-Student
Source: Moody's—page 13
ratio: total net assets subtract net investment in plant divided by full-time equivalent students
purpose: rough measure of college's ability to build reserves in relationship to changes in enrollment
computation

numerator = total net assets   **A**

total full-time students
add: total part-time students *.3333   **B**
denominator = total: full-time students   **A/B**

ratio

40 Return on Net Assets
Source: Moody's—page 14
ratio: change in net assets divided by total net assets (sum of net assets beginning and
end of year divided by 2)
purpose: identifies how well college is able to generate new net assets
computation

numerator = change in net assets   **A**

total net assets beginning of year
total net assets end of year
denominator = average net assets (beginning and end divided by 2)   **B**

ratio   **A/B**

APPENDIX C: RATIO BENCHMARKS

	ratio #	source	benchmarks	year 1	year 2	year 3	year 4	year 5	5 year change	year 4 & 5 change
Operations										
Revenue Flexibility Ratio	7									
Expense Flexibility Ratio	8									
Core Ratio	11	KPMG/Prager	40.40%							
Educational Support Ratio	12	KPMG/Prager	23.86%							
General Support Ratio	13	KPMG/Prager	20.89%							
Operations & Plant Ratio	14									
Annual Operating Margin	17	Moody's	1.69%							
Average Operating Margin	18	Moody's	1.73%							
Operating Margin Excluding Gifts	19	Moody's	-3.73%							
Tuition										
Net Tuition Ratio Total Institutional Aid	20									
Net Tuition Unfunded Aid	21									
Working Capital										
Cash Income Ratio	22	KPMG/Prager	7.54%							
Cash Expense Ratio	23	Guideline Only	25.00%							
Current Ratio	24	Weston	2.50%							
Available Funds Ratio	25									
Receivables Ratio	26									
Uncollectible Receivables	27									
Payables & Accruals Ratio	28									
Inventory Ratio	29									
Debt										
Viability Ratio	30	KPMG/Prager	> 1.25							
Debt Leverage Ratio		KPMG/Prager	> 2:10							
Actual Debt Service Coverage	32	Moody's	$2.08							
Average Actual Debt Service Coverage	33	Moody's	$2.03							
Average Peak Debt Service Coverage	34	Moody's	$1.66							
Risk or Interest Expenses Ratio	31	KPMG - NCHEMS	< 6.00%							
Long Term Assets										
Composition Ratio	35	KPMG/Prager	> 1.00							
Capitalization Ratio	36	KPMG/Prager	50% to 85%							
Age of Facility Ratio	16	KPMG/Prager	11.95							
Endowment Yield	37									
Free Expendable Resources to Operations	38	Moody's	0.19							
Total Financial Resources-per-Student	39	Moody's	$20,427							
Return on Net Assets	40	Moody's	8.46%							

Purpose: track financial performance against standard benchmarks. Ratios numbers tie into the numbering of ratios in the ratio appendix.

Note: benchmarks should be updated regularly and a separate benchmark should be identified for competitors.

APPENDIX D: CFI WORKSHEET

Primary Reserve (total expendable net assets/total expenses)

Numerator = total expendable net assets

+ unrestricted net assets
+ temporarily restricted net assets
- property, plant, equipment (net of depreciation)
+ long term debt

Total Numerator   **A**

Denominator = total expenses   **B**

Ratio Computation   **A/B**

Net Income Ratio using an Operating Indicator

Numerator = excess (deficiency) of unrestricted operating revenues minus unrestricted operating expenses

+ total unrestricted revenues and gains
+ net assets released from restriction   **A**

Denominator = total unrestricted operating income   **B**

Ratio Computation   **A/B**

Net Income Ratio using Change in Unrestricted Assets

Numerator = change in unrestricted net assets

+ total unrestricted revenues and gains
+ net assets released from restriction
+ unrestricted investment return in excess of spending rate   **A**

Denominator = total unrestricted income   **B**

Ratio Computation   **A/B**

Return on Net Assets Ratio

Numerator = change in net assets   **A**

Denominator = total net assets (beginning of year)   **B**

Ratio Computation   **A/B**

Viability Ratio

+ unrestricted net assets
+ temporarily restricted net assets
- property, plant, and equipment (net of depreciation)
+ long-term debt   **A**

Denominator = excendable net assets

Denominator = long-term debt   **B**

Ratio Computation   **A/B**

Strengths & Weights Worksheet

	Ratio divided by	Strength times	Weight =	CFI Score
Primary Reserve		/ 0.133	x 0.35	=
Net Income Operations*		/ 0.007	x 0.1	=
Net Income Unrestricted Net*		/ 0.013	x 0.1	=
Return on Net Assets		/ 0.02	x 0.2	=
Viability		/ 0.417	x 0.36	=
Totals & CFI SCORE				

* Use either form for calculation but not both forms

Source: KPMG/PRAGER pages 9–34

APPENDIX E: FINANCIAL AND MARKETING DIAGNOSTIC CHECKOFFS

(complements "Financial and Marketing Diagnostics" & Appendices on Ratios and Tables)

I. Financial Diagnostics

A. Operations

		checkoff
1.	Is the operating net or total net increasing or decreasing; if it is decreasing, why?	
2.	Are revenue and expense growth rates in balance?	
3.	If revenue is falling, why?	
4.	What is the trend for net tuition price relative to expense growth—rising, falling, or stagnant?	
5.	What is the trend for net tuition revenue relative to expensegrowth—rising, falling, or stagnant?	
6.	What proportion of revenue is gifts?	
7.	Do auxiliaries produce a positive net income?	
8.	If the expenses are growing faster than revenue, why?	
9.	Is the growth rate for core expenses less than non-core expenses; if so, why?	
10.	What is the trend in total compensation?	
11.	What is the tuition dependency rate?	
12.	How does operational performance compare to the competition?	

B. Operations—Drivers

		checkoff
1.	What is the enrollment—by level and by program?	
2.	What is the attrition rate—by level and by program?	
3.	What is the graduation rate—by level and by program?	
4.	How many employees—faculty, staff, and administration?	
5.	What is the cost of employees—faculty, staff, and administration?	
6.	How are employees allocated between core and non-core services?	
7.	What is the student-faculty ratio?	
8.	What is the average class size?	
9.	How many classrooms are there?	
10.	How is space allocated between core and non-core services?	
11.	How many parking spaces are there?	

C. Working Capital

		checkoff
1.	Are cash and short-term investments increasing over time?	
2.	Are cash and short-term investments growing as fast as expenses?	
3.	What is the source of the increase in cash—operations, increases inpayables and accruals, reduction in receivables, increase in short-or long-term debt?	
4.	Are cash and short-term investments greater than 16.0% of expenses? (a rough measure of one month of cash disbursements from expenditures)	
5.	Are receivables as a proportion of tuition increasing? Why?	
6.	Are uncollectible accounts as a proportion of receivables increasing? Why?	
7.	Are students billed monthly?	
8.	What is being done to collect outstanding bills?	
9.	Is inventory as a proportion of auxiliary sales increasing? Why?	
10.	Are payables and accruals as a proportion of expenses increasing? Why?	
11.	Are vendors, taxes, and benefits paid on time?	
12.	Is short-term debt increasing? Why?	
13.	Prepare a short-term debt list—terms, lender, payment schedule and reasons for borrowing.	
14.	Is the available funds ratio (cash & short-term investments to current liabilities) declining? Why?	

D. Permanent Capital

		checkoff
1.	Is long-term debt increasing?	
2.	List for long-term debt—terms, conditions, payment schedules, and uses? (include all forms—on- and off-balance sheet borrowing)	
3.	Is the debt leverage ratio less than 2:1? If so, debt may be excessive.	
4.	Does the college have a debt policy?	
5.	Is the return on net assets declining? If so, why?	
6.	Is the capitalization rate less than 50%? If so, it may limit future borrowing.	
7.	How does the return on investments (endowment) compare to a benchmark? (ex. S&P 500)	
8.	What is the investment policy of the college?	
9.	What is the pay out ratio for the endowment fund?	
10.	How is the pay out ratio computed?	
11.	Is there deferred maintenance? Is so, how much and what are the major categories?	
12.	Is there a long-term strategy for space utilization for the campus?	
13.	Does the college have sufficient parking?	
14.	Are new facilities designed and located to permit sale?	

APPENDIX E: FINANCIAL AND MARKETING DIAGNOSTIC CHECKOFFS

E. Financial Performance (refer to trend tables appendix)

		checkoff
1.	Have weights and growth rates for revenue and expenses been computed?	
2.	Have growth rates been computed for working capital?	

3.	Have these ratios been computed? (see ratio and tables appendix)
	  a. tuition dependency,
	  b. net tuition after unfunded institutional aid,
	  c. operating margin,
	  d. cash income,
	  e. cash expense,
	  f. current ratio,
	  g. available funds ratio,
	  h. receivables,
	  i. uncollectible receivables,
	  j. inventory ratio,
	  k. payables and accruals,
	  l. viability,
	  m. debt service,
	  n. interest expense,
	  o. composition,
	  p. capitalization,
	  q. age of facility,
	  r. free expendable resources to operations,
	  s. total financial resources per student,
	  t. endowment payout	

4.	Compute the preceding ratios for the previous five years and compare trends.	
5.	Is the primary ratio less than .40? (ratio less than .40 means that the college may not have the capacity to transform itself or to cover five months of expenses).[1]	
6.	Is net income with depreciation less than 2% of total revenue? (suggests that the college is living beyond its means and may not be building adequate reserves).[2]	
7.	Are net assets growing fast enough to exceed, whichever is greater —CPI or CPI for education expenses.[3]	
8.	Is the viability ratio less than 1:1? (When this ratio falls below 1:1; a college's to respond to adverse conditions from internal resources is jeopardized—ratio should fall in the range of 1.25 to 2.0).[4]	
9.	Compute the *CFI SCORE* for the college.	

F. Financial Distress —CFI SCORE < 3.

		checkoff
1.	Conduct strategic analysis of the college.	
2.	Is the current market viable? Why do students choose or not choose the college?	

3.	Can the institution produce new revenue or cut expenses to survive?
	  a. Are there new sources of revenue?
	  b. Can costs be cut through reorganization?
	  c. Can the college run a fund raising campaign? Who are the benefactors?
	  d. What is the condition of the plant?
	  e. Can debt be refinanced or reduced through gifts?	

4.	What is the college's strategic turnaround plan?	

G. Major Financial Distress

		checkoff
1.	Is the *CFI SCORE* < 1?	
2.	Has the state warned that licensing will be withdrawn?	
3.	Has the US Department of Education imposed financial conditions before student aid can be received?	
4.	Has an accrediting agency warned that accreditation will be withdrawn?	
5.	Does the college have sufficient cash or other investments to pay its bills?	
6.	Can the college meet its payroll?	
7.	Are payroll tax payments delinquent?	
8.	Are payroll benefits delinquent?	
9.	Is the college delinquent on debt payments?	
10.	Has the college considered a merger?	
11.	Does it have a survival/turnaround plan? Is it feasible?	
12.	Has the college declared financial exigency?	
13.	Is there a viable plan to close in an orderly fashion?	

II. Marketing Diagnostics

A. Competition

		checkoff
1.	Who are the major competitors?	
2.	What is their enrollment?	
3.	What is the market share for each competitor and the college?	
4.	How does the enrollment growth rate of the college compare to competitors?	
5.	How does the college's net price compare to the competitors?	
6.	What services do competitors provide students that the college does not?	
7.	Why do students choose a competitor?	
8.	What would the college have to change to compete with its competitors?	
9.	Are new competitors entering the market?	

APPENDIX E: FINANCIAL AND MARKETING DIAGNOSTIC CHECKOFFS

B. Market Analysis

	checkoff

1. What do you know about your students?
    a.   Why do they choose the college?
    b.   Why do some students not leave the college?
    c.   Can you give a description of the student market for the college?
    d. Can you give a description of the student market for each program?	

2. What are the yield rates for
    a.   Admissions (students applying/inquiries)?
    b.   Admitted students (admitted/applications)?
    c. Matriculated students (matriculated/admitted students)?	

3. Have students been surveyed to see what they would change or improve?	
4. What is the attrition rate for first year students?	
5. What is the graduation rate?	
6. How effective is the alumni office in building enrollment?	
7. What are the components of the marketing campaign and are they effective?	

8. Is the student market viable?
    a.   Is the population shrinking?
    b.   Is the college in an isolated rural area?
    c. Does the college offer programs that other colleges offer?	

9. Does the pricing policy bring in the students that the college wants?	
10. Does the pricing policy respond to the competition?	
11. What is the image of the college to the prospective student when they visit?	
12. Does the college have an effective public relations program?	
13. Develop a marketing program attuned to the reasons students would choose the college per George Dehne's themes—reduce risk of the choice, inform the prospective student on how the college fits them, reach the student through a variety of sources, and make sure product, price, and place are attuned to the promotion campaign[6]	

III Management and Oversight

		checkoff
1.	Does the college have an annual audit?	
2.	Does the board meet privately with the auditors to review financial management and performance?	
3.	Does the board review the financial aid audit?	
4.	Does the college conduct compensation and benefit tests to assure conformity with federal regulations?	
5.	Are personnel practices reviewed to assure conformity with regulations?	
6.	Does the college have unrelated business income that must be reported?	
7.	Are there policies on providing services by board members and by businesses owned by key administrators?	
8.	Are there policies on review of expense reimbursements and purchases by key administrators?	
9.	Does the college have a business policies and practices manual?	
10.	Is there a formal review and evaluation process for all levels of the college including the key administrators?	
11.	What is the college's Dunn & Bradstreet rating?	
12.	What is the strategic plan for the college —education, finance, and marketing?	
13.	Is the college on target—is it healthy and will it be around another 5 years?	

Notes

1. Ronald E. Salluzzo and Philip Tahey, Frederic J. Prager, and Christopher J. Cowen (1999). *Ratio Analysis in Higher Education, 4th edition*; KPMB LLP and Prager, McCarthy & Sealy, LLC: page 13.

2. See Ronald E. Salluzzo and Philip Tahey, Frederic J. Prager, and Christopher J. Cowen (1999). *Ratio Analysis in Higher Education, 4th edition*; KPMB LLP and Prager, McCarthy & Sealy, LLC: page 15.

3. See Ronald E. Salluzzo and Philip Tahey, Frederic J. Prager, and Christopher J. Cowen (1999). *Ratio Analysis in Higher Education, 4th edition*; KPMB LLP and Prager, McCarthy & Sealy, LLC: page 120.

4. See Ronald E. Salluzzo and Philip Tahey, Frederic J. Prager, and Christopher J. Cowen (1999). *Ratio Analysis in Higher Education, 4th edition*; KPMB LLP and Prager, McCarthy & Sealy, LLC: page 22.

5. Dehne, George C. (2001). *Student Recruitment: A Marketing Primer for Presidents*. GDA Integrated Services: Old Saybrook.; pages 10-15.

(track ratios over rolling 3 year period)	
Resource Sufficiency & Flexibility	**Ratio Description**
Primary Reserve Ratio	(unrestricted + temporary restricted net - net plant + long term debt) / total expenses
Operating Results	
Net Income Ratio—operating indicator	net unrestricted / unresticted operating income (gains + released from rest)
Net Income—change in unrestricted assets	change net asset / unresticted operating income
Cash Income Ratio	net cash by operating activities / (unrestricted income - gains)
Operating Income Ratio	(tuition and fees - scholarship allowances + state and federal grants and contracts + interest on loan receivables + other sources + auxiliary revenue - auxiliary expenses) / (total expenses - auxiliary expenses)
Net Tuition Dependency	(net tuition & fees - financial aid) / total revenue - (auxiliary expenses)
Net Tuition per FTE Student	net tuition & fees / full-time-equivalent students
Net Auxiliary Income Ratio	net / auxiliary revenue
Net Hospital Income Ratio	net / hospital revenue
Contributed Income Ratio	contributed income / total expenses - auxiliary expenses
Educational Core Income Ratio	(instruction + research + public service expenses) / total expenses - auxiliary expenses
Educational Support Ratio	academic support + student services / total expenses - auxiliary expenses
General Support Ratio	institutional support / total expenses - auxiliary expenses
Maintenance Ratio	plant / total expenses - auxiliary expenses
Deferred Maintenance Ratio	(outstanding maintenance requirements) / (unrestricted + temporarily restricted net assets - property, plant, & equipment + long-term debt)
Financial Asset Performance	
Return on Net Assets Ratio	change net assets / total net assets (beginning of the year)
Capitalization Ratio	modified net assets(remove intangible net assets; ex. good will) / modified total assets
Composition of Equity Ratio	financial assets / physical assets
Return on All Investments Ratio	total investment return(includes realized & unrealized gain / (cash, cash equivalents, investments, property, plant, and equipment (end-of-year - beginning of year/2)
Debt Management	
Viability Ratio	unrestricted + temporarily restricted net asset - property, plant, & equipment + long term debt
Debt Burden Ratio	debt service / total expenses
Debt Coverage Ratio	(unrstricted net assets + depreciation + interest) / debt service
Leverage Ratio	(unrestricted + temporarily restricted net assets) / long-term debt debt
Age of Facility Ratio	accumulated deprication / depriciation
Composite Financial Index	
Primary Reserve Ratio	(unrestricted + temporary restricted net - net plant + long term debt) / total expenses
Net Income	net unrestricted / unresticted operating income (gains + released from rest)
Return on Net Assets Ratio	change net assets / total net assets (beginning of the year)
Viability Ratio	unrestricted +temporarily restricted net asset - property, plant, & equipment + long term debt

APPENDIX G: MOODY'S LIST

(track over rolling 3 year period)	
Market Demand	**Ratio Description**
Selectivity	number of acceptances/number of applications
Net tuition per student	net tuition & fee revenue/full-time equivalent students
Educational expenses per student	total expenses & general expenses/full-time equivalent students
Total gifts per student	gifts(unresticted; temporarily restricted & permanently restricted) / full-time-equivalent students
Institutional tuition discount	unsponsored scholarships & fellowships/gross tuition & fee revenue
Total tuition discount	total scholarships & fellowships/tuition & fees
Capital	
Unrestricted financial resources to direct debt	((unrestricted net assets - net investment in plant)/direct debt
Expendable financial resources to direct debt	(unrestricted + temporarily restricted net asset) - net plant)/direct debt
Total financial resources to direct debt	total net assets - net plant/direct debt
Total cash & investments to direct debt	total cash & investments/direct debt
Direct debt to cash flow	direct debt/(operating margin + depreciation + interest)
Direct debt to total capitalization	direct debt/(total net assets + direct debt)
Actual debt service to operations	debt service/operatiing expenses
Peak debt service to operations	peak annual debt service/total operting expenses
Capital expense to operations	(depreciation + interests)/operating expenses
Age of plant	accumulated depreciation/depreciation expenses
Direct debt per student	direct debt/full-time-equivalent students
Balance Sheet	
Unrestricted financial resources to operations	unrestricted net asset - net plant/operating expenses
Expendable financal resources to operations	((unrestricted + temporarily restricted net asset) - net plant)/operating expenses
Free expendable financial resources to operations	((unrestricted+temporarily restricted net asset) - net plant - dir debt)/operating expenses
Expendable financial resources to total net assets	(unrestricted net assets + temp restricted net assets) - net plant)/total net assets
Total financial resources per student	total net assets - net plant/full-time-equivalent students
Operations	
Annual operating margin	[adjusted total unrestricted net income (adjustment = investment income equals 4.5% of prior year cash & investments and subtract net assets released for construction & acquistion of fixed assets) - total unrestreicted operating expenses] / adjusted revenue (see numerator)
Average operating margin	3 yr average of operating margin
Operating margin excluding gifts	adjusted total unrestreicted revenue - gifts - total unrestricted operating expenses/adjusted revenue
Actual debt service coverage	[annual operating surplus (deficit)+interest + depreciation]/(principle + interest)
Average actual debt service coverage	3 year average debt service
Average peak debt service coverage	[3 year average of operating surplus (deficit) + interest = depreciation]/(peak principle + interest)
Return on net assets	change in total net asets/(average total net assets ((begin of yr + end of yr net)/2
Return on financial resources (net assets minus net plant)	(total net assets - net investment in plant)/[(average = begin + ending of total net assets - net investment in plant /2)]

Bibliography

Books and Articles

Allen, Kimberly M. *The Response of Small Private Colleges to Financial Distress in the Nineties*. Master's thesis, 1999.

Ashby, Eric. *Adapting Universities for Technological Society*. San Francisco: Jossey-Bass, 1978.

Astin, Alexander. *What Matters in College?* San Francisco: Jossey-Bass, 1993.

Balderston, Frederick E. *Managing Today's University*. San Francisco: Jossey-Bass, 1975.

Baldridge, J. Victor, and Michael L. Tierney. *New Approaches to Management*. San Francisco: Jossey-Bass, 1979.

————, David V. Curtis, George Ecker, and Gary L. Riley. *Policy Making and Effective Leadership*. San Francisco: Jossey-Bass, 1983.

Barazzone Esther L. "Back from the Brink."

Bartlett, Thomas. "Amid National Boom in Enrollments, Some Liberal Arts Colleges See Declines." *Chronicle of Higher Education*, October 19. 2001.

Baumol, William J., and Sue Anne Batey Blackman. "How to Think About Rising College Costs." *Planning for Higher Education* 23, (summer 1995), pp. 1–7.

Ben-David, Joseph. *Trends in American Higher Education*. Chicago: University of Chicago Press, 1972.

Bernstein, Elizabeth, and Sarah Collins. "Colleges for a New Area." *Wall Street Journal*, October 5, 2001, pp. W1–W2.

Biggs, Barton M. "Revisiting the Case for Fire." *U.S. and the Americas Investment Perspectives*, Morgan Stanley Dean Witter, April 4, 2001, pp. 7–10.

————. "Venture Debacle." *U.S. and the Americas Investment Perspectives*, Morgan Stanley Dean Witter, April 18, 2001, pp. 5–6.

Biggs, Barton M. "What to Do about Tech. . . ." *U.S. and the Americas Investment Perspectives*, Morgan Stanley Dean Witter, April 24, 2001, pp. 9–10.

Birnbaum, Robert. "Value of Different Kinds of Colleges." In *Foundations of American Higher Education,* edited by James L. Bess. Needham Heights, Mass.: Ginn Press, 1991.

Blumenstyk, Goldie. "How a Publishing Empire Is Changing Higher Education." *Chronicle of Higher Education,* September 8, 2000.

Borrego, Anne-Marie. "Study Finds Strong Growth in For-Profit Higher Education."*Chronicle of Higher Education*, July 19, 2001.

Bowen, Howard R. *The Costs of Higher Education.* San Francisco: Jossey-Bass, 1981.

———. "What Determines the Costs of Higher Education?" In *ASHE Reader on Finance in Higher Education*, edited by Larry L. Leslie and Richard E. Anderson. Needham Heights, Mass.: Ginn Press, 1990.

Breneman, David W., and Chester E. Finn Jr. "An Uncertain Future." In *Public Policy and Private Higher Education*, edited by David Breneman and Chester E. Finn Jr. Washington, D.C.: Brookings Institution, 1978.

———, and Susan C. Nelson. *Financing Community Colleges.* Washington, D.C.: Brookings Institution, 1981.

———. "Higher Education on a Collision Course with New Realities." AGB Occasional Paper 22. Washington, D.C.: Association of Governing Boards of Universities and Colleges, 1993.

———. *Liberal Arts Colleges.* Washington, D.C.: Brookings Institution, 1994.

Brinkman, Paul T. "College and University Adjustments to a Changing Financial Environment." In *The Economics of American Universities*, edited by Stephen A. Hoenack and Eileen L. Collins. Albany: State University of New York Press, 1990

Brinkman, Paul T., and Larry L. Leslie "Economies of Scale in Higher Education: Sixty Years of Research." *Review of Higher Education* 10 (fall 1986): 1–28.

Brown, John Seely, and Paul Duguid. "Universities in the Digital Age." In *TheMirage of Continuity*. Washington, D.C.: Council on Libarary and Information Resources and Association of American Universities, 1998.

Brownstein, Andrew). "Tuition Rises Faster than Inflation and Faster than in Previous Year." *Chronicle of Higher Education*, October 27, 2000.

———. "Enrollment Shifts and Last-Minute Aid Requests Signal the Onset of an Economic Downturn." *Chronicle of Higher Education*, April 20, 2001.

Carr, Susan. "PBS Sticks to Its Strategy for Telecourses, Unfafraid of Competitionfrom the Internet." *Chronicle of Higher Education*, July 13, 2001.

Carnegie Commission on Higher Education. *Governance of Higher Education.* New York: McGraw-Hill, 1973.

"Chatham College Turnaround Lauded." *Pittsburgh Tribune-Review*, February 12, 2001.

"Education Enrollment." Chapter 2 in *Projection of Higher Education Statistics to 2010.* U. S. Department of Education, 2001. ces.ed.gov/pubs2000/projections/ chapter2.html.

Chatobar, Kent John. "Financial Ratio Analysis Comes to Nonprofits." *Journal of Higher Education,* March/April 1989, pp. 188–208.

Chishom, Mark, and Bethaviva Cohen. "A Review and Introduction to Higher Education Price Response Studies." In *National Center for Higher Education Management Systems.* Boulder, Colo.: publisher, 1982.

Clotfelter, Charles T., Ronald G. Ehrenberg, Malcolm Getz, and John J. Siegfried. *Economic Challenges in Higher Education.* Chicago: University of Chicago Press, 1991.

———. "Demand for Undergraduate Education." In *Economic Challenges in Higher Education,* edited by Charles T. Clotfelter, Ronald G. Ehrenberg, Malcolm Getz, and John J. Siegfried. Chicago: University of Chicago Press, 1991.

———. "The Familiar but Curious Economics of Higher Education: Introduction to a Symposium." *Journal of Economic Perspectives* 13, no. 1 (winter 1999): 3–12.

Cohen, Michael D., and James G. March. *Leadership and Ambiguity: The American College President.* New York: McGraw-Hill, 1974

Collier, Douglas J., and Cathleen Patrick. "A Multivariate Approach to the Analysis of Institutional Financial Condition." Unpublished report. Boulder, Colo.: NCHEMS, 1976.

"College Tuition and Fees." Bureau of Labor Statistics, Series ID CUSR0000SAS, May 24, 2001. At: http://data.bls.gov/cgi-bin/srgate.

"Coming to Market: A Growing Reliance on Student-Supplied Revenue." *Change* 32, no. 4 (July/August 2000): 53–56.

"Consumer Price Index: All Urban Consumers." Bureau of Labor Statistics, Series ID CUSR0000SEEBO1, May 24, 2001. At: http://data.bls.gov/cgi-bin/srgate.

Cowan, Ruth B. "Prescription for Small-College Turnaround." *Change* 25, no. 1 (January/February1993): 31–40.

———. "A Prescription for Vitality for Small, Private Colleges." AGB Occasional Paper 20. Washington, D.C.: Association of Governing Boards of Universities and Colleges, 1994.

Cowley, W. H. *Presidents, Professors, and Trustees.* San Francisco: Jossey-Bass, 1980.

Dehne, George C. "Another Look at the Future of the Private College." Old Saybrook, Conn.: GDA Integrated Services, 2001. At: www.gdais.com.

———. *Student Recruitment: A Marketing Primer for Presidents.* Old Saybrook, Conn.: GDA Integrated Services, 2001.

"Student Assistance General Provisions: Final Rule." U. S. Department of Education, 1997. *Federal Register*, Part IV, 34 CFR Part 668.

Doti, James L. "Tuition Discounting: Its Causes and Effects." Unpublished paper.

Drucker, Peter F. *The Practice of Management.* New York: Harper and Row, 1954.

———. *Management.* New York: Harper and Row, 1973.

Duryea, E. D. "Evolution of University Organization." In *Organization and Governance in Higher Education*, edited by Michael Peterson. Needham Heights, Mass.: Ginn Press, 1991.

"English and Scottish Education. Universities and Public Schools to the Time of Colet (1907–21)." In *Cambridge History of English and American Literature*, vol. 2, sec. 11.

"Exhibit 1-6: Percentage of Undergraduates Receiving Loans, Grants, and Work Study by Type and Sector of Institution and Attendance Status: 1995-96." In *Straight Talk about College Costs and Prices: Report of the National Commisson on the Cost of Higher Education*. Phoenix, Ariz.: Oryx, Press, 1998.

Feldman, Kenneth A., and Theodore M. Newcomb. *The Impact of College on Students.* Vol. 1. San Francisco: Jossey-Bass, 1976.

Feemster, Ron. "Faith in Financials." *University Business* 3, no. 3 (2000):

Financial Accounting Standards Board. "Statement of Financial Accounting Standards No. 93, Recognition of Depreciation by Not-for-Profit Organizations," no. 047, August 1987.

———. "Statement of Financial Accounting Standards No. 116, Accounting for Contributions Received and Contributions Made," no. 127-A, June 1993.

———. "Statement of Financial Accounting Standards No. 117, Financial Statements of Not-for-Profit Organizations," no. 127-B, June 1993.

———. "Statement of Financial Accounting Standards No. 124, Accounting for Certain Investments Held by Not-for-Profit Organizations," no. 155-C, November 1995.

Fisher, James L. *Power of the Presidency*. New York: American Council on Education and MacMillan Publishing Co., 1984.

Frances, Carol, and Sharon I. Coldren. *Assessing Financial Health*. San Francisco: Jossey-Bass, 1979

Getz, Malcolm, and John J. Siegfried. "Costs and Productivity in American Colleges and Universities." In *Economic Challenges in Higher Education*, edited by Charles T. Clotfelter, Ronald G. Ehrenberg, Malcolm Getz, and John J. Siegfried. Chicago: University of Chicago Press, 1991.

———. "Cost Inflation." In *Economic Challenges in Higher Education*, edited by Charles T. Clotfelter, Ronald G. Ehrenberg, Malcolm Getz, and John J. Siegfried. Chicago: University of Chicago Press, 1991.

Gose, Ben. "Enrollments Surge After Large Tuition Cuts at Private Colleges." *Chronicle of Higher Education*, July 19, 1996.

———. "Some Colleges Spend Summers Trying to Fill the Freshman Class." *Chronicle of Higher Education*, June 21, 1996.

Hamlin, Alan, and Curtiss Hungerford. "How Private Colleges Survive Financial Crises." *AGB Reports* 31, no. 3 (May/June 1989): 17–22.

"Harvard and Stanford to Offer Online Business Courses." *Chronicle of Higher Education*, January 5, 2000.

Hauptman, Arthur M. *The College Tuition Spiral*. New York: American Council on Education and College Board, 1990.

———. "Five Strategic Responses to the Financial Challenges Facing Colleges and Universities." AGB Occasional Paper 33. Washington, D.C.: Association of Governing Boards of Universities and Colleges, 1997.

Hawkins, Brian L., and Patricia Battin. *The Mirage of Continuity*. Washington, D.C.: Council on Library and Information Resources and Association of American Universities, 1998.

Hebel, Sara. "Tax-Repeal Plan Could Cause Drop in Gifts." *Chronicle of Higher Education*, June 23, 2000.

Healy, Patrick. "Why Two Public Universities Courted a Small Private College." *Chronicle of Higher Education*, March 27, 1998.

"Higher Education Enrollment." Projections of Educational Statistics. U. S. Department of Education, National Center for Education Statistics, 2001.

Hoffer, Eric. *The True Believer*. New York: Harper Perennial, 1951.

Hopkins, David S. P., and William F. Massy. *Planning Models for Colleges and Universities*. Stanford, Calif.: Stanford University Press, 1981.

Hubbell, Loren Loomis, and Lucie Lapovsky. "Tuition Discounting in Challenging Times." *Business Officer* 34, no. 8 (February 2002): 24.

"Illustrative Summary of Inflation Measures Affecting Education and Libraries." 1998. At: www.rschassoc.com/inflation.html

"In Search of Strategic Perspective: A Tool for Mapping the Market in Postsecondary Education." *Change* 29, no. 6 (November/December 1997): 23–39.

"In the Matter of Upsala College." *Student Financial Assistance Proceeding: Compliance and Enforcement Division of the Office of Postsecondary Education of the U.S. Department of Education*. Docket No. 93-148-St, May 17, 1994.

James, Estelle. "Decision Processes and Priorities in Higher Education." In *The Economics of American Universities*, edited by Stephen A. Hoenack and Eileen L. Collins. Albany, N.Y.: State University of New York Press, 1990.

Jaschik, Scott. "Ivy League Agrees to End Collaboration on Financial Aid." *Chronicle of Higher Education*, May 29, 1991.

Jencks, Christopher, and David Riesman. *The Academic Revolution*. Garden City, N.Y.: Doubleday Anchor Books, 1969.

Keller, George. *Academic Strategy*. Baltimore, Md.: Johns Hopkins Press, 1983.

Klein, Eva, and John H. Augustine. "Debt Financing and Management." In *College and University Business Administration*, edited by Caroline M. Grills. Washington, D.C.: National Association of College and University Business Officers, 2000.

Lapovsky, Lucie, and Loren Loomis Hubbell. "An Uncertain Future." *Business Officer* 34, no. 8 (February 2001): 39.

Lenington, Robert. *Colleges Are A Business!* Phoenix, Ariz.: Oryx Press, 1996.

Lifelong Learning. Washington, D.C.: University Continuing Education Association, 2000.

Lindbloom, Charles. *The Policy Making Process.* Cambridge, Mass.: Harvard University Press, 1968.

Lively, Kit. "Gifts to Education Hit Record $28-Billion in 2000." *Chronicle of Higher Education,* May 24, 2001.

———. "For Private Colleges Without Large Endowments Bearish Markets Bring Anxiety and Caution." *Chronicle of Higher Education,* April 20, 2001.

Mabry, Tristan. "College Tuition Outpaces Inflation Again." *Wall Street Journal,* March 12, 1999, p. A-2.

"Management Ratios FS-9899 Private Institutions Financial Statistics and Ratios." Boulder, Colo.: John Minter Associates, Inc., 2001.

Mangan, Katherine S. "Business Enrollments Boom at For-Profit Colleges." *Chronicle of Higher Education,* October 10, 1999.

Mansfield, Edwin. *Microeconomics.*: New York: W.W. Norton, 1992.

Martin, James, and James E. Samels & Associates. *Merging Colleges for Mutual Growth.* Baltimore, Md.: Johns Hopkins Press, 1994.

Massy, William F. "Remarks on Restructuring Higher Education." In *Straight Talk About College Costs and Prices: Report of the National Commission on the Cost of Higher Education.* Phoenix, Ariz.: Oryx Press, 1998.

———. "A New Look at the Academic Department." In *The Higher Education Research Program.* Philadelphia: University of Pennsylvania,

Maurice, S. Charles, Owen R. Phillips, and C. E. Ferguson. *Economic Analysis.* Homewood, state: Richard D. Irwin, Inc., 1982.

McMurtrie, Beth. "Jesuit Colleges Try to Bring Their Values to Online Education." *chronicle of Higher Education,* May 12, 2000.

McPherson, Michael S., and Morton Owen Schapiro. "The Effect of Government Financing on the Behavior of Colleges and Universities. In *Paying the Piper,* edited by Michael S. McPherson, Morton Owen Schapiro, and Gordon C. Winston. Ann Arbor: University of Michigan Press, 1993.

———, and Morton Owen Schapiro. "Preparing for Hard Times Shows Wisdom Not Pessimism." *Chronicle of Higher Education,* April 20, 2001.

———, Morton Owen Schapiro, and Gordon C. Winston, eds. *Paying the Piper.* Ann Arbor: University of Michigan Press, 1993.

Mercer, Joyce. "Death Throes at Upsala." *Chronicle of Higher Education*, April 24, 1995.

Meisinger, Richard J. Jr, and Leroy W. Dubeck. "Fund Accounting." In *ASHE Reader on Finance in Higher Education*, edited by Larry L. Leslie and Richard E. Anderson. Needham Heights, Mass.: Ginn Press, 1990.

Mingle, James R., and Donald M. Norris. "Institutional Strategies for Responding to Decline." In *Challenges of Retrenchment*, edited by James R. Mingle et al. San Francisco: Jossey-Bass, 1981.

Moody's Rating Approach for Private Colleges and Universities. New York. Moody's Investors Service, 1999.

Moody's Seminar on Higher Education. NACUBO 2001 Annual Meeting, July 28, 2001, New York City.

Moore, Kathryn, M. "University." *Encyclopedia Britannica*, 2001.

Mortimer, Kenneth P., and T. R. McConnell. *Sharing Authority Effectively*. San Francisco: Jossey-Bass, 1982.

Mundel, David. "Whose Education Should Society Support?" In *Does College Matter?* edited by Lewis C. Solmon and Paul J. Taubman. New York: Academic Press, 1973.

Nelson, Susan C. "Financial Trends and Issues." In *Public Policy and Private Higher Education*, edited by David Breneman and Chester E. Finn Jr. Washington, D.C.: Brookings Institution, 1978.

O'Neill, James M. "An Exacting Education in Economic Realities." *Philadelphia Inquirer*, January 28, 2001, pp. 1–7.

Organizational Paradigm Shifts. Washington, D.C.: National Association of College and University Business Officers, 1996.

Private Colleges and Universities Outlook 2001/02 and Medians. New York: Moody's Investor Service, 2001.

Pulley, John L. "Researchers See a Widening Gap between Rich and Poor Colleges." *Chronicle of Higher Education*, July 31, 2001.

———, and Anne Marie Borrego. "Wealthiest Colleges Lost Billions in Endowment Value in Last Year." *Chronicle of Higher Education*, October 19, 2001.

Redd, Kenneth E. "Becoming an Expert Juggler." *Business Officer* 34, no. 8 (February 2001): 34–38.

Reed, William S. *Financial Responsibilities of Governing Boards*. Washington, D.C.: Association of Governing Boards of Universities and Colleges and National Association of College and University Business Officers, 2001.

Reynolds, Alan. "The Real Cost of Higher Education: Who Should Pay It and How?" in *Straight Talk About College Costs and Prices: Report of the National Commission on the Cost of Higher Education*, pp. 103–15. Phoenix, Ariz.: Oryx Press, 1998.

Riesman, David R. *On Higher Education*. 1980. 2nd ed. New Brunswick, N.J.: Transaction Publishers, 1998.

Rudolph, Frederick. *The American College and University*. New York: Random House Vintage Books, 1962.

Ruch, Richard S. *Higher Ed, Inc*. Baltimore, Md.: Johns Hopkins Press, 2001.

"Salem State Has Interest in Buying Bradford College." *Boston Business Journal*, March 3, 2000.

Salluzzo, Ronald E., Philip Tahey, Frederic J. Prager, and Christopher J. Cowen. *Ratio Analysis in Higher Education*, 4th ed. KPMG LLP and Prager, McCarthy & Sealy, LLC, 1999.

Simon, Herbert. "The Job of a College President." *Educational Record* 58 (winter 1967): 69.

Snow, C. P. *The Masters*. New York: Charles Scribner's Sons, 1951.

Splete, Allan, and Robert C. Dickeson. "Five Boards that Lit a Spark." *Trusteeship*, January/February 2001, pp. 30–31.

"Spring Garden College Fails to Meet Payroll." *Chronicle of Higher Education*, June 6, 1992.

"Spring Garden College Will Close in Fall." *Chronicle of Higher Education*, July 8, 1992.

National Commission on the Cost of Higher Education. *Straight Talk about College Costs and Prices: Report of the National Commission on the Cost of Higher Education*. Phoenix: Oryx Press, 1998.

"Through a Different Lens: A New Angle on the Price Spiral in Higher Education." *Change* 32, no. 1 (January/February 2000): xxiii.

Townsley, Michael K. "Brinkmanship, Planning, Smoke, and Mirrors." *Planning for Higher Education* 19 (summer 1991): 27–32.

———. "A Model Predicting Financial Health for Private Colleges and Universities." Unpublished report, 1992.

———."A Strategic Model for Enrollment-Driven Private Colleges." *Journal for Higher Education Management* 8, no. 2 (winter/summer 1993): 57–66.

———. "Deficit Prevention: Budget Control Model for Enrollment-Dependent Colleges." *Business Officer* (October 1994): 40–44.

———. *The Effect of Competitive Structure on Price Elasticity in Local Markets of Higher Education in the Commonwealth of Pennsylvania.* Ph.D. diss., University of Michigan, 1994.

Trow, Martin. "American Higher Education: Past, Present and Future." *Foundations of American Higher Education*, edited by James L. Bess. Needham Heights, Mass.: Ginn Press, 1991.

Tugend, Alina. "MIT and U. of Cambridge Announce $135 Million Joint Venture." *Chronicle of Higher Education,* November 19, 1999.

Varian, Hal R. *Intermediate Microeconomics.* New York: W.W. Norton, 1987.

Van Der Werf, Martin. "The Death of a Small College." *Chronicle of Higher Education,* May 12, 2000.

———. "Vermont's Trinity College Survives a Scare, but Its Future Remains Uncertain." *Chronicle of Higher Education,* May 12, 2000.

———. "Vermont's Trinity College Announces Plan to Shut Down." *Chronicle of Higher Education*, May 12, 2000.

———. "Colleges Turn to Debt to Finance Their Ambitions." *Chronicle of Higher Education*, March 19, 2001.

———. "More Colleges Are Seeing the Virtues of Merging." *Chronicle of Higher Education.* March 23, 2001.

"Vermont's Trinity College Seeks a Merger." *Chronicle of Higher Education*, August 6, 1999.

"Vermont's Trinity College Survives a Scare, but Its Future Remains Shaky." *Chronicle of Higher Education.* May 12, 2000.

"Vermont's Trinity College Announces Plan to Shut Down." *Chronicle of Higher Education*, May 12, 2000.

Vichas, Robert P. *Handbook of Financial Mathematics, Formulas, and Tables.* Englewood Cliffs, N. .: Prentice-Hall, 1979.

Welzenbach, Lanora F. "Administration of Endowment and Similar Funds." In *College and University Business Administration*, edited by Lanora F. Welzenbach. Washington, D.C.: National Association of College and University Business Officers, 1982.

Weston, J. Fred, and Eugene F. Brigham. *Managerial Finance*. 7th ed. Hillsdale, N.J.: Dryden Press, 1981.

Wildavsky, Aaron. *Budgeting*. 2nd ed. New Brunswick, N.J.: Transaction Books, 1986.

Williams, Thomas. "The Proper Mix." *Business Officer* (March 1999), pp. 34–37.

Williamson, Oliver E. *Markets and Hierarchies*. New York: Free Press, 1975.

Winston, Gordon C. "College Costs: Subsidies, Intuition, and Policy." In *Straight Talk About College Costs and Prices: Report of the National Commission on the Cost of Higher Education*. Phoenix: Oryx Press, 1998.

———. "Subsidies, Hierarchy. and Peers: The Awkward Economics of Higher Education." *Journal of Economic Perspectives* 13, no. 1 (winter 1999): 13–36.

Zemsky, Robert. "The Lattice and the Ratchet." *Policy Perspectives* (Pew Higher Education Research Program) 2, no. 4 (June 1990): 1–8.

———, and Penney Oedel. *The Structure of College Choice*. New York: College Entrance Examination Board, 1983.

Interviews and E-Mails

Barazzone, Esther. President, Chatham College, Pittsburgh, Pennsylvania. October 5, 2001.

Crouch, William. President, Georgetown College, Georgetown, Kentucky. September 13, 2001.

Chopko, David. Vice President November 19, 2001.

Dehne, George. President, George Dehne & Associates, Old Saybrook, Conn. August 27, 2001.

Doti, James. President and Donald Bren Distinguished Professor of Business and Economics, Chapman University, Orange, Calif. October 10, 2001.

Fisher, James L. Baltimore, Md. September 5, 2001.

Kirk, Greg. Partner, Deloitte & Touche, Philadelphia, Pa. August 9, 2001.

McPherson, Michael. President, Macalaster College, St. Paul, Minn. August 31, 2001.

Miller, Scott. President, Wesley College, Dover, Del. August 10, 2001.

Minter, John, President, John Minter and Associates. January 15, 2001 (E-mail).

Nelson, John. Senior Vice President, Moody's Investors Services, New York, N.Y. August 7, 2001; November 8, 2001 (E-mail).

Richman, Naomi. Senior Vice President, Moody's Investors Services, New York, N.Y. August 7, 2001.

Stevens, John. Senior Vice President and Chief Operating Officer, Kaludis Consulting, Washington, D.C. September 11, 2001, and September 18, 2001.

Stokes, Peter. Executive Vice President, Eduventures, Inc., Boston, Mass. September 17, 2001.

Tahey, Philip. Williamsburg, Virginia. January 15, 2002.

Williams, Thomas, President, Noel-Levitz, Iowa City, Iowa: Interview September 24, 2001.

Wirt, Gary. Vice President and Director of Admissions, Goldey Beacom College, Wilmington, Del. October 11, 2001.

Wilgenbush, Nancy. President, Marylhurst College, Portland Oreg. August 28, 2001.